MOTORCYCLE DESIGN AND TECHNOLOGY

Motorcycle Design and Technology

Gaetano Cocco

MOTORBOOKS

First published in 2004 by Motorbooks, an imprint of MBI Publishing Company, Galtier Plaza, Suite 200, 380 Jackson Street, St. Paul, MN 55101-3885 USA

GIORGIO NADA EDITORE s.r.l.

Editorial coordination
Antonio Maffeis
Sergio Nada

Translation
Zakiya Hanafi
(The Royal Cambridge school of English)

Illustrations
Andrea Rossi Raccagni

©1999 Giorgio Nada Editore, Vimodrone (Milan)
Previously printed in Italy

Motorbooks titles are also available at discounts in bulk quantity for industrial or sales-promotional use. For details write to Special Sales Manager at MBI Publishing Company, Galtier Plaza, Suite 200, 380 Jackson Street, St. Paul, MN 55101-3885 USA.

ISBN-13: 978-0-7603-1990-1
ISBN-10: 0-7603-1990-1

Printed in the United States of America

On the front cover: Aprilia's 2004 Mille R Factory demonstrates motorcycle dynamics. *Kevin Wing*

We would like to thank the following people for their help in writing this book:

Professor Vittore Cossalter, for his indispensable scientific support; Mr. Alan Cathcart, for his supervision of the English translation; Dr. Laura Bastianetto, for her help in writing the text; all the racers, test riders, mechanics, and designers in the Racing Department and in the Technical Department who have contributed to creating the wealth of Aprilia's technical knowledge.

CONTENTS

I would firstly like to thank my friend and long-term Aprilia staff member Gaetano Cocco for having conceived of and written this book, an important, much-needed work that fills a significant gap in the international motorcycling literature.

This is a book written for both motorcycling enthusiasts and youngsters hoping to become designers or technicians within the two-wheeled world. It draws on the wealth of experience accumulated by Aprilia over years of research, design and development of both road and race bikes. Today this know-how has been made available to all those interested in cultivating their passion for motorcycles through the study of the scientific and technical aspects of the field.

However, it would be overly simplistic to consider *How and Why: Motorcycle Design and Technology* as a form of technical manual for specialists of the present or the future. In reality this work describes with admirable simplicity and clarity the physical principals and laws that determine the behaviour of a two-wheeled vehicle, making them accessible to all. The secrets of acceleration and braking, banking in curves, broadslides and wheelies are all revealed here.

Mysteries are solved by this book. There are certain things that we know we cannot do . . . and others we do without knowing how. We do not need to study in order to learn how to ride on two wheels: it is something we master naturally, instinctively, exploiting our innate sense of balance.

This book instead teaches our minds how to ride a motorcycle. It explains scientifically how to obtain maximum performance and safety from two wheels. Those who read this book and are accustomed to mounting up and riding a motorcycle without giving it much thought will thus find themselves struck by sudden illuminations, flashbacks to moments and situations experienced in the past, a fall perhaps the reasons for which have never been fully understood.

For this reason I recommend this book to all. By illustrating the dynamics involved, Cocco

helps us to understand and better control our machines without, I believe, taking away any of the pleasure enjoyed by those who love the experience of riding a thundering motorcycle.

As a boy my great dream was that of one day becoming a motorcycling World Champion. I have to confess that I have always aimed high. Experience, however, has taught me that for certain people obstacles act as potent stimuli: thus the greater the dream, the greater the commitment and the determination to see that dream realised. This is as true of business enterprises – such as Aprilia – as it is of sporting goals; as valid for an entrepreneur as it is for a motorcycle rider.

Of course, in order to realise our dreams determination alone is not enough: we also need a degree of good fortune (and to tell the truth, it sometimes takes an awful lot). My own good fortune – and that of Aprilia – lies in having managed to gather around me in a few short years a young, resourceful staff, highly motivated by their passion for motorcycles and enthusiasm for racing.

I hope that this book will serve to transmit to the young people of today and those of the future eager to enter the fascinating world of the motorcycle, a little of this passion and enthusiasm that represent the true wealth of Aprilia. And to prepare them to tackle the challenges that await them in the third millennium.

Ivano Beggio

INTRODUCTION: A BOOK ABOUT MOTORCYCLES

WHY

To explain the fundamental parameters that influence the function and behavior of the main parts of the motorcycle, with the idea of enhancing your riding pleasure.

WHO THIS BOOK IS FOR

For anyone who has never ridden a motorcycle and who would like to join the world of bikes. It is never too late . . .

For young motorcycle enthusiasts.

For old hands with years of experience, who have motorcycles under their skin.

For aces with nerves of steel, who are at the same time style-conscious.

For well-informed technical experts who have plenty of know-how in the sector.

In a word, this is a book for everyone.

HOW

By means of a guided tour, even the most demanding and informed reader will be able to benefit from a complete presentation of technical back-up for a number of concepts that have never been so thoroughly explained.

The first part of the text examines the physical phenomena that make handling and control of the motorcycle possible; at the same time, it discusses the geometrical parameters that determine the dynamic behavior of the vehicle.

In the second, more informal part, we provide a complete illustration of the main components of the motorcycle and their basic functioning.

The final touch is added by lots of drawings, figures, and illustrations to help the reader visualize the topic at hand.

To make understanding of the concepts more interesting, they are often explained by comparing motorcycles to cars, showing both the similarities and fundamental differences between the structure and behavior of the two vehicles.

At heart, the real aim of this book is to allow the reader to hit the saddle with more awareness and understanding, to help truly bond with the motorcycle and, at the same time, to offer a little more active safety to the riding experience.

Beach riding is one of the most evocative images of the spirit of freedom that the motorcycle represents. The technical description of a "single-track" vehicle, as the motorcycle is called in the literature, is tied to the same image, precisely because of the characteristic single impression that it leaves behind when it passes over sand.

As we shall see, this peculiarity is the source of everything that makes the study of this vehicle so undeniably complex, and yet, at the same time, so surprising and fascinating.

The fact is, the means of transport that we generally use in our day-to-day movements, and which are so familiar to us that we drive them with ease, can all be essentially reduced to two categories: two-wheel and four-wheel vehicles.

The first category includes the bicycle and the motorcycle, which are equivalent, in terms of kinematics; the second category, obviously, includes the automobile, which is certainly the most studied vehicle today, with the largest bibliography.

Let us pause right here for further reflection. Without doubt, the most macroscopic difference between an automobile and a two-wheel vehicle involves the problem of balance:

• A crucial, if banal, consideration to keep in mind is that when a car is stationary, with or without passengers on board, it mantains a stable equilibrium, whereas a motorcycle at a standstill tends to fall over unless it is appropriately supported by the rider or propped up on a stand.

• A few simple observations bring to light some fundamental differences in approaching the two vehicles in a state of motion:

• A young person at the wheel for the first time in a car will quickly and intuitively grasp that when the steering wheel is turned in one direction, the car turns towards the same direction; beginner drivers are soon able to guide a car quite accurately in the direction they want to go in;

• Whereas even an adult inevitably has to face the potentially embarrassing difficulties associated with trying to ride a bicycle for the first time—beginner riders are pratically forced to drop their feet to the ground in order to keep their balance while trying to make the bike go in the right direction.

At first they will find themselves teetering around to stop from falling over; but before long, they will catch on to the fact that the faster the bike goes, the easier it is to keep their balance.

Handling and control of a two-wheel vehicle is, in fact, anything but simple and intuitive, as we shall see. It may be surprising to discover that our riding behavior is often dictated by complex "riding strategies" that our brain has unconsciously elaborated.

It is precisely our familiarity with the vehicle and our feeling of mastery over it that make it seem like such a part of us; so much so that we may lose sight of a question that is anything but banal: what are the physical phenomena that allow a rider to keep the motorcycle upright, to travel in a straight line and then to go around corners?

The first part of the book explores all of these themes, avoiding potentially complex and overly rigorous explanations in order to get to the heart of the matter in an accessible way.

With this goal in mind, we will identify the geometrical parameters that have the greatest effect on the dynamic behavior of the motorcycle. In other words, we will look into how such fundamental quantities as the center of gravity height, the wheelbase, and the trail value go about determining a motorbike's 'character.'

We will also attempt to explain how to go about controlling a motorcycle in various situations, so as to develop rider awareness of the satisfaction and pleasure that a bike offers its rider once the right handling techniques have been mastered.

There is no doubt that a motorcycle is a functional means of transport, but it is also, and especially, a thrilling source of enjoyment.

The second, simpler and more descriptive part of this book is devoted to illustrating the basic components of the machine.

Our intention is certainly not to offer yet another technical parts manual, but rather, to particularly focus the reader's attention on the design criteria derived from the ideas presented in the following chapters.

As we all know from personal experience, the hardest part about learning to ride a bicycle comes with the first impact; in the same way, the novelty and scope of the concepts in this opening chapter could present an initial challenge to the reader. Once this "obstacle" is overcome, the chapters that follow will be much easier to read and understand.

As we have already hinted, the inexperienced rider of a two-wheel vehicle (whether a motorcycle or a bicycle) must first tackle the problem of keeping his or her balance while controlling the direction of forward motion.

We will start, then, by describing and analyzing the factors that come into play and that can help our rider simply keep the bike in a vertical and "stable" position while traveling in a straight line.

These factors are essentially:

- **inertia effects;**
- **gyroscopic effects;**
- **righting effect due to trail.**

INERTIA EFFECTS

The stabilizing effect due to inertia forces is intuitively easy to grasp and explain.

The product of mass multiplied by the velocity of a body gives the quantity of motion of the body.

The greater this value is, the less influence external forces will have on the trajectory.

Let us imagine traveling on a motorcycle at a fairly constant high speed, for example, 100 km/h. If, for example, the vehicle also acquires a velocity of 10 km/h perpendicular to the original trajectory thanks to a gust of wind, the resultant velocity will be that indicated in Figure 3.1a by the arrow V_{res}.

In angular terms, the variation of the direction of travel (now determined by the resultant velocity) will be very slight, as clearly indicated in the figure.

If, instead, the motorbike proceeds at a much slower speed, for example, 10 km/h, the same component velocity determined by the gust of wind will bring on, in angular terms, a considerable variation in the direction of travel, as illustrated in Figure 3.1b.

We can see, then, that as the velocity increases, small directional variations orthogonal to the original direction will bring on ever smaller angular variations in the direction.

We can therefore state that the greater the forward velocity, the more difficult it is to shift the vehicle from its initial straight-line trajectory.

The same concept can be applied to mass.

It is obvious from common experience that the heavier a body is, the more it resists changes to its conditions of motion, that is, to its speed and direction.

In fact, instead of two equal vehicles that proceed at different speeds, let us consider two

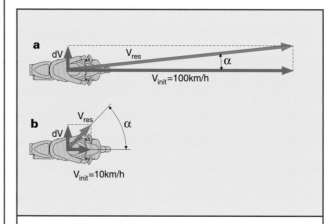

Fig. 3.1: as the velocity increases, small directional variations orthoganal to the original direction will bring on ever smaller variations in the direction.

V_{init} = initial velocity
V_{res} = resultant velocity
dV = variation in velocity
α = angular variation in velocity

vehicles whose weights are significantly different: for example, a scooter and a large touring bike that proceed at the same speed. Allow us to apply at an instant the same disturbing force. The resulting variation in velocity for each body will be inversely proportional to its mass.

In conclusion, then, by increasing the *velocity* and *mass* of a motorcycle it is easier to maintain a straight-line trajectory.

GYROSCOPIC EFFECTS

To provide a rigorous explanation of the laws of physics that produce gyroscopic effects would be too long and too complex for our purposes. Let us simply say that every time a body spins rapidly on its axis and at the same time is put into rapid spin around a second axis, what arises is what in the literature is referred to as a "**gyroscopic effect**" or, rather, a moment that acts around a third axis perpendicular to the other two.

Daily life offers many common examples of gyroscopic effects: to stay close to our subject of two-wheel vehicles, for example, try giving a good spin to a bicycle wheel while holding it between your hands, as in Fig. 3.2. Raise and lower the wheel straight up and down, keeping it axially parallel to itself. You will notice no opposing action on your hands. In other words, the opposing vertical force needed to perform the action will never be more than the weight of the wheel itself.

Try now instead to turn the axis of the wheel quite quickly in a clockwise motion around the vertical axis, as if you were steering handlebars. In this case you will notice that your arms are affected by a couple that tends to rotate them around the longitudinal axis.

Figure 3.3 is meant to help visualize what we have described.

A number of observations can be made at this point:

- the faster the wheel is made to rotate, the more obvious the effect will be;
- by tilting the axis faster or slower, the intensity of the reaction will differ significantly.

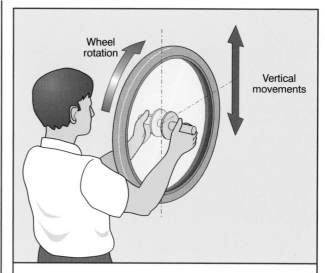

Fig. 3.2: raise and lower your arms; the only opposing action you will feel is that of the weight of the wheel.

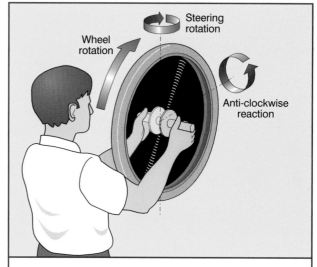

Fig. 3.3: you will notice the force of a couple acting on your arms.

In fact, the mathematical expression that quantifies gyroscopic moment is the following:

Equation 3.1

$$M_{gyr} = I_r \bullet \omega_r \bullet \omega_s$$

where:

I_r is the moment of inertia of the wheel around the spin axis;

ω_r is the rotation velocity expressed in radiants/second;

ω_s is the velocity with which the axis is rotated on the plane of the wheel, expressed in radiants/sec.

If the hands-on demonstration of the gyroscopic effect came as a surprise to you, this demonstration of how to halt the gyroscopic effect in the case of two oppositely rotating shafts might come as an even bigger surprise. This time, hold up two bicycle wheels on the same axis and spin them in opposite directions. No opposing actions will be felt as you turn their axes.

And now, finally, we get to the motorcycle.

We will offer a brief description of the three main gyroscopic effects that come into play in motorcycle systems:

- The first, called the **steering** moment, relates to the front wheel as it is being turned; this is practically identical to the situation described in the previous example. The wheel is spinning around its own axis and at the same time is being turned by the rider when changing directions. The moment that is created in this case tends to lean the bike away from the direction towards which it is being steered, making turns more difficult (Figure 3.4).

- The second, producing a stabilizing effect and referred to as the **roll** moment, concerns the vehicle as a whole, assuming the steering were blocked; whenever the entire bike leans to one side (rolls), with the wheels continuously rotating around their axes, the moment that is generated tends to roll the whole vehicle around an axis that is perpendicular to the ground (in popular terms, we say the bike yaws); if the rider maintains the handlebars straight, the reactions of the tires tend to right the vehicle (Figure 3.5).

- The third, called the **yaw** moment, also produces a stabilizing effect and is created during turns: it is produced by the wheels spinning around their own axes and at the same time in rotation around the center of the curve;

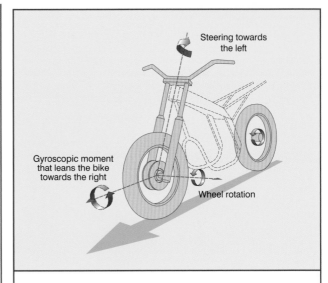

Fig. 3.4: steering moment.

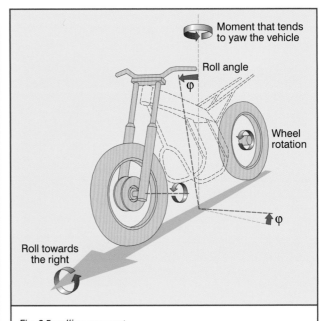

Fig. 3.5: rolling moment.

the moment generated in this case tends to keep the bike in a vertical position (Figure 3.6).

Just to understand each of these phenomena separately is a rather complex task. Since *they produce rotation effects, these, in turn, go on to trigger other gyroscopic phenomena.* As a result, while the motorbike is in motion, the various combinations that are created are exceedingly complex to describe, to quantify, and thus, to explain.

Without going into too much detail, we can simply say that the dynamics of the motorcycle include numerous gyroscopic phenomena which heavily influence how the vehicle rides.

Gyroscopic phenomena contribute, in any case, to transforming the motorcycle from an apparently "acrobatic" vehicle into what is, in reality, a perfectly controllable means of transportation.

In any case, the faster the vehicle goes, the more the gyroscopic effects help to keep the motorcycle upright and moving in a straight-line.

In addition to the wheels, there is another element not to be overlooked which is responsible for generating a significant gyroscopic effect: that is *the engine,* with its rotating parts, which is usually characterized by a crankshaft parallel to the axis of the wheels, rotating in the same direction.

Considering, for example, the crankshaft and the flywheel of a 600 cc enduro bike engine, we can note the following:

• Their combined weight is comparable to the weight of a wheel, including rim and tire;

• The diameter (which, along with the mass, determines the axial moment of inertia) is clearly smaller;

• The rotational speed, instead, can be very high, varying between 800 r.p.m., when the motor is idling, up to 7000 r.p.m. at maximum revolution speed;

• As a consequence, the gyroscopic effect is also very variable: a small value when idling, but a large one when the motor is revved up.

Furthermore it is independent of the speed of the motorcycle.

As we have seen this is not the case with the wheels. In first gear, at low speeds, the gyroscopic effect of the wheels is of little importance, but when the motor is running at top speed the gyroscopic effect relating to its rotating masses is strong.

After all these theoretical observations, we propose a practical demonstration which, if approached with the right sensitivity, makes it

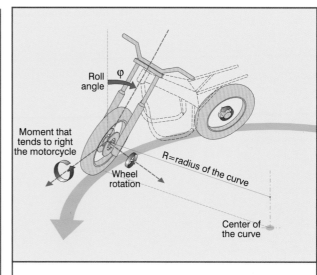

Fig. 3.6: yawing moment.

possible to feel how the gyroscopic effect of the engine contributes to keeping the motorcycle upright and moving in a straight-line.

Take an enduro bike at walking pace (4-5 km/h) down a steep, rough path, like a flight of steps or a rocky, wet trail.

Do it once with the motor off and then again in neutral, keeping the engine revved up. *Going down a slope with the motor revved up you will notice that the motorbike is steadier and more stable.*

For the same reason, we can state that when a motor is provided with a large flywheel and is kept revved up, it is easier to keep the bike balanced in a stationary position (so-called "sur place").

Another observation - one which we do not recommend trying, but which can be put to the test by wheelie enthusiasts - is that when the lifted front wheel begins to slow down or stop rotating, it becomes more and more difficult to keep the bike balanced.

RIGHTING EFFECTS

Up until now we have examined two stabilizing factors that do not depend on the general geometrical characteristics of the vehicle, that is to say, they are independent of the quantities that are generally considered fundamental in defining the handling ability of a motorcycle: for example, the rake angle, the position of the center of gravity, the wheelbase, etc.

The **righting effect** is, rather, a parameter that is heavily influenced by the geometrical characteristics of the steering unit of the bike; and it is dependent on a number of parameters. The correct combination of these factors gives rise to a more or less satisfying perception of stability.

This phenomenon is thus worth studying in detail.

Premise: all motorcycles, regardless of the structure of their particular suspension, are characterized by a front steering wheel; that is, a front wheel that is free to rotate around an axis, which is called, in fact, the **steering axis** (Figure 3.7).

If, then, the front suspension is designed with a telescopic fork structure, it is easy to identify the steering axis, because it coincides with the axis of the guide bearings inside the slider around which the fork rotates. This steering axis, present in all kinds of automobile-type suspensions, is inclined with respect to the vertical at an angle called the **rake (or castor) angle**. The following section, departing from this premise, is generally valid for all cases.

The distance between the point of intersection of the steering axi*s with the ground and the* point of contact of the front wheel with the ground (also known as 'contact patch') *is called* **trail** (designated simply as **t** in Figure 3. 9).

Generally, the wheel axis does not lie on the steering axis; rather, it lies at a distance of measurement referred to as offset (**d**) (Figure 3. 10).

In the following section, then, for simplicity's sake, we will suppose that *the steering axis passes through the center of the wheel (zero offset).*

Looking at the next figure, imagine being seated on a motorcycle traveling in a straight-line at a constant speed. Let us suppose that a slight irregularity in the road causes a rotation of the steering towards the right.

The point of contact wheel-to-ground will shift, sliding to the left with respect to the axis of the motorcycle (see Figure 3.11). We know from physics that whenever there is a relative sliding movement, a force of friction is also created, going in the opposite direction.

This force will therefore act on the tire and will go on to determine a moment with respect to the steering axis whose arm, (the length of the

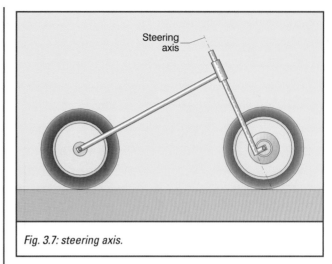

Fig. 3.7: steering axis.

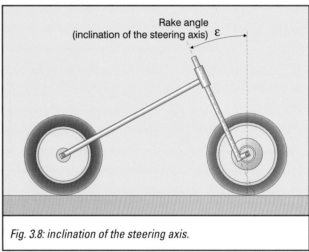

Fig. 3.8: inclination of the steering axis.

perpendicular distance from the line along which the force is applied) is proportional to the **trail**.

This moment tends to right the wheel, creating an effect that keeps the vehicle upright and moving in a straight-line.

This effect, called the **righting effect** in the literature, is of crucial importance for how the bike handles. We will use this section to analyse what the most influential parameters are that determine it.

The situation we are studying and a breakdown of the velocity are illustrated in Figure 3.12, where: **V** is the vector of the front wheel travel speed, which can be further broken down into two components:

• **the first** ($\omega_f R_f$), lies on the plane of the wheel and will be equal to the product of the radius R_f multiplied by the rotation speed;

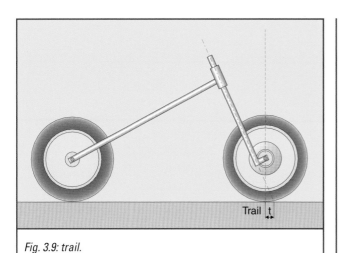

Fig. 3.9: trail.

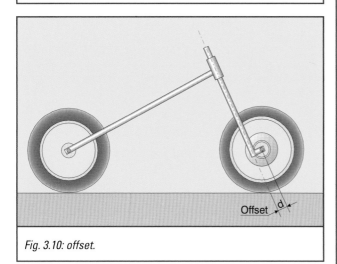

Fig. 3.10: offset.

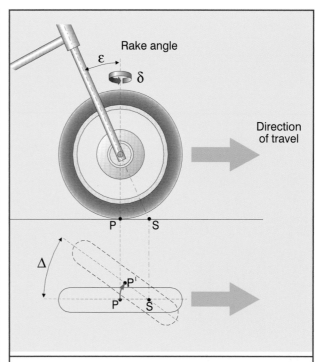

Fig. 3.11: turning the wheel towards the right (with zero roll), the point of contact shifts to the left of the direction of travel.
S= Point at which the steering axis intersects with the ground.
P= Point of contact between wheel and ground
P¹= Point of contact after steering is turned.

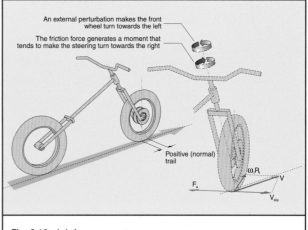

Fig. 3.12: righting moment.

• **the second** (V_{slip}), is perpendicular to the first and corresponds to the velocity of sliding wheel-to-ground.

In the case of a negligible angle of roll in the rear end (the motorcycle is roughly vertical), it can be demonstrated that the final relation that the righting moment value expresses is the following:

Equation 3.2

$$M = t_n \cdot (F_f \cdot \cos \beta - N_f \cdot \sin \beta)$$

where:

t_n is a geometrical measure, to be exact, a value proportional to the trail of the bike and it represents the orthogonal projection onto the steering axis;

β represents the angle of roll of the front wheel;

F_f and N_f are two forces: F_f is given by the relation:

Equation 3.3

$$F_f = m \cdot \frac{v^2}{R} \cdot \frac{b}{\sin \Delta} + f \cdot N_f \cdot \tan\Delta$$

and represents the side force acting on the tire, while N_f represents the vertical load on the front wheel and is represented by the following expression:

Equation 3.4

$$N_f = mg \cdot \frac{b}{wb} - F \cdot \frac{h}{wb}$$

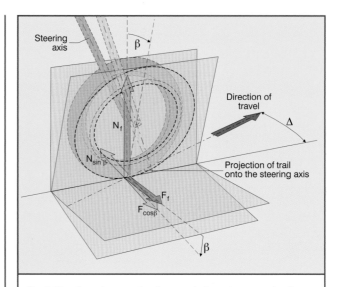

Fig. 3.13: *when the steering is turned, there is a reaction from the ground at the point of contact between wheel and ground.*

where, in both:

Δ corresponds to the actual steer angle of the wheel;

wb is the wheelbase of the motorcycle, or, the distance between the two wheel axles;

mg is the weight, while b is its distribution. The smaller b is, along with the wheelbase, the more load there will be on the front wheel;

f is the coefficient of friction tire-ground;

V represents the velocity of the vehicle;

R represents the radius of curvature of the trajectory taken;

F is the force on the ground of the vehicle's traction.

Focusing our attention now on the expression of the righting moment (Equation 3.2), we observe that the factor between parentheses ($F_f \cdot \cos_\beta - N_f \cdot \sin_\beta$) is generally positive, so during normal use of the bike it is the trail, which appears as a factor of amplification, that determines the positive or negative sign of the moment. If the righting moment is positive, which is clearly the case in most instances, it helps to keep the bike upright and moving in a straight-line.

When the righting moment has a high, positive value it means that, when traveling in a straight-line, the motorcycle is directionally very stable. That is to say, the steering head always tends to "straighten" itself after having encountered a perturbation such as a pothole, or simply after an involuntary turn of the handle bars.

Making use of a good righting moment can be an advantage when you are traveling on the freeway and on high-speed roads, but it can become a limitation for city use or on narrow, winding mountain roads where it should be easy to maneuver the bike and vary its path of travel.

This is where we begin to discern the inevitable need to compromise between **stability** and **ease of handling**.

If *the righting moment is negative,* the rider must intervene by adjusting the steering and by shifting his or her weight in order to keep the bike balanced.

The formula that expresses the value of the righting moment (Equation 3.2) is rather complicated, as anyone who has thought it over will agree.

M = trail · dynamic factor

In a more simplified way it can also be expressed in this form:

where:

M naturally, represents the righting moment;

$trail$ is the geometrical characteristic introduced at the beginning of this section and represented in Figure 3.9;

a – rake angle	1 – weight
b – wheel radius	2 – speed of travel
c – offset	3 – coefficient of friction tire-ground

M = trail • dynamic factor

dynamic factor represents a factor that depends on the characteristics of the vehicle and on its conditions of motion.

In order to cut straight to the heart of the phenomena and to avoid complicated analytical explanations, we will describe the influence of the righting moment and the "dynamic factor" only in terms of the three main factors that come into play in determining them.

TRAIL

When the trail is negative, or rather, when the steering axis meets the ground behind the point of contact wheel-to-ground, the direction of the force of friction will remain unchanged. But the sign of the moment acting on the steering will be inverted, tending to favour rotation of the front end towards the direction of steering (and the consequences of this could be disastrous, even for the most experienced rider).

Clearly, from what we have seen, all models of motorcycles are designed with this consideration in mind to give a quite high, positive value for trail, between 40 and 110 mm. Nevertheless, during normal use of the bike there may occur situations in which the trail value suddenly drops.

Let us suppose that the vehicle comes up against a step. Take a look at the Figure 3.15:

In static conditions, trail is equal to CP, but in the instant of impact with the step, it suddenly diminishes to C'P'. When the irregularity in the surface is large enough, trail can even take on a negative value (see Figure 3.16).

Motorcyclists should be aware of this, especially when cornering: the righting effect can be diminished whenever the bike is traveling over rough or uneven surfaces. A rapid succession of changing trail values can bring on sudden changes in the righting moment, causing temporary loss of control of the vehicle.

By applying a few geometrical transformations we can also express trail as:

Equation 3.5

$$t = R_f \cdot \tan \varepsilon \cdot \cos\delta - \frac{\sqrt{1 - (\sin\delta \cdot \sin\varepsilon)^2}}{\cos\varepsilon} \cdot d$$

where:

R_f represents the radius of the front wheel;
ε inclination of the rake angle;
δ the turning of the steering;
d offset.

In this case, too, we see that the formula is capable of producing both positive and negative values when the final term is bigger.

Let us go on, *keeping a zero rake angle,* to analyze the influence of various factors, modifying them one at a time so as to understand each one individually.

a) inclination of the rake angle (ε)

Just like all the other parameters, when you increase the angle of the steering axis you increase the value of trail (see Figure 3.17).

Generally we can state that *the steeper the inclination of the rake angle, the more the motorcycle is directionally stable.*

Now we understand why motorbikes that are mainly for highway or use in wide-open spaces, like **custom** bikes, have a steep rake angle, starting from 28 degrees and reaching 40 degrees on some American beach bikes. Motorcycles meant for competitive or sports-oriented uses are characterized

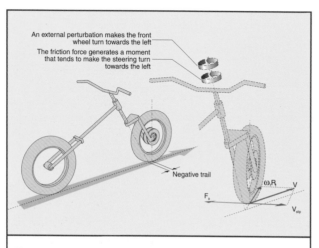

Fig. 3.14: righting moment and negative trail.

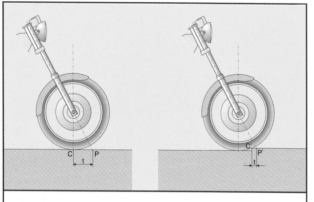

Fig. 3.15: abrupt trail variation due to an obstacle.

instead by smaller rake angles (some Grand Prix bikes have as little as 21 degrees.)

b) wheel radius (R_f)

Keeping all the other parameters constant, we note that by increasing the radius of the wheel, we also increase the trail. If you substitute your front wheel rim with a different wheel diameter, it can bring about large differences in the behavior of the vehicle.

The motorcycle is so sensitive to the trail value that just by changing the height of sidewalls of your tires you will notice a difference in the handling. Clearly, the diameter of the wheels has a profound effect on the comfort level of the bike:

• let us suppose that there is a hollow in the surface of the road, as illustrated in Figure 3.18. We can see that the wheel with the bigger diameter does not sink as far down into the hole as the smaller wheel, so the rider is less aware of it. At the same time, obviously, speed and acceleration will also be less affected, making it easier to adjust the suspension settings.

When traveling over a raised bump, instead, the distance that the two wheels must be raised, even if they have different diameters, will always be the same for both. What changes, though, are the vertical velocities and acceleration values placed on the wheels.

As shown in Figure 3.19, the larger the wheel diameter is, the greater the distance AO' between the projection onto the ground of the wheel center and the point of contact with the obstacle. Thus, with equal speed of travel, the wheel will take longer to go up over the bump (as we can see, when the center of the wheel is directly vertical above the obstacle, the wheel must be raised the distance represented by Z).

By using wheels with a large radius, then, the velocity and acceleration values of the unsprung masses will be diminished, which, as we will see in the next chapter on suspension, is all to the benefit of a comfortable ride.

Scooters are a classic example of this principle: their 10-inch wheel rims are perfectly functional on smooth surfaces, on badly paved roads and on rough terrains, but they give a less comfortable ride than a bike with wide wheels. This is why big-wheel scooters were introduced, to ride well on bumpy pavement and on cobblestone streets.

On the other hand, the adoption of big rims for scooters brings with it certain limitations: a reduction in the storage space under the seat and a design form that is more conditioned by the size of the wheels.

In terms of design, the best choice of wheel diameter to use for any particular model thus becomes a question of optimizing a number of different factors. The final decision will be based primarily on the kind of motorcycle that is desired and the degree of comfort that is considered acceptable.

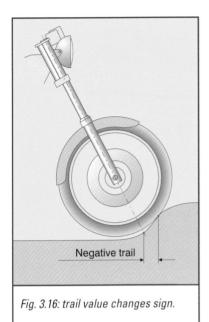

Fig. 3.16: trail value changes sign.

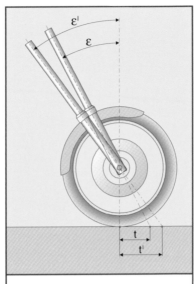

Fig. 3.17: various rake angles (inclination of the steering axis).

c) offset

$$t = R_f \cdot \tan \varepsilon \cdot \cos\delta - \frac{\sqrt{1 - (\sin\delta \cdot \sin\varepsilon)^2}}{\cos\varepsilon} \cdot d$$

All motorcycles currently in production have their wheel center forward of the steering axis, as we have already discussed.

It is clear that, as offset (d) appears in the equation 3.5

as a multiplicative factor of the negative term, when it increases, trail decreases.

Generally, the offset is created by means of the triple clamps (see Figure 3.20).

Sometimes, in motocross bikes, part of the offset is obtained directly by means of the fork, through the particular form of the axle mounting lugs (see Fig. 3.21).

In fact, this makes it possible to lengthen the sliders of the fork legs, allowing them a greater range of travel.

Varying combinations of offset and rake angle determine the amount of trail.

Naturally, it is possible to obtain the same amount of trail using different combinations of rake angle and offset.

When needed, it is possible to come up with solutions that create zero offset or zero rake.

For most everyday applications, we generally find offset values that range from 25 to 40 mm. In combination with the right rake angle, we are able to produce the amount of trail desired.

Bicycles also have offset: in their case, it is produced by the curvature of the front fork.

The objective here is not to maintain some pre-set steering head geometry, but rather, more simply, to allow a certain amount of flexibility to the fork, and thus to transmit less force onto the frame when the wheel goes over a bump-this improves the riding comfort (remember that bicycles do not have a suspension).

Let us now return to the diagram on page 21 and proceed to analyze the three main factors that determine the "dynamic factor."

DYNAMIC FACTOR

As we have said, the term "dynamic factor" used here indicates a rather complex analytical expression that depends on the geometrical parameters of the vehicle, but especially on the forces that act on the front end (hence, the adjective "dynamic"). These forces (the reader is encouraged to consult Equation 3.2, Equation 3.3, Equation 3.4) are heavily influenced by:

1) the weight of the vehicle (including that of the rider) and its distribution;
2) the speed of travel;
3) the coefficient of friction between the tire and the ground.

Let us analyze each of these factors separately:

1) weight and its distribution

As the weight increases, the dynamic factor and, along with it, the righting moment, also increase in absolute value (regardless of the sign).

This means that when the moment is negative, a heavy bike leans and falls over more easily; conversely, if the moment is positive, for example,

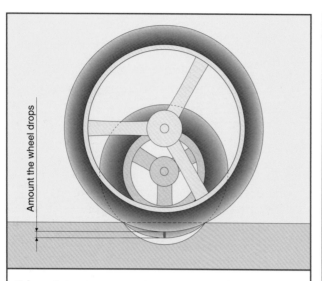

Amount the wheel drops

Fig. 3.18: influence of the wheel radius when passing over a hole.

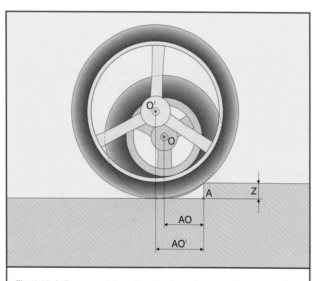

Fig. 3.19: influence of the wheel radius when passing over a rise.

at high speeds, it is easier for the vehicle to keep upright and moving in a straight-line.

The importance of the weight distribution onto the two axles of the motorcycle is of great interest in this context: its value is indicated in the figure by the letter b, which specifically represents the distance between the rear wheel axis and the center of gravity projected along the axis of the ground.

A small value for b indicates a center of gravity shifted towards the rear wheel, conversely, a high value for b indicates a forward center of gravity, that is, shifted more towards the front of the bike.

The distribution of the bike's weight is one of the most important parameters in achieving ease of handling. The balancing of the motorbike is carefully worked out during the design and testing phases of a new model and, in fact, the correct distribution of weight always constitutes an endless source of discussion.

A large load on the front wheel makes it difficult to slide the wheel sideways when turning the handle bar in a stationary position or at low speeds; in other words, the motorbike is difficult to handle in these circumstances, while at high speeds, when the aerodynamic effect also tends to raise the front end, the same heavy load guarantees a good contact with the ground and, thus, greater stability.

On the contrary, it can easily be seen that a zero load on the front end leads to a lack of righting moment and, thus, greater difficulty in maintaining control over the vehicle.

In any case, the correct distribution of weight depends on the kind of motorcycle and especially on its intended use, or rather, on the range of speed within which it is likely to be used.

A road racing bike, for instance, which always takes turns at a high speed (generally higher than 60 km/h) should have adequate weight on the front end, since possible handling problems at low speeds (20 to 30 km/h) are relatively unimportant.

Of course, the weight of the rider cannot be overlooked. We have said that a motorcycle can weigh between 70 kg for a low-powered bike, up to 220 kg for a supersport bike, and the weight is often distributed 50/50 between front and rear.

The average weight of a rider, including motorcycle gear, can be estimated to be around 75 kg., or in other terms, the relation between the weight of the rider and the weight of the motorcycle can vary between approximately 1:1 to 1:3.

From this observation it becomes clear that the position the rider assumes within the rider-plus-motorcycle unit is relevant to the weight distribution; in fact, the rider is easily able to increase or decrease the front-wheel load (up to as much as 5 to 7 kg.) by shifting positions, thus noticeably varying the balance and behavior of the whole bike.

Take the case of a motocross bike: the whole vehicle is specifically designed for the rider to be able to easily shift through a full range of positions.

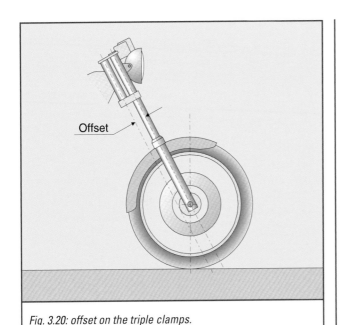

Fig. 3.20: offset on the triple clamps.

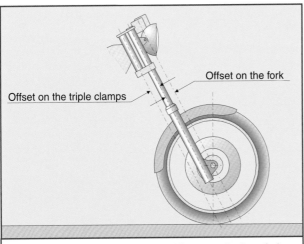

Fig. 3.21: distribution of offset shared between the front fork and the triple clamps.

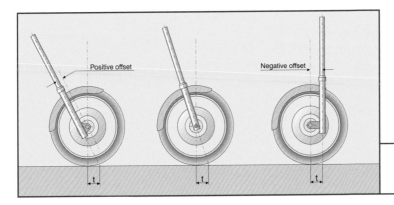

A motorcycle rider is not, therefore, an easily moulded, inert mass attached to the seat (that is, rigidly fixed to the chassis). Since he or she has the power to heavily influence the bike's weight distribution by shifting around according to what the situation and the characteristics of the vehicle demand, the rider must be considered a body characterized by an adequate number of degrees of freedom.

This vastly complicates development of all the mathematical models used to describe bike maneuverability and handling that are currently being developed by motorcycle manufacturers. In fact, it is very difficult to simulate the behavior of a rider, for example, during the various phases of cornering.

It also explains why in the racing world we often hear that a bike was "made-to-measure" for a specific racer: it is the only way to make the machine efficient. A different racer on the same machine might very well not be comfortable and could require a different attitude in order to get the best results from the bike.

Generally when a rider mounts a bike, in sitting position *his or her weight falls mainly on the rear end,* bringing the distribution up to 60% over the rear: this percentage rises even more with a passenger on board and with *extra luggage* loaded onto the rear.

We have already observed that with a *lighter front load,* the righting moment diminishes, and that a significant overall weight has a negative effect on the "agility" and, consequently, on the handling ability of the vehicle. It makes sense, then, to pay attention when you take on a passenger because the performance of the bike can be noticeably altered.

Baggage placed on top of the fuel tank has less of an influence on the variations in weight distribution since it is generally located near the center of gravity or even adds slightly to the load on the front wheel.

2) speed

This works in favour of the stability of the motorcycle, as would be clear if we analyzed Equation 3.3, in which the

Fig. 3.22: the same amount of trail can be created with various rake angles and offset values.

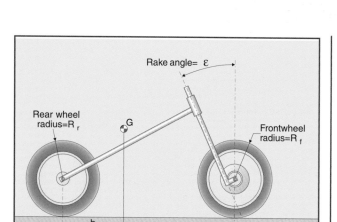

Fig. 3.23: center of gravity and weight distribution.

speed of travel of the vehicle appears in the expression of lateral force.

This consideration, too, helps to explain why even at maximum speeds now attainable by high-powered bikes (over 280 km/h) the rider still retains a feeling of mastery.

The formula for the righting moment shows that for each motorcycle, as a function of its geometrical parameters, there exists a minimum speed at which the righting moment is rendered positive (for positive trail).

In simple terms, at very low speeds (walking pace) *the stabilizing moment is insufficient* to keep the bike upright and riders must count on their own ability to control the motorcycle by turning the steering and by shifting their body weight. As the speed increases, the righting moment helps to keep the bike upright and the rider's efforts become easier.

All modern motorcycles designed for road use become stable at moderate speeds; in any case, if

you try out various vehicles you will notice that they behave differently at a walking pace.

3) coefficient of friction

It is easy to describe the influence that the coefficient of friction has on the "dynamic factor" and, thus, on the righting moment.

When the coefficient of friction is high, the bike rides better.

With a zero coefficient of friction it would not be possible to control the vehicle; just think about when the bike passes over an icy or oily patch on the road.

We will go more into this and the workings of the coefficient of friction in the chapter on tires.

In this chapter we have dealt with the factors that allow riders to keep their balance on a motorcycle while traveling in a straight-line.

Of course there are many more aspects, with far more complicated effects, than one would expect.

To be specific, we have seen that *when the velocity increases, the stabilizing forces tend to increase in equal measure,* so that even inexperienced riders realize that they feel much less clumsy when they manage to work up to a good speed rather than keeping the bike at a walking pace.

This is not meant to suggest that everybody should launch themselves onto the road at the speed of light!

Even though it is true that by increasing your speed you can take advantage of greater stability in terms of maintaining a straight-line trajectory, high-speed handling has it own dangers: remember that the speed at which you must react to unexpected, sudden obstacles increases along with the speed of the vehicle, while your reaction time, unfortunately, remains the same.

CHAPTER 4
CONTROL OF THE MOTORCYCLE WHEN CORNERING

In Chapter 3 we analyzed all the aspects that keep a motorcycle upright while moving in a straight line as well as the main factors that make the vehicle directionally stable.

We now propose to explain how to corner in the direction you want while at the same time maintaining control over the vehicle.

To understand how a two-wheel vehicle like a bicycle or a motorcycle goes around a corner at the rider's command is actually quite complex. What we are asking, in essence, is how one goes about introducing a variation in side force necessary to change directions; and how a motorcycle, a single-track vehicle, then, with no supporting points on its sides, is able to turn without falling over.

Airplanes have wing profiles, which can be appropriately tilted to provide a "push" on the air, a necessary component for changing directions; spaceships can count on the thrust of their rockets to do the same thing.

Let us look for a moment at two phenomena that play a very important role in allowing motorcyclists to corner. They are:

- **centrifugal force;**
- **gyroscopic effects.**

CENTRIFUGAL FORCE

What is the centrifugal force? It is a pseudo-force that opposes a rotating motion, acting at the center of gravity of the body under consideration.

Its direction is given by the conjunction between the center of gravity and the center of curvature of the trajectory of the mass; it is directed radially toward the outside of the curve.

The intensity of such a force is expressed in the well-known relation:

Equation 4.1

$$F_c = \frac{M \cdot V^2}{R}$$

where:

M is the mass of the motorcycle;
V is the velocity of the motorcycle;
R is the radius of curvature of the trajectory

GYROSCOPIC EFFECTS

Let us once again take up the concept of gyroscopic effect, introduced in the previous chapter, and add a few new observations to it.

With straight arms, hold up a bicycle-wheel axle as illustrated in Figure 4.2, as if you were riding on a bicycle; turn the wheel in front of you, imagining that its axle is the handlebar.

As we have seen, raising and lowering this axle parallel to itself, no extraneous forces are felt on your hands because the sole force to be opposed is the weight of the wheel itself.

Try now to "steer" firmly towards your **left**, as if you were cornering in that direction.

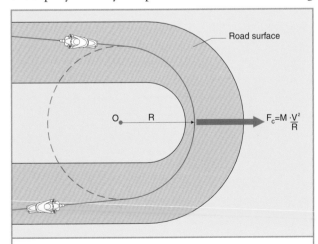

Fig. 4.1: cornering.

R= radius of curvature

O= instantaneous center of curvature of the trajectory

F_c = *centrifugal force*

Centrifugal force
G_m G=overall centre of gravity
Body force
G
G_m°
G
G_p
G_m°

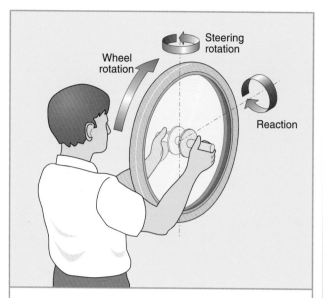

Steering rotation

Wheel rotation

Reaction

Fig. 4.2: gyroscopic effect when turning the steering.

The effect may come as a surprise to you: what you will feel is the action of a couple on your arms that tends to make them tilt clockwise with respect to the direction of imagined travel.

TURNS

At this point, keep in mind the concepts of centrifugal force and gyroscopic effect as they have just been presented, because **we are ready to go around our first corner, for example, to the right.**

Putting the wheel back onto the bicycle, mount the bike and pedal until you work up to a good speed. At this point, perform the maneuver just described above in the section on gyroscopic effects: that is to say, **a rapid but brief turn of the handlebars to the left.**

That's right, we are quite serious: remember that our intention is to corner to the right, but trust us for a moment and see what happens.

Since the bicycle is changing directions, both a centrifugal force and a gyroscopic effect are created, with the following consequences:

- *the centrifugal force* that acts on the center of gravity, being directed outwardly away from the curve, will tend to overturn the bike, leaning it towards the right;

- *the gyroscopic effect* will give rise to a comparable effect, as a consequence of the pull of the handlebars to the left, creating a couple that will lean the vehicle ever more towards the right (clockwise with respect to the direction of travel).

Unless something else intervenes at this point to create a new state of equilibrium, the situation will inevitably deteriorate and the bike will fall over. And yet, it is just as we are losing control of the bike that we are also about to go around the corner!

We have said that our bike is leaning towards the right and that the rider also feels a sensation of falling towards the right. Let us now turn the steering, making a slow rotation to the **right**: this places the bicycle on a circular path (or rather, in a curve towards the **right**), giving rise to a centrifugal force that will bring about a new state of balance, as described in Figure 4.3.

The force of the bike's weight, tending to make the motorcycle fall inwardly, combined with the centrifugal force, will give rise to a resultant force along the axis that connects the point of contact wheel-to-ground with the center of gravity.

What we are describing is a state of balance.
Please note that we are presently describing a corner towards the **right**, *even though the maneuver began with a turn of the handlebars towards the* **left**.

This explains why even adults who mount a bicycle for the first time find it difficult to make a proper turn without placing a foot on the ground to support themselves.

That initial impulse of turning the handlebars in the opposite direction to the corner you want to take would seem to be an unconscious mechanism developed by the brain as it elaborates a sophisticated control system of which we remain largely unaware. Nobody, it seems, has ever learned to ride a bicycle by analyzing the process in a rational way.

This impulse gradually becomes a conditioned reflex and every time we ride a bicycle or a motorcycle, that mechanism is triggered automatically.

As we can clearly see from Figure 4. 3, once we are in a corner, a state of balance is achieved that accounts for that familiar feeling of mastery over the motorcycle.

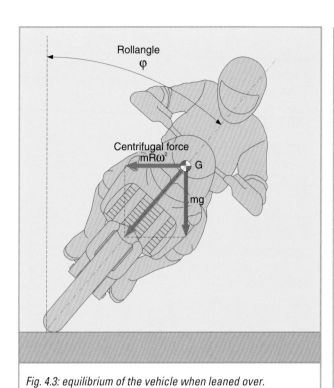

Fig. 4.3: equilibrium of the vehicle when leaned over.

Roll angle (also called angle of lean and banking angle): the angle between the verticle and the axis of the motorcycle.

The next time you take a ride on your motorbike, focus your attention on the aspects we have just analyzed: you will be able to perform your first turn while keeping aware of the mechanics involved in cornering.

As we can see, then, even a relatively simple mechanical object such as a bicycle reveals a riding dynamic that is intuitive in nature and anything but banal. Two different phenomena—the centrifugal force and gyroscopic effects—compete to allow the vehicle to follow a curved path.

Obviously, at very low speeds the gyroscopic effect is practically nil and handling will be most strongly affected by the centrifugal force.

The faster you go, the greater the contribution of the gyroscopic effect. However, since both phenomena act in the same direction, when you pass from low to high speeds your handling should remain unchanged.

Someone might object that the theories described above are inconsistent or incomplete: in reality, in fact, you could just as well *ride the motorcycle without having your hands on the handlebars at all* and still describe a perfect curve.

The fact is, however, that the "technique" remains the same, but it is applied in different ways since, in this case, we are affecting the banking angle of the motorcycle.

Let us suppose we are moving in a straight line with our hands off the handlebars: in order to steer the motorcycle to **the right** we will lean the bike slightly to the left. The steering head will follow the movement of the frame, leaning in the same direction and will create that small angle opposite to the direction of the curve that is necessary to corner in the traditional way.

At this point we lean our weight towards the right and we find ourselves cornering in exactly the same position as in the previous illustration.

There are, therefore, two "techniques" for establishing your trajectory:

you can corner by acting exclusively on the steering, applying appropriate couples to the handlebars by turning it; or you can control the vehicle entirely by leaning your body from side to side, without using your hands.

Obviously, in real life, motorcycles are ridden in a number of different ways, almost always making use of a "mixture" of the two techniques. One version or another will be adopted depending on the riding style of the driver, on the type of motorcycle, and on the particular riding situation.

Riding Styles

It should be easy now to understand why it is possible to ride motorcycles with such radically different, individual styles, such as those you see in track racing or cross-country competitions:

• Some racers are extremely agile and prefer to lean more on the motorcycle, making little use of the steering;

• Other racers, using a more compact style, tend to form a single body with their motorcycle, making more use of the steering.

Both styles are perfectly valid and in competitions winning riders come from either school. The various approaches can be summarized by the three types proposed in Figure 4.4.

In all these cases, the motorcyrcle-plus-rider unit creates the same angle of roll with respect to the ground, so that the spend at which the corner is taken remains identical.

The first rider does not shift with respect to the chassis: the center of gravity of the unit formed by the motorcycle + rider remains on the plane of the motorcycle; the second rider prefers to remain more vertical, so the roll angle of the motorcycle will have to increase the angle $\Delta\varphi$; the last rider leans towards the inside of the curve, banking the motorcycle at a smaller angle than the other two.

Let us look at the parameters that may influence the riding style of any individual rider:

Influence of the type of motorcycle:
• Motorcycles characterized by a strong righting effect and by high inertia on the rotation of the front end, or by what is known as "heavy" steering, are operated primarily by banking the motorcycle;

• Motorcycles that are difficult to roll to the right or left are primarily operated by acting on the steering.

Influence of the riding situation:
• When braking, with the weight of the motorcycle more loaded onto the front wheel and causing a strong righting effect, it is better to bank the motorcycle or lean your body;
• On the contrary, when accelerating in a curve, with the front end unloaded and a weak righting moment, it may be better to use the steering.

No mathematical model can determine the absolutely best way to ride for any particular circumstance or type of bike; in fact, you will note that during the course of one long corner a rider may pass from one style to another.

In any case, we had stopped to consider the situation of a motorcycle balanced in a cornering path.

Let us go on to see how we may change the radius of curvature of the trajectory, or widen or tighten a cornering path.

You can act on the steering or on the banking of the motorcycle in order to vary the curvilinear trajectory, in exactly the same way as you do in the initial phase; or you can vary the speed.

Let us suppose we are cornering with a certain steering angle and roll angle: *by reducing the speed,* you diminish the centrifugal force and therefore the motorcycle tends to fall inward, at an ever greater angle.

In order to keep your balance you must increase the steering angle; therefore, traveling on a curve with a smaller radius R, bringing the centrifugal force up again (see Figure 4.1), you are able to

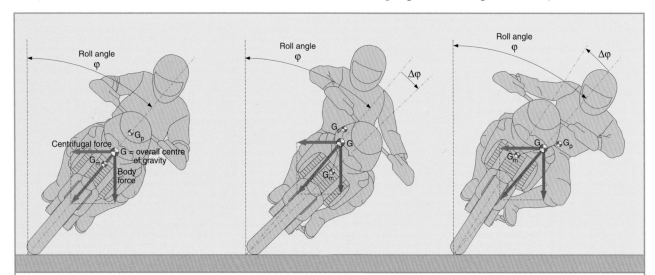

Fig. 4.4: different riding styles, at the same speed, can create the same (overall) angle of roll.

bring the bike into balance. At the same time you will have tightened the corner.

In the same way, by increasing the speed, the motorcycle will tend to right itself because of the greater centrifugal force; to keep your balance you must diminish the steering angle (which means a bigger radius of curvature R), and thus you widen the corner.

And this is exactly the maneuver needed to come out of a corner.

In both these cases the motorcycle is being exceptionally direct and user-friendly in satisfying the rider's needs:

• supposing, in fact, that while going around a corner the turn suddenly sharpens and the rider backs off the throttle, therefore slowing down; the result will be that the motorcycle will tend to tighten its curve, thus keeping to the path;

• in the opposite case, with a widening, gentle curve, by accelerating and increasing the speed, the motorcycle will automatically "open up" its trajectory.

The natural instinct of the rider is rewarded with a "user-friendly" response on the part of the motorcycle.

By appropriately combining your use of the motorcycle's steering, banking and speed, and by continuously changing this mixture in your handling response, you will be able to perform well-controlled, gentle corners.

ROLL ANGLE AND MAXIMUM SPEEDS

We have seen from Figure 4.3 how a state of balance is achieved when cornering: clearly, when the velocity is increased during a curve, so is the centrifugal force and, thus, correspondingly, the roll angle.

It is possible to increase the roll angle, and therefore the speed, up to the point that the transversal force on the ground (proportional to the tire's coefficient of friction) will be strong enough to counterbalance the centrifugal force.

This simple observation explains why it is important to use tires with good adhesion in order to perform sharply banked corners, and, on the other hand, the difficulty of performing them on a damp or wet surface.

Let us analyze the simple case of a coefficient of friction equal to 1: in this situation the bodyforce is equal to the transversal force (given that the force of friction is equal to the bodyforce because of the coefficient of friction) and thus, the possible roll angle is 45 degrees.

The speed on a circular path with radius R, and the motorcycle's angle of inclination are strictly, univocally, related to each other.

There is only one precise angle of inclination that allows you to maintain your balance at any particular speed when cornering.

In fact, referring once again to Figure 4.3, we see that:

Equation 4.2

$$\tan\varphi = \frac{V^2}{R^2 \cdot g}$$

Fig. 4.5: vehicle leaned over.

27

or rather:

Equation 4.3

$$\varphi = arctan \frac{V^2}{R \cdot g}$$

where:

V represents the vehicle's speed of travel;

R represents the radius of curvature of the trajectory;

g indicates gravitational acceleration.

There is also a maximum cornering speed limit: this is reached when the centrifugal force is equal to the opposing force of friction on the ground; or rather:

Equation 4.4

$$\frac{m \cdot V^2}{R} = f \cdot m \cdot g$$

with:

f = coefficient of friction and
m = vehicle's mass

we can show that:

Equation 4.5

$$V_{max} = \sqrt{f \cdot g \cdot R}$$

Surprisingly, as we can see, the angle of inclination of the bike and its maximum speed do not depend on the weight of the motorcycle.

Therefore, bikes with different weights can take the same curve at the same speed.

Why, then, should racing bikes be as light as possible?

The answer is simple: the relation given in Equation 4.4 is valid only *in a constant state*, that is, when the motorcycle is already in a corner and is neither accelerating nor decelerating, a static situation that is only possible in theory.

Experienced motorcyclists are already aware that when cornering at a high speed they are constantly adjusting the steering or banking angle for a number of reasons: to keep the bike on course, to respond to variations in the radius of the curve, to compensate for irregularities in the road surface, to counterbalance gusts of wind or other external disturbances. As we can see, any static condition will necessarily last only a brief instant.

Sophisticated data acquisition systems, monitoring second by second the rake angle, the angle of lean and the speed of the motorcycle, confirm that whenever there is a static situation during cornering, it is actually of extremely short duration. What really happens is a continuous series of small adjustments that the rider performs without even being aware of doing so.

During transients (variations in trajectory or attitude), on the other hand, a light motorcycle is characterized by shorter intervention times. This means that cornering is made more efficient, since the rider can more easily and rapidly make all the adjustments he or she wants to; this results in an overall faster process.

Furthermore, it is apparent that by decreasing the weight of the vehicle it will accelerate more using the same amount of power. A lighter weight will obviously provide comparable advantages *during braking*.

ONE-WHEEL CORNERS

Let us now examine how wheelie enthusiasts are able to do those flashy and risky tricks down our neighbourhood streets, both on mopeds and on high-powered bikes.

The front wheel is lifted off the ground, so the righting moment contributed by the trail value disappears; the only thing the rider in this situation can make use of is the gyroscopic effect of the front wheel, as long as it continues to spin, and with it, the centrifugal force.

So the maneuver turns out to be rather complicated to explain in physical terms; obviously though, since you can't count on your usual steering moves, only extremely skilled, perceptive riders are able to impose the desired trajectory on a vehicle that may weigh tens of kilos, going at high speeds.

There are a number of driving methods used for cornering, but they always pass through a series of

Centrifugal force
G_m
G=overall centre of gravity
Body force
G
G_m
G_p G_p
G_m

transients. That means it is the initial conditions that are most important: in concrete terms, *the result of cornering in a wheelie depends on how the bike is initially stood on its end, because the motorcyclist's means of control once it is in position are effectively limited.*

As a result, your capacity to vary the trajectory becomes restricted and slow, making any encounter with an obstruction a more risky proposition.

If the motorcycle is brought into a wheelie while proceeding at a medium or high speed, the front wheel continues to spin and therefore, thanks to the gyroscopic effect, when you rotate the steering, it is easier to adjust the trajectory of the motorcycle.

One-wheel riding experts, you will probably have noticed, constantly 'jiggle' the steering head in order to go in the direction they want.

AVOIDANCE PATHS

Let us suppose that a motorcycle is moving in a straight line when the rider must suddenly make a quick, hard corner in order to avoid an obstruction such as, for example, another vehicle suddenly appearing from the side of the road. The maneuver will be similar to what we have described at the beginning of the chapter.

Looking at Figure 4.7, let us suppose that the rider decides to put the obstructing vehicle to the left (in other words, to pass it on the right). The tracks on the ground will describe a curve traced first to the left (segment AB in the illustration and necessary, as we have seen, in order to initiate a corner), and then, next, the avoidance tracks will go off to the right.

Let us now analyze the behavior of an automobile having to avoid the same obstructing vehicle. As soon as it is sighted, the car driver can make a turn to the right.

For the motorcyclist, however, there will be a delay in making the same maneuver, equal to the time necessary to cover the distance between point A and point B.

The more agile the bike is, the shorter the delay time will be and the more sharply curved the avoidance tracks will be.

That is why major motorcycle manufacturers concentrate so much of their research on making their bikes faster, of course, but also on making them easier to handle.

Fig. 4.6

Ease of handling, as a concept, is linked not only to achieving better times on the racing circuit, or to obtaining a more nimble ride up a mountain pass, but also to improving everyday use of the vehicle: maneuverability is seen as an active instrument for creating a safer bike.

It is clear, in other words, that the less effort required to handle a motorcycle, the safer it is to use, or rather, the easier it is to minimize dangers on the road.

In order to reassure motorcyclists about the safety of their machines, it might be opportune to add that the avoidance tracks of an automobile must be much wider than those of a two-wheel vehicle, because of the bigger transverse width of a car compared to a motorcycle. Not only that, it is quite easy for motorcyclists to go around tighter corners.

Furthermore, when the motorcycle rider corners towards the right, he or she leans towards the inside of the curve, reducing the cumbersome transversal bulk and making it even easier to avoid the obstruction.

We have already discussed gyroscopic effects in relation to the ease or difficulty of rotating the front end around the steering axis.

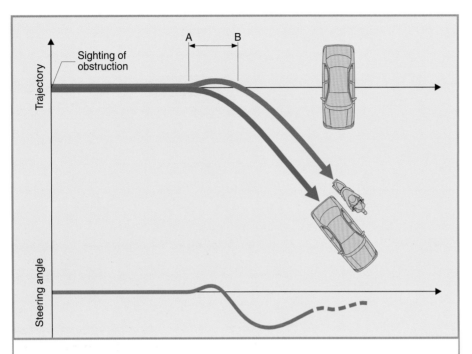

Fig. 4.7: avoidance maneuver tracks: comparison between an automobile and a motorcycle, with progression of motorcycle steering angle (not exact quantities).

Let us see which rotating parts contribute to the inertia of a turning front wheel:

• The tire has a significant effect, since its mass, which is considerable, is essentially concentrated around the external diameter;

• The rim, usually made of an aluminum alloy;

• The brake discs, almost always made of stainless steel, a material with good mechanical properties and, at the same time, rust-proof.

The following chart shows a few values for weight and inertia on a wheel for a medium-powered road bike:

In the racing world, track speeds are always very high, so to reduce the moment of inertia (and therefore, the gyroscopic effect) and to make the motorcycle easier to handle and ride, some very sophisticated and costly technologies are put to use:

• Rims are made of magnesium alloys and in some cases even include composite materials;

• Brake discs may be made out of carbon, extremely light with small diameters, held in place by delicate aluminium structures;

• Tires are created with technologies capable of keeping weight down while still providing exceptional performance and endurance.

The following chart reproduces the previous table, showing the weights of the components of an Aprilia 250 GP Replica.

Sportbike riders with a certain awareness will have already realized how it is possible for a tiny decrease in the inertia of the rotating parts to bring on a big change in the bike's behavior.

Hence the importance of reducing the mass and the inertia of the rims and of all the rotating parts, to improve riding comfort and performance, both when accelerating and braking.

A FEW IMPORTANT OBSERVATIONS
Lowering effect on the center of gravity when rotating the steering: cornering made easy

Take a look at the following figure: it simply represents a disk that is made to spin around an axis that is *not perpendicular to the ground*: if the center of the disk were forced to remain at its original height from the ground, then P, the point of contact with the ground, would have to lift up.

This consideration can be directly applied to the front wheel of a motorcycle that spins around the axis of steering; in this case, however, it will not be lifted up from the ground as illustrated in Figure 4.8, because the force of gravity will make it maintain contact with the ground: *a rotational turn of the steering head lowers the entire front end and, in short, the whole motorcycle.*

Parts	weight (kg)	percentage (%)	moment of inertia (kg m²)	percentage (%)
rim 17" · 3.50	4.3	37	0.11	27
tire 120/60	4.1	35	0.27	66
two brake discs=300mm	3.2	28	0.03	7
Total	11.6	100	0.41	100

This lowering effect is greatest at the front wheel and decreases as it moves towards the rear end, disappearing at the point of contact between rear wheel and ground.

This effect may not be immediately obvious to you, but it is easily demonstrated: position your motorcycle with the engine off so that you can see the steering-axis from above: at this point, turn the handle bars, for example, to the left. You will see that the whole motorcycle pitches slightly forward.

The lowering of the center of the front wheel is provided by the relation:

Equation 4.6
using standard symbols.

$$\Delta V = \left[1 - \sqrt{1 - \left(sin(\delta)^2 \cdot sin(\varepsilon)^2 \right)} \right] \cdot R_f - d \cdot sin(\varepsilon) \cdot \left(1 - cos(\delta) \right)$$

In effect, you will have often noticed that when a bicycle (which has the same steering geometry as a motorcycle) is standing still, the handlebars tend to fall to the right or left because, as we have seen, the force of gravity lowers the center of gravity of the front end.

This effect is especially evident when the terrain offers very low friction (for instance, on ice) and when the tires are well inflated so they slide sideways easier.

This is due to the fact that when a motorcycle (or a bicycle) is stopped, in order for the wheel to turn, it must slide sideways across the ground; this movement is easier or more difficult to perform depending on whether there is a high or low coefficient of friction between the tire and the ground.

When the speed increases, these sideways movements become easier because true dragging movements are always facilitated when the tires are rolling.

Sideways drag during steering also occurs with automobiles and it is decisively worsened by the weight of the end and the width of car tires, to the point that *in the case of parked cars, the steering wheel is often difficult to turn,* making it necessary to adopt power-steering.

We have said that as the speed increases, sideways dragging motion becomes easier to perform; this is very easy to demonstrate in cars without power-steering: when stopped, it is difficult to turn the wheel, while when the car is moving the steering-wheel becomes instantly easier to manage.

There are plans to install a more sophisticated kind of power-steering in some cars that would progressively limit its power as the speed increased, thus allowing the driver to maintain a solid steering sensation.

In any case, the effort required to turn the steering gear when the vehicle is stopped is equally evident on motorcycles, and the effort required increases along with the load placed on the front end.

The motorcycle's tendency to lower when turning the steering head also explains why during tight corners taken at low speeds (for example, on winding mountain roads), some models show a

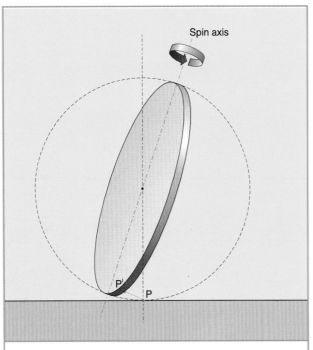

Fig. 4.8: a disk spinning around an axis that is not orthogonal to the ground will lift up its contact point.

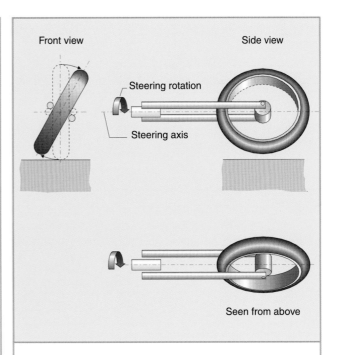

Fig. 4.9: horizontal axis of steering: a rotation around the steering axis does not give rise to any useful steering ingredient; it offers, instead, only considerable sideways tire drag and significant lowering of the wheel center.

Note that: with the same handlebar steering angle, the larger the rake angle (e), the smaller the effective steering angle at ground level.

tendency to fall into the curve: the righting effect due to the velocity (remember the gyroscopic and inertial effects) is unable to counterbalance the tendency of the center of gravity to lower.

Furthermore, since this is a slow corner, the pull on the steering is quickly accomplished, while the inertial effect tends to continue to lower the motorcycle.

According to what we have seen, distribution of weight plays, once again, a truly important role: a center of gravity close to the front of the bike amplifies these sorts of effects, both in positive and negative ways.

Effective Steering Angle

One does not usually think much about it, but you might have realized that the angle given to the steering head by the motorcyclist does not correspond to an equal effective steering angle at ground level.

This fact, too, is partly attributable to the inclination of the steering axis with respect to the vertical.

The following figure, which presents an extreme situation, gives an idea as to how much influence this phenomenon has: let us imagine, for example, zero offset and zero angle of roll.

With the axis of steering vertical and the roll angle nil, the steering action made by the rider coincides with that made by the motorcycle, while with the axis of steering horizontal to the ground, the bike's effective steering angle is zero.

In practice, the bigger the rake angle, the bigger the curve radius the motorcycle makes with the same amount of handlebar turn; in other words, the more effort required to corner the bike.

In general, the relation that links the effective steering angle to the angle put on the steering head is the following:

Equation 4.7

$$\Delta = arctan \left[\frac{sin(\delta) \cdot cos(\varepsilon + \mu)}{cos(\varphi)\,cos(\delta) - sin(\varphi)\,sin(\delta)\,sin(\varepsilon + \mu)} \right]$$

a function describing the angle δ, created by the rider turning the handlebars, the rake angle ε, the roll angle of the rear end φ and the angle of pitch μ.

As an example, we include a figure that represents the effective steering angle as a function of the steering head angle, with a number of values for the roll angle.

It is much easier to understand the simplified formula:

Equation 4.8

$$\Delta = \frac{cos(\varepsilon)}{cos(\varphi)}\,tan(\delta)$$

using symbols with the standard meanings.

The effective steering angle Δ and the steering rotation δ only coincide when the angle of roll is equal to the angle of inclination of the steering head. In all other cases, if the roll angle is less than the angle of the steering rotation, then the effective steering angle is less than the one placed on the steering head; and viceversa in the opposite case.

The preceding observations allow us, therefore, to conclude that:

the narrower the rake angle (therefore the bigger cos (e) is), the more reaction is felt from the steering head, both in response to the rider's own interventions and in response to external disturbances.

Influence of the motorcycle's wheelbase on the radius of the curve

The length of the motorcycle, as we have seen from the formulas describing the stabilizing effect,

is a very important parameter whose influence can be described by means of simple observations.

Figure 4.11 (based on a simplified case of zero trail and roll angle) makes it clear that a motorcycle with a long wheelbase, equal to the effective steering angle, will perform a curve with a radius that is bigger than for a motorcycle with a smaller wheelbase.

This is made evident, quite obvious to us all, by the fact that to go around a tight corner with a

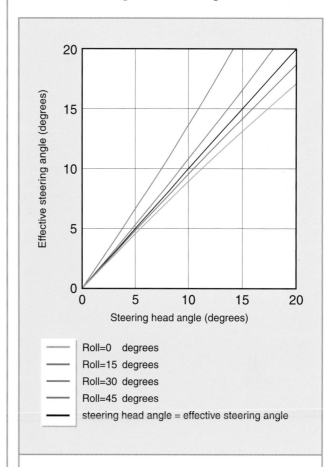

Fig. 4.10: effective steering angle as a function of the angle on the steering head (with pre-set angle of roll values).

33

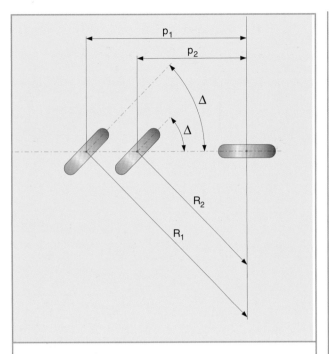

Fig. 4.11: with an equal effective steering angle, motorcycles with longer wheelbases correspond to wider radii of curvature (the vehicle corners less tightly). Note that: roll has been ignored.

long motorcycle, you have to rotate the steering head a lot, or pull hard on the handlebars.

These simple considerations help us to understand why road racing bikes, which have to move about in narrow spaces and make quick, hard corners, have a very modest wheelbase distance, while super touring bikes, designed for longer, more wide-open spaces, have much longer wheelbases.

Let us suppose now that a gust of wind, a pothole, a lengthwise joint in the asphalt or some other kind of disturbance brings on the situation illustrated in Figure 4.12, in which the rear wheel has been shifted a certain distance S.

The corresponding steering angle diminishes as the wheelbase is lengthened.

So with the same disturbance, the rider with a longer wheelbase will feel less oscillating movement on the handlebars, and therefore, will have a perception of greater stability on the motorcycle.

Hence, motorcycles with a long wheelbase are considered less "twitchy".

Influence of the roll angle on the effective radius of the curve

The longer the motorcycle's wheelbase, the more steering is necessary in order to go around a corner.

Let us go on to analyze more closely what happens when a motorcycle describes a curvilinear trajectory.

As we have seen, the motorcycle leans inwardly: we say that it bends or rolls (an actual case is illustrated in Figure 4.13).

The center of instantaneous rotation of the vehicle is, thus, lower than the plane of the road surface; projecting it vertically and connecting the point where it meets the ground with the projection of the motorcycle's center of gravity onto the ground, we thus obtain *the radius of curvature with respect to the ground* which *turns out to be less than the theoretical value* (center of instantaneous rotation-center of gravity).

This is a phenomenon worth taking into account: Grand Prix motorcycles reach and surpass a 45-degree banking angle; this makes the effective radius of the curve on the circuit 0.7 times smaller than the theoretical radius.

This fact explains a peculiar sensation that you feel on the motorcycle: that of having to put very little effort into steering (compared, for example, to how much effort is required to steer a car) relative to the radius of the curve you are performing; this sensation is amplified the faster you go around the corner.

We have all unconsciously put this characteristic of the motorcycle (or the bicycle) to use. Have you ever noticed that you naturally lean the bike a lot when guiding it by hand when you want to turn in a narrow space?

As far as handling is concerned, the practical effect of what we have described is the following:

When you are beginning to corner and you want to take it with a constant radius, the more you lean the motorcycle, the less, gradually, you have to operate the steering.

This observation is especially true for racing bikes which (since they have tires with a high coefficient of friction), are able to lean deeply into a corner.

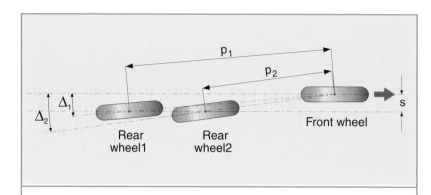

Fig. 4.12: a long wheelbase gives greater stability in the presence of external disturbances.

Equation 4.9

$$sin\,(\Delta\varphi) = \frac{(t \cdot sin\,\varphi_i)}{h - t}$$

where:

t is the radius of cross-section of the tire;

$\Delta\varphi$ is the angle of roll with (ideal) punctiform tires;

h is the height of the center of gravity.

This reduction of the radius of curvature due to roll aids the rider greatly when he or she has to avoid an obstacle; as illustrated earlier, given that the motorcycle is leaning towards the inside of the curve, less of the motorcycle's girth overhangs into the outside area of the curve.

This brings us back to what we have seen regarding the tracks that an avoidance path leaves behind; it also confirms with what ease a motorcyclist is able to avoid an obstruction by taking a very tight curve and maintaining limited transversal bulk.

Influence of tire width on the angle of roll

There is another interesting phenomenon linked to the width of the tires: we have already analyzed the balancing conditions of the motorcycle when cornering with lense-shaped tires (single point of contact between wheel and ground).

For every particular curve radius and speed of travel, as we have seen, there is a consequent roll angle as illustrated by the relation Equation 4.4 and from Figure 4.3.

If we now examine a tire width greater than zero, but to be more realistic, with a circular cross-section, *the point of contact with the ground shifts towards the inside of the curve* and the axis that joins that point with the center of gravity no longer coincides with the axis of the motorcycle, with which it forms the angle $\Delta\varphi$.

This angle is easily obtained from the following relation:

In order for the motorcycle to maintain its balance, it will have to be leaned over more deeply, passing from angle φ_i, in the case of negligible tire width, to the angle $\varphi_i + \Delta\varphi$, so that the axis between the point on the ground and the center of gravity is inclined at an appropriate angle.

As a result of this, then, the bigger the cross-section of the tire, and equally, the greater the speed at which you enter the corner, the more you must lean the bike into the curve.

This is hardly unimportant if we remember that some supersport street bikes have tire widths of 190mm (the same size as the tires on medium-to-large automobiles!).

With the flattening of the rear tire during usage, the point of contact shifts more towards the inside of the curve, making the motorcycle even less manageable.

We hope these observations will have convinced you to be rather cautious about substituting your original tires and rims with bigger-sized replacements. A wider cross-section on your tires can obviously provide you with a stronger "grip" on the road when cornering, but, as we have seen, it would require alterations to a number of geometric design parameters specific to each vehicle, such as *trail*.

Today's motorcycles are laid out to achieve their best possible performance within the conditions they are designed for; outside of these conditions, their performance may not be at its best.

We also advise you to replace your tires immediately when you notice that the center section is

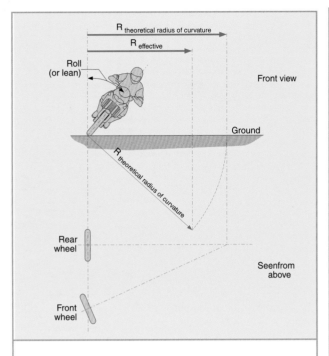

Fig. 4.13: effective radius of curvature.

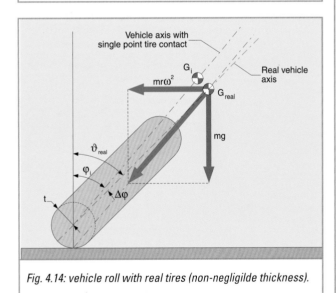

Fig. 4.14: vehicle roll with real tires (non-negligilde thickness).

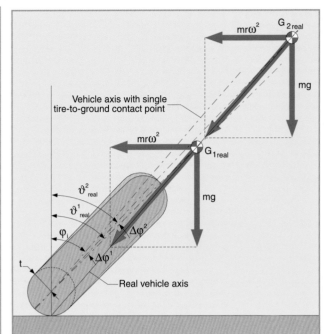

Fig. 4.15: where: $\Delta\varphi^2$ is smaller than $\Delta\varphi^1$
keeping the same values for:
• radius of curvature R;
• speed of travel in the corner V;
• vehicle mass m;
when the center of gravity is raised (h1>h2) the motorcycle
does not have to be leaned as far over.

worn down, since the problem described above becomes worse with wear.

Influence of the center of gravity height on the angle of roll

Even though it might sound strange at first, we have seen that the height of the center of gravity also has an influence on the motorcycle's roll angle.

Taking up the preceding formula (Equation 4.9), we see that an increase in the angle of roll $\Delta\varphi$, in the case of negligible tire thickness, depends on the height of the center of gravity as much as it does on the radius of the wheel.

By raising the center of gravity along with the radius of curvature and the speed of travel, the motorcycle does not have to be as steeply banked.

A rather surprising fact, indeed!

We can easily see from Figure 4.15 that the increment $\Delta\varphi_i$ of the theoretical angle gets smaller as the height of the motorcycle's center of gravity is raised.

CHAPTER 5

EQUILIBRIUM OF FORCES ACTING ON A MOTORCYCLE IN STRAIGHT-LINE MOTION

This is the first of three chapters that are intimately linked together: the final goal is to understand how the attitude of the motorcycle varies according to its motion, for example, when accelerating or braking.

What does the word "attitude" mean? We hear it used especially in the racing world.

It is certainly not an easy term to explain because it gathers together and concentrates into one word a set of both geometrical and other quantities and dimensions that go into defining the vehicle's configuration and, consequently, its behavior in various riding situations.

We have already seen the influence of some important parameters -such as the rake angle, the trail, the wheelbase, the position of the suspension and the distribution of weight- on a motorcycle traveling at a constant speed in a straight line.

The parameters that we have focused on, however, are not constant (the speed hardly ever is either); rather they change, even to a significant extent, in response to the riding conditions, since the suspension system and the transmission of engine power are sensitive to both vertical loads and horizontal loads such as traction and braking.

For example, as we know from daily life, when the brakes are applied, the front end tends to lower; as a consequence, this affects the trail, the rake angle and wheel loads with respect to the initial conditions; or rather, *the attitude and, therefore, the behavior of the motorcycle itself are altered.*

In order to predict what attitude the vehicle will assume in any particular circumstance, we will follow this sequence of steps:

• In this chapter we will analyze the motorcycle as if it were a single rigid body, without suspension, and we will proceed to work out the forces

that act exten-ally on our system when a (horizontal) force from traction or braking is applied;

• In the next chapter (Chapter 6: *How forces are transmitted*) we will see how such forces are transmitted within the motorcycle system; or rather, we will analyze the stresses that bring on suspension movements;

• In the chapter that follows (Chapter 7: *Motorcycle attitude*) we will synthesize what we have discovered in order to determine the particular position assumed by the chassis, that is to say, the attitude of the vehicle, under various conditions.

POWER NECESSARY FOR MOTION

The power necessary to make the vehicle move forward on a **level** surface at a **constant speed** is given by the sum of the power necessary to overcome the rolling resistance of the tires and the aerodynamic drag.

Equation 5.1

$$P_{necessary} = V - (F_R + F_A)$$

where:
V is the forward speed of travel;
F_R is the force of the rolling resistance of the tires ;
F_A is the force of aerodynamic drag.

Let us examine these two factors separately:

• the rolling resistance of the tires

is primarily due to tire deformation and the forces interacting between tire and street. It is estimated that, altogether, the force of the rolling resistance of the tires is less than 2% of the vehicle's body force.

In order to push a vehicle weighing 2000 N (200 kg) by hand, then, only a moderate force of less than 40 N (4 kg) should be required.

In reality, however, as any rider who has had to push their motorcycle in search of gas will tell you, the force needed is actually greater because of all the forces of friction created by the bearings, the chain against the engine and drive sprockets, and by the possibly minimal residual braking couples on the discs.

In any case, note that the rolling resistance of the tires *in proportion to the total resistence is only significant when the wheels are rotating at low speeds*; and its importance diminishes radically at higher speeds.

• aerodynamic drag

Using a simplification, we can say that the resistance of aerodynamic force is proportional to the square of the speed of travel, using a few coefficients. Obviously, its contribution becomes more important as the speed increases.

For more information on the influence of aerodynamics, see the chapter on to this subject.

If the street is not level, in addition to the rolling resistance of the tires and the aerodynamic drag, we must add another force needed to overcome the component of weight parallel to the velocity: $F_P = mg \cdot \sin(\alpha)$.

The power necessary to climb up the slope is equal to:

Equation 5.2

$$P_P = V - mg \cdot \sin(\alpha)$$

using standard symbols.

Given that the amount of power available to a motorcycle is generally quite large, it is therefore theoretically possible for a sportbike to make it up almost any slope.

That is not the case in the real world. You might have heard about a spectacular, well-

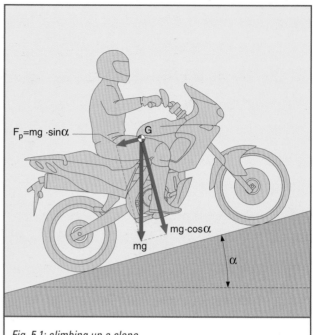

Fig. 5.1: climbing up a slope.

known competitive event that first started in the United States and later spread to Europe, in which the winner is the rider able to reach the highest point on a very rough or sandy steep hill. The bikes are stopped eventually because their rear wheels spin without being able to transmit power to the ground, or else because the front wheel lifts up and the bike tumbles over backwards (see Figure 5.2).

This provide us with is an excellent example of how the *power **available** to the vehicle is not always **usable**.*

Let us look at the limits that condition the motorcycle's ability to go up a slope:

• adhesion limit

At times it is not possible to transmit the necessary force to the ground, due to an inadequate coefficient of friction.

The maximum transmittable power is equal to the load bearing on the driving wheel, multiplied by the coefficient of friction; past this limit, the wheel will spin uselessly.

Equation 5.3

$$P_{max\ transmittable} = V \cdot N_r \cdot f$$

f = coefficient of friction;
N_r = load bearing on the rear driving wheel.

When riding conditions offer a low value for the coefficient of friction, on a wet, icy, or sandy surface, for example, the motorcycle will have difficulty in transmitting the force to the ground needed to climb up a steep slope.

The formula shown above explains motorcyclists' instinctive response when their rear wheel starts to slip: they lean their weight backwards, putting more load onto the driving wheel.

• the vehicle's tumble limit

When the projection of the body force applied to the center of gravity of the motorcycle-plus-rider unit falls behind the rear tire impression, it is impossible to keep the bike balanced.

The motorcycle tumbles over backwards. This is something you can easily witness if you ever watch the incredible slopes that racers scramble up during the hill scramble competitions we mentioned earlier.

The racers' instinctive response of leaning forward is explainable by the fact that the center of gravity of the system also shifts forward with their movement.

CONSTANT MOTION

We will now consider the vehicle as if it were a **rigid body**, or rather, as if the suspension were blocked.

Furthermore, we will exclude aerodynamic drag, by supposing that the motorcycle is traveling at a slow speed.

At a constant, moderate velocity we can easily calculate the vertical reactions on the tires:

La plus belle sortie
shoire d'énerver encore un tantinet les furieux qui montent [et

Fig. 5.2: the prize in these spectacular competitions goes to the rider who is able to reach the highest point on a very rough or sandy steep hill.

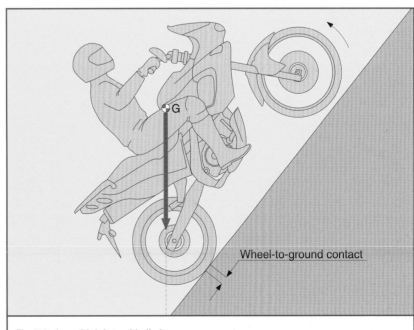

Wheel-to-ground contact

Fig. 5.3: the vehicle's tumble limit.

Equation 5.4

$$N_f = mg \cdot \frac{b}{wb}$$

$$N_f = mg \cdot \frac{wb - b}{wb}$$

where:

N_f represents the load on the front wheel;
N_r represents the load on the rear wheel;
b the distance between the point of contact between rear wheel and the projection of the center of gravity onto the road;
wb the motorcycle's wheelbase.

These reactions depend essentially on the position of the center of gravity, as well as, obviously, the net weight of the vehicle.

More specifically, *the more forward the center of gravity is, the more load there will be on the front end and vice versa*. In the case of a center of gravity

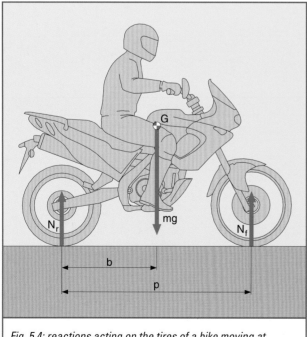

Fig. 5.4: reactions acting on the tires of a bike moving at constant speed.

positioned in the middle of the wheelbase, the load distribution will be divided 50% between front and rear.

Naturally, in the case of constant motion, the engine transmits a power equal to what is strictly required to overcome tire resistance; when the engine transmits a power greater than this, the motorcycle accelerates.

THE MOTORCYCLE UNDER ACCELERATION

We are accelerating; we shall apply a driving force **T** to the point of contact between wheel and ground, excluding the rolling resistance force of the tires, while a resistance force **R** (the force of inertia, actually) shall be applied at the center of gravity.

For this system to be in a state of equilibrium with respect to its preceding conditions, we must calculate a variation in the vertical loads acting on the wheels.

The same component is referred to in the literature as **weight transfer**, and is given by the expression:

Equation 5.5

$$N_{trans} = T \cdot \frac{h}{wb}$$

The loads on the wheels can therefore be expressed by the following relations:

Equation 5.6

$$N_r = mg \cdot \frac{b}{wb} - T \cdot \frac{h}{wb} \quad \text{or:}$$

Equation 5.7

$$N_r = Ns_r - N_{trans}$$

$$N_r = Ns_r + N_{trans}$$

where Ns_f and Ns_r indicate, respectively, the verticle reaction on the front and rear wheels in static conditions.

Thanks to the *weight transfer*, the application of a push lightens the load on the front and increases the load on the rear (the sum of the verticle reactions, in fact, remains constant).

Let us note that the presence of a weight transfer allows a greater force to be transmitted to the ground.

Let us pause for a second on Equation 5.5 in order to draw out a few more considerations:

The weight transfer obviously turns out to be directly proportional to the force of traction and to the height of the center of gravity.

It is important to keep this fact in mind: motorcycles with a high center of gravity and a short wheelbase will easily lose their front wheel adhesion and will have a strong tendency to lift the front wheel under acceleration.

We are now in the position to summarize what we have discussed so far, in the form of an illustration that will be of use to us in the following sections:

• Let us place a sum of the force of traction and weight transfer onto the rear: the result will be balanced by the sum of the resistance force and the weight transfer on the front (Figure 5.6). The line of action of both these resulting forces will be inclined with respect to the horizontal at **an angle whose tangent is equal to h/wb.**

$$\tau = arctan\left(\frac{h}{wb}\right)$$

The ratio h/wb describes the tangent of an angle τ which is referred to as **the angle of** weight **transfer**, which constitutes an important indicator of the motorcycle's behavior.

A motorcycle with a large angle τ will be characterized by large weight transfers. In other words, **a motorcycle with a high center of gravity and short wheelbase will be more "jumpy".**

What we mean by "jumpy" in this case is a vehicle that will be subject to strong rebound reactions in response to small accelerations or deceler-

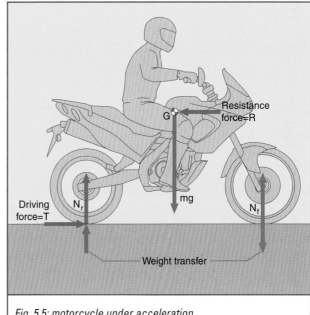

Fig. 5.5: motorcycle under acceleration.

ations. This could be a nuisance for touring bikes which are meant, instead, to offer a completely relaxing ride.

One indicator of a vehicle's acceleration power is its weight-to-power ratio: *the smaller this is, the greater the acceleration will be with the same amount of power provided by the engine.*

We might do well at this point to propose a **comparison between motorcycles and automobiles.**

While waiting at a traffic light, when the light changes to green you will notice that small displacement motorbikes are perfectly capable of "burning up the turf" and leaving behind them automobiles with engine displacements even 10 times bigger than their own.

Let us analyze the weight/power ratio in a few different motorcycle and automobile classes: as we can see, compared to that of cars, both low- and high-powered motorcycles have a weight/power ratio that favors their acceleration capacity.

The answer to why there is such a notable difference lies in the different design philosophy of the two types of vehicles.

Motorcycles are almost always designed for sport uses, so that research aims at developing ever

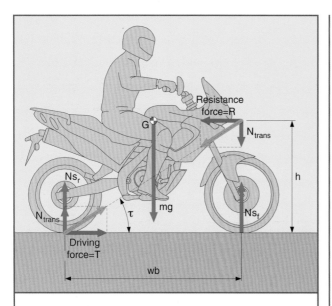

Fig. 5.6: weight transfer angle (body force is balanced by the static reactions on the tires).

better performance results; cars, on the other hand, may be designed according to various priorities, such as riding comfort, low fuel consumption, high loading capacity and a long engine life.

Furthermore, the way the automobile transmission is conceived (the way the gears shift) often privileges low fuel consumption over powerful acceleration.

Cars often have five gears, the last one serving to "rest" the motor; while all of the motorcycle's six gears, which are spaced very close to each other, are for acceleration purposes.

Beyond these rather general and, therefore, probably overly simplistic considerations, it would seem more interesting to propose a few thoughts regarding **environmental issues.**

The motorcycle is a vehicle designed to transport two mounted passengers with limited baggage, making up a very simple structure that weighs relatively little as well.

The automoble, on the other hand, is generally designed to transport five passengers who are completely protected from outside agents. This entails using a huge quantity of materials along with, generally, far more resources.

In terms of energy consumption, then, the difference between the two means of transport becomes even more evident if you consider that a person who uses their economy car to go to work every day has to accelerate and brake and keep up to speed a vehicle weighing, let us say, 1100 kg. The same person riding a medium-powered motorcycle, on the other hand, only has to "move" a mass that is up to ten times smaller.

WHEELIES

When, under acceleration, we reach the limit in which the front load (N_f) diminishes to zero, we create the conditions that lift the front end off the ground, known in popular terms as a **wheelie**.

Breaking down, then, the expression for N_f:

Equation 5.8

$$N_f = mg \cdot \frac{b}{wb} - T \cdot \frac{h}{wb} = 0$$

we obtain the value for the maximum possible traction force, or rather, the value at which, at a constant speed, the motorcycle will "stand up on its end:"

Equation 5.9

$$T_{max} = mg \cdot \frac{b}{h}$$

When the front wheel lifts up, so does the height of the center of gravity; this means that, maintaining the same initial push, *the motorcycle will tend to "pull-up" (to use an aeronautical term) and then overturn backwards.*

In other words, *the push needed to keep the motorcycle in a wheelie is less than the push necessary to pull it up in the first place.* You must pay special attention, then, to how you control your throttle in these circumstances.

Traditional motorbikes, therefore, have limited acceleration possibilities.

In fact, in competitions based on acceleration times, with extremely high-powered engines, the motorcycles are especially designed to be very long and low in order to limit their tendency towards front end lifting.

Type of vehicle	displacement [cc]	weight with rider [kg]	power [kW(CV)]	weight/power ratio [kg/CV]
AUTOMOBILE				
compact	1200	980	53.7 (73)	18.25
medium sized	2000	1415	97 (132)	14.6
high powered	2800	1570	142 (193)	11.13
sportscar	3200	1515	236 (321)	6.41
high-powered sportscar	3500	1500	280 (380)	5.35
MOTORCYRCLE				
low powered	125	215	24 (33)	9
medium powered bike	600	272	70 (95)	3.88
high powered bike	1100	300	100 (138)	3
superbike	900	265	98 (133)	2.755

In addition to high acceleration **power** wheelies, there is another way to lift the front wheel into the air while keeping the motorcycle in a precarious state of balance.

Having lifted the front wheel off the ground by accelerating the vehicle and, especially, by leaning your body weight backwards to shift the balance, you will be able to maintain the bike in this delicate, pulled-up position.

To do so, the overall bodyforce of the motorcycle-plus-rider unit must always fall within the rear wheel impression, which is obviously a very small area.

That is why only experienced riders with high sensitivity and a great sense of balance are able to perform this maneuver.

What we are describing is comparable to the situation of a marble balanced on top of a mound, an extremely precarious state of affairs.

By adroitly combining these two kinds of power and balancing wheelies it is possible to keep the bike standing up on its rear wheel for a long time.

World-class records testify to covering tens of kilometers with the bike heeled over on its back wheel.

In spite of the possibility of accomplishing this sort of record, which, for safety reasons, is performed on indoor circuits far away from traffic, we remind you that: controlling the motorcycle during wheelies is **extremely dangerous**, not only because of the tenuous balancing conditions, but also because, even though it is possible to swerve in order to avoid unexpected obstacles (discussed in the section on one-wheel cornering), it is not always possible to manage quick, hard corners as the circumstances may require. Furthermore, forward visibility may be reduced, since the field of vision is at the same height as the motorcyclist's head.

To study phenomena associated with braking, we will apply the same approach taken in the preceding sections: deceleration, in fact, is nothing other than negative acceleration.

Clearly, when braking, the weight transfer is increased onto the front wheel and taken off the rear wheel; the weight transfers, which are generated in direct correspondance to acceleration and deceleration, are larger compared to a car's, since the center of gravity is higher and the wheelbase distance is shorter than an automobile's.

The large weight transfer characteristic of motorcycles means that the braking apparatus must be **much more powerful** on the front.

In fact, as soon as the motorcyclist applies the brakes, the load tends to transfer to the front, while the rear load is diminished, and along with

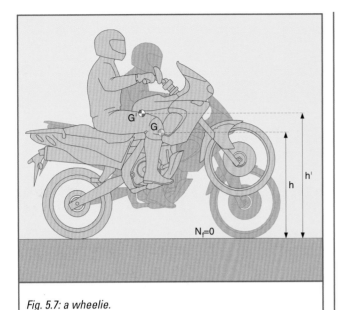

Fig. 5.7: a wheelie.

Fig. 5.8: balancing in a wheelie.

Fig. 5.9: unstable equilibrium.

it, the possibility to use it for braking. Big, powerful rear brakes would only cause the wheel to lock for no useful purpose, causing an unjustifiable burden on the total weight of the vehicle.

As a consequence, all high-powered sportbikes are endowed with good-sized front braking systems, with two discs as big as possible, compatible with the practical need to be able remove the calipers from the rim, while at the rear wheel there is only one disk of much smaller dimensions.

This is not to say, however, that rear brake use is always without purpose, and now we will see why.

Let us imagine braking solely with the rear brake: if a small irregularity in the terrain or a steering adjustment causes the vehicle to be misaligned, the braking force generates a moment that tends to right it, helping to maintain the vehicle on a straight-line trajectory.

Single applications of the rear brake can therefore bring on an important stabilizing effect.

Braking only with the front brake, on the contrary, could provoke a situation that is difficult to handle: the moment generated by the braking force tends to further rotate the vehicle, with an obvious destabilizing effect.

DECELERATION LIMITS

Calculating the possible braking limit for a motorcycle turns out to be quite complex.

Just as for acceleration, the limit can be reached **either from lack of adhesion or from excessive weight transfer**, resulting in the back wheel lifting off the ground.

Let us imagine braking in a "panic", or an emergency application of the brakes, using solely the front brake.

At the beginning of the braking action, the front wheel load is equal to approximately 40% of the total weight of the vehicle, so that a decisive, hard "grab" on the brakes could cause the front wheel to lock.

In this case, the deceleration limit is given by the tire's adhesion to the ground.

This is clearly possible only if the action of the front braking apparatus is very powerful and quick.

After the first deceleration impulse, the load transfer is increased onto the front wheel, which considerably limits the likelihood of the wheel blocking and at the same time makes it possible to decelerate much more.

Decelerating even more and increasing the braking force on the ground, we reach the limit (**F$_{max}$**) at which the weight on the rear wheel reaches zero, causing it to begin to lift off the ground and, thus, creating a dangerous situation.

In this case, too, like that of a front wheelie under acceleration, when you reach **F$_{max}$** you must "let up" on the brakes so as not to topple over.

SUMMARY

The relation between height of the center of gravity and the wheelbase of the vehicle (h/wb) and the relative weight transfer angle turn out to be crucial parameters in the design and behavior of the vehicle.

For example, a motorcycle that is capable of powerful acceleration or deceleration will have to be characterized by a very small weight transfer angle in order to avoid toppling too easily.

This means a very long motorcycle with a low center of gravity—not the best features for easy handling.

Obviously, a prototype "acceleration" bike with a long wheelbase of 1800 mm, for example, will hardly give a particularly brilliant performance winding through a slalom obstacle course.

Motorcycles with a short wheelbase and a high center of gravity, on the other hand, turn out to be agile and easily handled in spite of limitations on their maximum acceleration potential.

Let us focus on a few practical differences that arise when riding motorcycles with different weight transfer angles.

Motorcycles with large weight transfer angles:

• These vehicles allow you to change the weight distribution on the wheels according to the needs of the moment in extremely quick times, or rather, *these motorcycles respond instantly to your commands.*

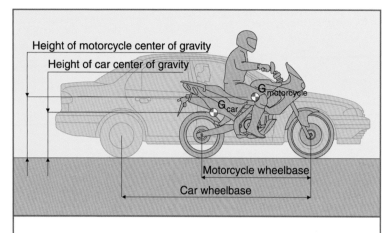

Fig. 5.10: there is greater weight transfer on a motorcycle than on a car.

• For offroad riding, this easily allows the front wheel to be slightly lightened when going over a bump, with only a moderate twist of the throttle;

• Similarly, for track racing, it makes it possible to go around corners to the limits, with only small adjustments on the accelerator or the

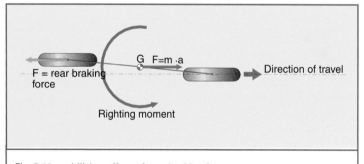

Fig. 5.11: stabilizing effect of rear braking force.

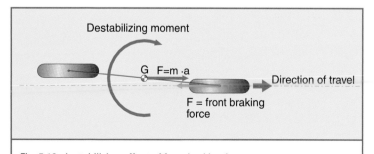

Fig. 5.12: destabilizing effect of front braking force.

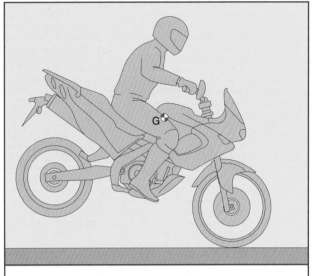

Fig. 5.13: toppling over during braking.

brakes in order to shift the load onto the wheel that needs the most adhesion at the moment.

Motorcycles with small weight transfer angles:

• Turn out to be exceptionally fine at breathtaking "take offs" and for passing other racers at the end of a straight-line course;

• They can also be adapted to long-distance touring, since their responses to accelerating or braking actions are muted, allowing a more restful ride.

At present, when designing a sportbike more priority is given to a motorcycle that responds quickly to commands rather than to developing the most powerful acceleration and deceleration, since it is a quick response that obtains:

• The best times on the track for racing bikes;

• Satisfying ease of handling and, therefore, a

high degree of safety and riding pleasure for sport streetbikes.

This explains why when Grand Prix motorcycles are braked violently, their rear end lifts up, and even at high speeds they lift up their front wheel under acceleration.

Let us not forget either that there is a considerable moving "ballast" aboard a motorcycle, constituted by the rider, who can greatly alter the distribution of weight.

Riders are constantly shifting their weight on their motorcycles. This relatively small movement is especially noticeable during motocross events when racers lean their weight back when braking and forward when accelerating; this is how the load gets increased onto the appropriate axle, allowing the bike to reach very high positive or negative acceleration values.

The motorcyclist, in fact, is completely absorbed by the act of riding:

• **mentally**, the rider's attention must be focused on controlling the vehicle by commanding the throttle, brakes, and handlebar;

• **physically**, the rider's expenditure of energy is considerable, given that every maneuver the bike makes must be accompanied by a corresponding body movement.

The more sports-oriented the riding is, the more total mental and physical involvement is required of the rider, especially in cross-country competitions where a lot of physical energy is expended, but in any case:

to ensure a productive, safe ride you must be fit and healthy.

By respecting these needs you are making a fundamental, active contribution to your riding safety.

CHAPTER 6
HOW TRACTION AND BRAKING FORCES ARE TRANSMITTED WITHIN THE MOTORCYCLE SYSTEM

In the preceding chapter we determined the motorcycle's state of equilibrium when traction and braking forces are applied to it.

As we know very well, however, the motorcycle is hardly made up of a single rigid body. The best way to represent the motorcycle in terms of aerodynamics is to consider it a system made up of a sprung mass—defined roughly by the frame, the rider, the passenger and the engine- linked through a system of suspensions, or two elastic elements, to two unsprung masses, that is, the wheels.

So, the forces applied to the system will be transmitted from the wheels to the chassis, by means of the suspension. The suspension varies its configuration according to the load that traverses it, thus determining the attitude of the vehicle.

These are the kinds of topics we will be analyzing in this chapter. We will be looking at how the suspension behaves in relation to the geometrical configuration of the motorcycle, depending on the loads applied to it.

TRANSMISSION OF DRIVING FORCE FROM ENGINE TO WHEEL

In most cases, the engine is attached rigidly to the frame; the rear wheel, attached to the fork, is able to oscillate along with it in order to absorb irregularities in the road surface. In fact, the wheel shifts position with respect to the frame, and for this reason, in order to transmit the torque of the engine power, we need a transmission system that both allows and absorbs movements between wheels and frame.

The two methods universally adopted are:
- *chain/gear or belt-drive;*
- *shaft-drive.*

Scooters are a special case and will be treated separately.

One might wonder why there are no motorcycles with front traction or integrated traction (with power being transmitted to both ends). This is probably due to the following reasons:

1. As far as **front traction** is concerned:

- it is quite difficult to transmit the power of an engine rigidly attached to a front wheel which must not only oscillate but must also be able to turn for steering purposes.
The kind of solutions found for automobiles are certainly applicable but at the price of considerable bulk, added weight, complications and cost;

- furthermore, as we have seen, when the motorcycle is under acceleration it tends to lighten at the front end, often resulting in the front wheel lifting off the ground.
Even without taking this situation to an extreme, when accelerating, the load bearing on the front wheel is lightened, diminishing the engine's capacity to transmit power to the ground.
Remember, too, that the front wheel's loss of adhesion is very dangerous, since it jeopardizes the effectiveness of the righting moment. When coming out of a turn, under acceleration, slipping of the front drive wheel could easily cause you to lose control of the vehicle.

- another aspect concerns the fact that the motorcycle could end up understeering because of the amplified effect of any drift on the front tire, including the effects discussed in the chapter on tires.

2. As far as **integrated traction** is concerned:

• Clearly, this would be an accomplishment that would bring about increased push transmitted to the ground, very useful for motorcycles needing the most traction that they can have.
Trials bikes, for example, which make difficult maneuvers in sometimes very low friction conditions, could benefit enormously from this sort of solution.
The same reasoning could be extended to 500 cc Grand Prix superbikes which have a problem with front wheel slippage during acceleration.
In any case, we can only repeat the difficulties described above in connection with front drive transmission: increased weight, bulk, mechanical complexity.

We must also remember that the trajectory of the front wheel is different from that of the rear wheel; when you want to corner, this could turn out to be a problem: the difference in the speed of rotation could be absorbed by the slip of the tires but in the case of a very sharp curve, for example, and with good friction on the surface, this would be unlikely.

It would probably be necessary to come up with a differential able to compensate for the different rotational speeds and which could appropriately regulate the distribution of power between the front and rear wheels under any riding conditions.

At the moment, all of these complications are quite outside the design philosophy of the motorcycle, which must be a serviceable and functional

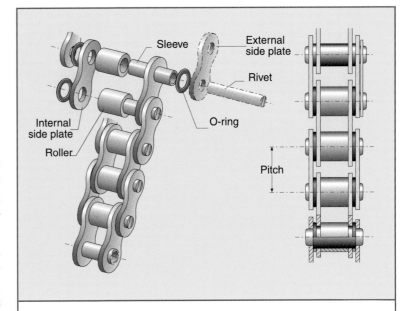

Fig. 6.1: motorcycle chain transmission.

vehicle, but at the same time remain lightweight and be mechanically simple.

Chain/Gear Drive
Chain/gear-driven transmission is the most widely-used system in the motorcycle world.

Its development has been carefully tended to, and there have been some rewarding improvements based on recent innovations:

• As far as smoothness is concerned, self-lubricating chains have reduced power loss to a quantifiable 3% to 5%. Systems with guaranteed grease levels, thanks to special rubber rings, have made it possible to get long distance output from even high-powered bikes (Figure 6.2);

The system of transmitting the torque is very simple (Figure 6.2).

• The chain is engaged by an engine sprocket placed on the output shaft of the engine and on a rear wheel sprocket (usually with a bigger diameter than that of the engine sprocket), situated on the rear wheel axle and forming a fixed part of it.

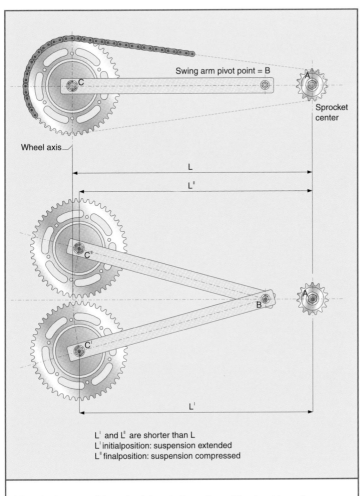

Swing arm pivot point = B

Sprocket
center

Wheel axis

L

L"

C"

B

A

C'

L'

L' and L" are shorter than L
L' initialposition: suspension extended
L" finalposition: suspension compressed

Fig. 6.2: the overall length of the chain varies with wheel travel

The fact that the chain is not always tight clearly *creates some problems for continuity of motion.*

Let us suppose that we are traveling in a straight line, having given a lot of play to the chain.

When the rider accelerates, the engine rotation speeds up and, as a consequence, the inertia effect caused by all its rotating parts also increases, with the following effects:

• At first, the slack on the chain is taken up without the rear wheel having to proportionally increase its rotation speed;
• Only after having taken up the slack, with the chain now tightly extended, will it transmit the driving force to the wheel, which, naturally, will undergo a sudden acceleration;
• The increase of driving force to the wheel will obviously provoke a sudden acceleration of the motorcycle.

The riding sensation that comes from this state of affairs is a series of jerking motions that are very annoying, especially during a relaxing stretch or when caught in an urban traffic jam.

Since the engine sprocket is not on the axis of the swingarm pivot, the chain's total length must vary during the range of wheel motion.

This length is greatest when the engine spocket, the fork axis and the wheel axis are aligned (in terms of the suspension, this is obviously the case at mid-travel).

The chain, therefore, must adapt appropriately to these changing lengths, which is to say, it must have minimal play at the greatest length and be somewhat slack in other conditions.

Given the same suspension, long swingarms shorten the amount of play (Figure 6.2).

Too much play on the chain therefore gives rise to a jerking motion.

The way to deal with this problem is to have your swingarm length checked regularly (if you are already familiar with motorcycles you will know that the mounting between the swingarm and the wheel is built to allow easy adjustments); this is how to obtain the right amount of play on your chain.

Take the following steps:
After removing the connection between the suspension and the swingarm, lift the rear wheel until the axis of the the engine sprocket, the swingarm and the wheel are in alignment. As we have already

mentioned, this configuration places the greatest distance between the engine and final drive sprockets; at this point, regulate the length of the swingarm in such a way as to obtain minimal chain play.

This sequence of operations is not easily performed but by referring to the manufacturer's instructions (usually reproduced on the swingarm), you will in any case be able to obtain adequate results.

Be careful, however not to overdo how much play you cut out: by pulling it too tight you may provoke the following harmful effects:
- Cause high enough tension in the chain to lengthen it and, consequently, damage it in a short amount of time;
- Damage the engine sprocket bearing;
- Impede correct functioning of the suspension.

From a design perspective, in order to keep chain play down to a minimum, swingarm pivots are positioned as close as possible to the engine sprocket, and, at the same time, an effort is made to make the swingarms very long.

In any case, during the design process of a touring or street bike, in order to facilitate a smooth ride on a straight course, the three pivots are either completely or nearly in alignment, so that when the rider opens or closes the throttle, there will be little slack to take up and, thus, minimal jerking motion.

Since the primary objective of Grand Prix bikes is always maximum performance levels, they are not expected to be especially comfortable to ride; so the idea for these bikes is to have the three pivot points of the suspension configuration line up when the racer is coming out of a curve and starting to "open up the throttle." This is when power delivery must be at its most regular and smooth; even the smallest impulse too much could be enough to push the bike beyond its adhesion limit.

Cush-drive systems made of rubber, placed between the sprocket and the rear wheel, play the important role of damping sudden jerking movements due to chain slack, gearshifts, and irregulari-

ties coming from the fact that the engine does not produce a continuous torque.

Cush-drive systems are therefore very important both to improve riding comfort as well as to protect the inner parts of the engine, such as the gears, from sudden yanks and uneven gas delivery.

Finally, we note that the reason the engine sprocket shaft and the swingarm pivot do not coincide is substantially due to manufacturing difficulties, but there is no reason in the future why some sort of innovative solutions may not be found for this.

Belt-drive

For **belt-drive**, the functioning is completely analogous to chain-drive, and, in theory, a chain-drive could be substituted by a belt-drive. Obviously, appropriate attention must be given to the dimensions of the pulleys or rollers, which must have a radius bigger than a certain minimum value; and their size must be adequate to the torque that is to be transmitted by the engine.

An obvious but rather limiting consideration for many bikes with a braced swingarm, making these models unsuited for belt-drive, is that a belt cannot be opened up like a chain for assembly in the factory.

Shaft-drive

Shaft-driven transmissions are generally characterized by a structure containing the following elements:

- A transmission shaft, up to the swingarm pivot, longitudinal to the motorcycle;
- A universal joint coinciding with the swingarm pivot;
- A transmission shaft parallel to the swingarm;
- A pair of bevel gears that rotate the motion 90 degrees.

In this system, play is eliminated from the transmission system, apart from that of the universal joint and coupling.

The loss of power in the pair of bevel gears is roughly 4% to 5%, depending on the precision with which they have been manufactured.

If the output shaft of the engine's transmission is transversal to the axis of the motorcycle (which is the case for most motorcycles), then it is necessary to add another pair of bevel gears at the base of the swingarm to rotate the motion 90 degrees, with further power loss.

The same considerations regarding the importance of a cush-drive system, which can even be built into the engine, hold true in the case of shaft-driven transmission as well since it is an extremely rigid structure requiring an accurate damping system to protect against sudden movements.

A COMPARISON BETWEEN GEAR/CHAIN SYSTEMS AND SHAFT-DRIVEN SYSTEMS

Let us examine the differences between the two types of transmission.

Weight: shaft transmission is overall heavier than chain drive; furthermore, the last pair of gears is placed right on the rear wheel axle, which notably increases the inertia of the unsprung masses and, consequently, causes a theoretically less comfortable ride on bumpy surfaces.

Duration and maintenance: shaft transmission has a clear advantage in that is practically everlasting and only requires a minimum of servicing.

Cleanliness and safety: clearly a better solution is provided by shaft transmission which never dirties the motorcyclist or passengers with oil, and is safer because it has no visible moving parts. Furthermore, if a chain is neglected or poorly regulated it may jump off its track between the engine and final drive sprockets and jam the motorcycle.

Bulk: shaft transmission is no more bulky in itself than normal chain transmission, but, so as to avoid two 90-degree motion returns, the adoption of an engine with a longitudinal crank shaft is a necessary premise. In the case of some engine configurations that are designed to have a longitudinal engine axle (such as engines with boxer or opposed cylinders, and 90-degree V-Twins) a shaft transmission is obviously the best solution.

For these kinds of engines *the inertial effect due to the crank shaft creates a curious state of affairs* that you can easily put into practice and experience yourself. In a stopped position and out of gear, firmly open up the throttle: you will be surprised by the creation of a sideways toppling couple that gives a truly startling sideways push to the motorcycle.

When you are in motion this effect is hardly noticeable.

Ability to vary the gear ratio: it is very easy to substitute the engine sprocket and/or the final drive sprockets in order to vary the final gear ratio in chain drives; the last pair of gears on a shaft transmission are more expensive and to ensure good working order, it is best to get the parts directly supplied from the manufacturer.

Conclusions: no one system is absolutely better than another; every kind of motorcycle lends itself to one solution or another.

Sportbikes, which need to be light and uncomplicated mechanically, are built with chain drive.

For touring bikes and models which require easy servicing and maintenance, a shaft transmission is generally preferred.

EFFECT OF THE TRANSMISSION OF DRIVING FORCE TO THE GROUND

(known as "chain pull" effect in the motorcycle world) Having seen the systems for transmitting the torque from the engine to the wheel, we can now go on to examine the effect of applying this force to the suspension.

Let us give a schematic version of a normal transmission system, (Figure 6.3):

We have described how the force of traction *T* creates a weight transfer from front to rear. The change in the load on the rear wheel tends, obviously, to compress the suspension.

Keep this in mind as we go on to examine another rather curious and surprising force that exists along with it, yet goes in the opposite direction.

Let us calculate the moment of the forces acting on the transmission system at a particular point where the force of the chain pull produces zero moment (Figure 6.4). This point, which we will call the **pole of the moments** (**PofM**), is located at the intersection of the straight line passing through the tight segment of the chain and the straight line formed by the swingarm axis.

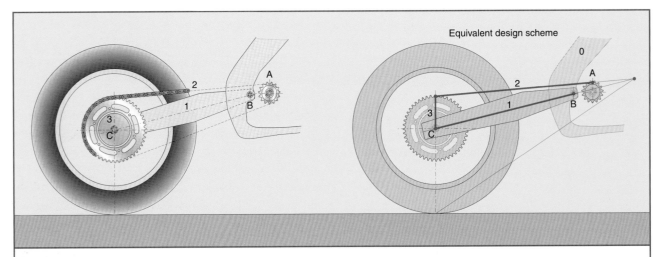

Fig. 6.3: standard system for transmitting driving force
• element 0 is the frame;
• element 1 is the swingarm;

• element 2 is the tightened segment of the chain
• element 3 is the wheel plus sprocket, which effectively form a single body.

The angle formed by the straight line passing from the **PofM** to the point on the ground P and the surface of the ground, is called the **chain pull angle** and will be indicated by the Greek letter σ.

As we can see from the figure, the *force of traction tends to make the suspension extend, thus lifting the rear end of the motorcycle; the larger the chain pull angle, the bigger the lift!*

In practice **σ** takes on fundamental importance as a design parameter, because it determines the bike's attitude when driving force is transmitted to the ground. Small variations in the angle can make the same motorbike handle quite differently, since the rear suspension is heavily affected by its influence.

Let us see in what way:

A large chain pull angle brings on a big change in the suspension behavior depending on whether the rider is accelerating or not.

A forceful burst of speed rebounds the suspension, so only a very soft, barely preloaded spring is needed to maintain the attitude and pass over holes in the road.

When the rider closes down the throttle, the rebound effect on the rear suspension disappears, so the rear end tends to squat a lot.

Seeing how important this angle is, Grand Prix

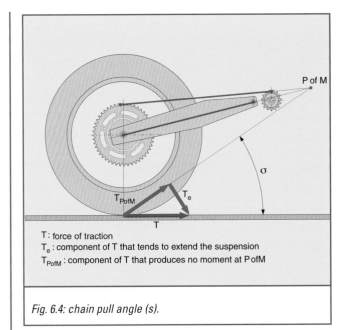

T : force of traction
T_e : component of T that tends to extend the suspension
T_{PofM} : component of T that produces no moment at P of M

Fig. 6.4: chain pull angle (s).

bikes are usually built so that the swingarm connection is designed to allow the height to be adjusted, to adapt the motorcycle to the particular track and rider.

We should point out that the **PofM** is not a fixed point on the chassis: it varies from second to second with the vertical travel of the wheel. To be more specific, when the wheel rises, the **PofM**

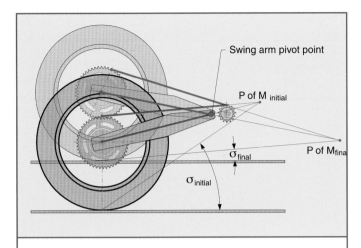

Fig. 6.5: chain pull angle varies with wheel travel.

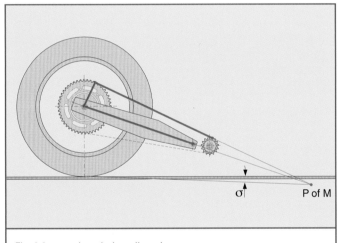

Fig. 6.6: negative chain pull angle.

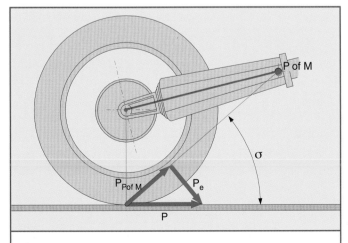

Fig. 6.7: chain pull angle with universal transmission.

lowers and the angle σ diminishes.

The parameters that determine the end points of the **PofM** are:

- the position of the engine sprocket shaft;
- the position of the swingarm pivot;
- the length of the swingarm;
- and the diameters of the engine and final drive sprockets.

If, paradoxically, the swingarm were of infinite length (and thus, the chain as well), the angle σ would never change (Figure 6.5).

In theory, one should also be able to obtain a zero chain pull effect.

Modifying the geometry of the motorcycle, or to be more specific, the swingarm and engine sprocket axes, one would be able to position the **PofM** on the line formed by the ground.

Under these conditions, the force transmitted to the ground would create no action on the suspension: in other words, with zero angle σ, the transmission of power to the ground does not bring about any lifting of the rear end of the motorcycle.

If we gave completely free play to our imagination, we could create a transmission system that tends to compress the suspension during acceleration, with the design scheme for example, in Figure 6.6.

With a shaft driven transmission the situation simplifies to the following:

The **PofM** *coincides with the swingarm pivot and the angle* σ *is the angle between the ground and the line joining the point of contact between wheel and ground with the swingarm pivot (Figure 6.7).*

In this case the variation in the height of the **PofM** coincides with the lowering of the frame. It is intuitively easy to grasp that angle σ is bigger with chain transmission; in fact, if you think about it, motorcycles with simple shaft transmissions, especially old models, tend to lift up their rear end under rapid acceleration.

In order to reduce this problem, which caused undesireable variations in attitude according to the

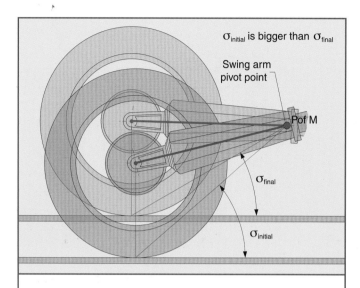

$\sigma_{initial}$ is bigger than σ_{final}

Swing arm
pivot point

P of M

σ_{final}

$\sigma_{initial}$

Fig. 6.8: variations in the chain pull angle with wheel travel

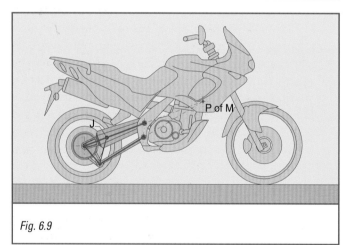

P of M

J

Fig. 6.9

size of the torque, more complex solutions were developed to allow the **PofM** to be positioned at the desired height, thus eliminating the trouble.

As we can see, this solution goes back to a four-bar linkage system with all its attendant advantages.

The only added complication is that a second joint must be placed at the point J in Figure 6.9, entailing an increase in weight and cost.

OTHER CONSIDERATIONS ON THE "CHAIN PULL" EFFECT

Up until now we have analyzed the behavior of the transmission system assuming that all the power is transmitted to the ground. Let us suppose instead that **friction is eliminated**, either because of the presence of water or oil on the road surface, or more simply, because the wheel has lost contact with the ground (after a jump or a hollow).

Under these conditions, the chain accelerates the rear wheel without being opposed by any force other than the inertia of rotation. This set of conditions is illustrated in Figure 6.10.

As the diagram makes clear, the chain pull tends to rebound the suspension in according to the *angle* $\boldsymbol{\eta}$.

The effect illustrated in the figure can be easily experienced.

Solidly placing the motorcycle on its main stand with the rear wheel raised off the ground, remove the shock absorber and stretch a bungy cord from the luggage rack, for example, to around the rear fork.

Put the wheel back into its standard position as if the shock absorber were mounted, pushing against the tension of the elastic cord.

Turn on the engine at this point, put it in gear and give a sudden twist to the throttle: *you will notice the rear suspension extending and, consequently, the wheel moving farther away from the frame.*

When accelerating a motorcycle on the road, then, because of the chain pull effect, the suspension will rebound, according to:
• The angle of chain pull $\boldsymbol{\sigma}$ when there is perfect adhesion between tire and ground,
• The angle $\boldsymbol{\eta}$ when there is no contact with the ground, or zero adhesion.

Generally, the angle $\boldsymbol{\sigma}$ is bigger than the angle $\boldsymbol{\eta}$.
Because of the difference between these two angles, the attitude of the motorcycle varies greatly during passages from maximum adhesion to zero adhesion conditions and vice versa.

We will take this topic up again when discussing the highsiding phenomenon in Chapter 7, on motorcycle attitude.

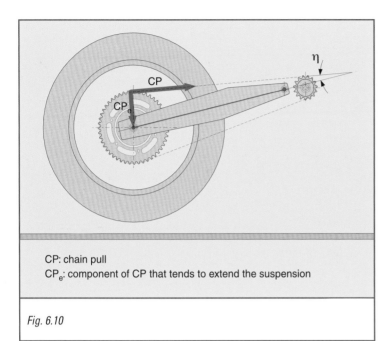

CP: chain pull
CPₑ: component of CP that tends to extend the suspension

Fig. 6.10

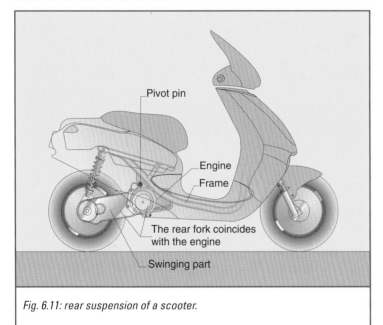

Pivot pin

Engine
Frame

The rear fork coincides
with the engine

Swinging part

Fig. 6.11: rear suspension of a scooter.

THE SCOOTER

The scooter represents a special case in the motorcycle world: its peculiarity derives from the fact that its engine is not mounted rigidly onto the frame as it is for all the other motorcycles, but rather, it rests on a fulcrum at a single point, free to oscillate around itself.

In this way the scooter engine takes over the function generally assumed by the swingarm as an oscillating part, and, at the same time, the automatic gear shift, using a belt-drive, transmits the driving force all the way to the wheel, also acting, then, as a transmission system.

The engine, like the swingarm, also offers a point of linkage for the shock absorber and, at its rear end, supports the wheel (Figure 6.11).

What is accomplished, then, is a very rational structure which manages to eliminate one part, the rear fork, and remove at source, so to speak, all the motorcycle problems associated with the cost and regulation of the transmission. This also frees up a considerable amount of space, permitting more carrying compartments.

The scooter's practicality, with maintenance reduced to a bare minimum, the ease of riding with an automatic gear shift, and the extreme rationality of the system are some of the characteristics that have assured the success of the scooter as a vehicle perfectly suited to transportation needs in big urban centers.

To return to our discussion on the effect of the transmission of power on the rear suspension and, thus, on the attitude, *the scooter behaves like a motorcycle with shaft drive*; the point where the engine fulcrum rests on the frame becomes the center of instantaneous rotation of the suspension system.

For manufacturing reasons, in some scooters the engine-frame fulcrum is located rather high with respect to the ground, causing a significant "chain pull" effect; these scooters are characterized by visibile lifting of the rear end under acceleration. Since the maneuverability demands made on the scooter are rather limited, this phenomenon turns out to be of little importance, or, at the most, a surprising effect.

The solution offered by the scooter, in which the swingarm and the engine are one part, is ingeniously simple, but it gives rise to a rather complex technical question, that is, how to mount the engine.

The main requirements to satisfy are the following two:

• Isolate the frame from vibrations;
• Allow the suspension to function properly.

Let us take the case of a 50 cc scooter, representing one of the most popular models in current use: like almost all scooters, it is supplied with a single-cylinder engine and, because of cost and bulk, does not have a countershaft.

When rotating, then, a lot of very big and noticeable primary vibrations are produced; so if the engine were mounted to the frame with a simple pin joint, the repercussions on the rider's comfort would be absolutely unacceptable.

Let us analyze the frequency band of this disturbance. The engine rotation range is between 1200 rpm minimum to over 7000 rpm maximum speed, to which there is a corresponding frequency band that ranges from 20 to over 100 Hz.

This is a rather high frequency range that causes low amplitude vibration in the motor-cyrcle; in fact, these are the frequencies that create the tingling sensation you feel on your skin when gripping the handlebar.

Road surface irregularities generate lower frequency disturbances with, at the same time, higher amplitudes.

In order to reconcile the demands made by these two families of disturbances with such diverse characteristics, it is necessary to mount the engine to the frame using a sophisticated suspension system with two degrees of freedom:

• The classic coil-spring shock absorber that goes to work on road surface irregularities,

• While a system of connecting rods (in order to have two degrees of freedom at least one push-rod must be used) more rigidly attached to the frame serves to filter the high frequency vibrations.

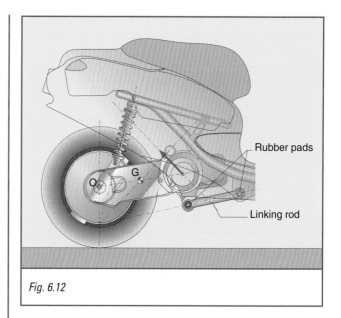

Fig. 6.12

The attachment of the engine unit to the frame is often made using rubber dampers that reduce the vibrations transmitted to the chassis.

These rubber supports must also be appropriately sized and positioned; in fact, if they are too stiff they will continue to transmit vibrations; if they are too elastic, on the other hand, they will make the whole structure too elastic, possibly causing handling problems in the form of visible oscillations of the engine-wheel set.

The most common design scheme adopted for most low-powered scooters is shown below (Figure 6.12). Note how the axis of the connecting rod extension is placed in a position so as to not generate loads on the damper caused by forces acting on the suspension.

The same sort of problems discussed in regard to a 50 cc scooter are present to an even worse degree in high-powered scooters.

The more high-powered the engine, the bigger the vibrations that need to be absorbed and the force that must be transmitted from the wheel to the frame.

Moreover, given the higher performance in terms of acceleration and speed, the elasticity of the whole engine support system must be contained, so as not give rise to instability problems.

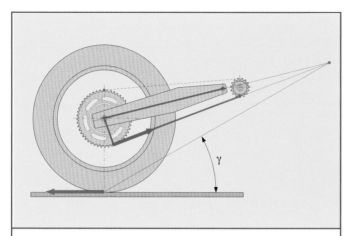

Fig. 6.13: chain pull angle when downshifting.

BEHAVIOR OF THE TRANSMISSION WHEN DOWNSHIFTING

Let us get back to the motorcycle. In the preceding sections we analyzed the transmission of power only under acceleration; let us now look at what happens under **deceleration or when downshifting**, or rather, when the transmission acts as a brake.

The lower part of the chain is now the tight segment and the engine acts as a true brake, slowing down the motorcycle.

Under these conditions, in every way analogous to the preceding situation des-cribed above, this time a brake pull angle will be determined (referred to as **γ**), while the suspension will tend to be compressed (Figure 6.13).

This gives rise to a very peculiar response on the part of the motorcycle. Especially with high-powered engines with little back gearing, by down-shifting abruptly you can easily make the rear wheel perform a little jump.

Let us describe this phenomenon: the reverse-torque produced by the engine braking transmits a large, sudden braking force which *tends to abruptly compress the suspension.*

This means that the wheel tends to lift up and the frame tends to sink down. If the clutch is suddenly let out, the movements between the frame and the wheel are inversely proportional to their respective masses (remember what was said about the inertia

effect). The motorcycle, in any case, being heavier than the wheel, does not sink much, while *the wheel is lifted off the ground*. While in the air, it is then further slowed down by the reverse-torque and when it touches back down onto the ground, a large braking effect is once again generated, resulting in a new, abrupt compression of the suspension.

This series of actions can set off an annoying chattering response from the rear wheel that is dampened in time by the shock absorber or by the rider, who can pull the clutch lever or decelerate less.

A chattering response when downshifting is most felt from engines with big reverse-torque capacity such as large single-cylinder or four-stroke, twin-cylinder engines.

If these sorts of propulsion systems are mounted onto sportbikes, which have little rear load during braking, in order to avoid that annoying wheel-hopping problem it becomes almost obligatory to apply some sort of system to limit the transmission of the reverse-torque.

EFFECT OF THE TRANSMISSION OF A BRAKING FORCE TO THE GROUND

As we have said, the transmission of the engine power to the motorcycle only comes about through the rear wheel, while the braking force can be applied to both the wheels. Let us see the effect of applying a braking force onto the wheels of a motorcycle. The transmission of the forces and their effects can be analyzed using the same method used for the driving force.

Rear Wheel Braking

The rear brake caliper can be attached in two different ways:
- *Mounted directly onto the rear fork;*
- By means of *a connecting push rod to the frame.*

Both designs, which have a significant effect on the suspension response, can be illustrated in the following way:

- Mounting of the brake torque arm **directly onto the rear fork** (Figure 6.14).

This set-up is analogous to a shaft: the wheel and the brake mounting form a single body with the rear fork.

The force applied to the ground during braking will go in the opposite direction to the force of traction; and the reaction, too, will be the opposite: *the suspension will tend to be compressed, according to the size of the angle* λ.

It is important to note that the functioning remains the same, no matter where the point of attachment is between the brake caliper mount and the rear fork.

The only variation that might be noticeable from shifting the point of linkage to the rear fork would be constituted by forces internal to the system.

• Attachment of the brake torque arm **by means of a connecting push rod linked to the frame** (Figure 6.15).

This case is very similar to chain/gear-drive and the compression effect on the suspension can be regulated on the basis of the position of the point of linkage to the frame.

This linkage system is clearly heavier, more costly and more complicated compared with direct anchoring onto the rear fork, but it does allow the possibility of reducing the suspension compression to a desired level and, partially, too, the wheel-hopping response.

In practice, this solution presents the following limitations:

• Quite small benefits, with the disadvantages of added weight and cost;
• The possibility of positioning the point of anchorage to the rear fork where you want it to be is often limited by other mechanical obstructions such as the exhaust header passing through.

In any case, if a strong, abrupt force is applied to the rear brake there is likely to be a chattering response from the rear wheel.

General Observations

If the rear braking force is applied gently, the motorcycle will tend to slightly squat at the rear end, which gives a more yielding steering action; at the same time, a lessened forward pitching movement offers a more comfortable ride, especially for the passenger.

The rear suspension settings take on *great importance*:

• Too much preload on the shock absorber spring causes easy wheel strain, with rapid deformation; moreover, when the suspension is extended, it is difficult to absorb small bumps in the road surface;
• The retarding force of the hydraulic brake must be strong enough to rapidly dampen the chatter response whenever it is provoked.

What follows is a reproduction of an unusual design used for some racing bikes during the 70's:

the brake disk is coaxial to the engine sprocket and the caliper is fixed directly onto the engine or onto the frame; the braking force is entirely transmitted by means of the chain.

This arrangement presents the following undeniable advantages:

• Strong braking force from a lightweight disc. The engine sprocket rotates much faster than the final drive sprocket, usually 2 to 3 times as fast, and as a result, the braking force applied to the wheel equals that developed by the brake disc rotating on the engine sprocket, multiplied by the same ratio.
  With this setup, even with a smaller diameter disc (which is therefore much lighter), we are able to obtain the desired amount of braking force;
• The weight of the unsprung masses is reduced: the weight of the disc, the caliper, and the anchoring bears on the frame, and not on the wheel, which is an unsprung mass;

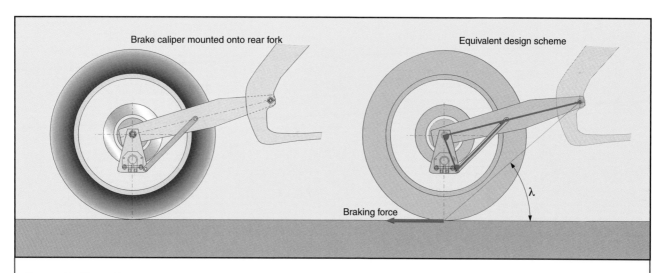

Fig. 6.14: braking with torque arm directly attached to rear fork.

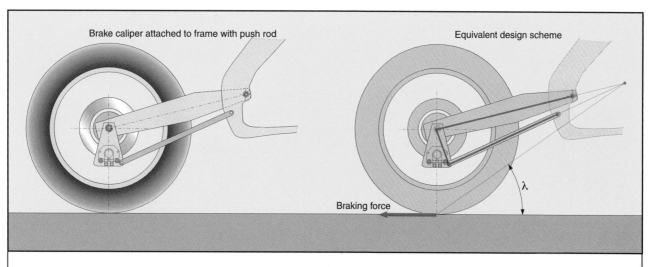

Fig. 6.15: braking with torque arm attached to frame with connecting push rod.

• Concentration of the masses around the center of gravity.

Due to safety reasons, technical regulations subsequently banned this design scheme. *Whenever the chain broke, the motorcyclist was left without a rear brake.*

Front Wheel Braking

The transmission of the braking force to the suspension depends greatly on the geometrical characteristics of the suspension and, even more importantly, on the trajectory taken by the wheel.

Let us ignore for the moment that along with this force there will also be a weight transfer that, as we have seen, tends to compress the front suspension; in the figure only the *braking force* is taken into consideration, and it is immediately evident that it will differ widely in the three cases.

In the first case (case **a**, Figure 6.17, that of an ordinary telescopic fork), the trajectory of the point on the ground P is necessarily parallel to the

Fig. 6.16: brake disc co-axial to sprocket.

fork axis and passes directly through the center of the wheel; the application of a braking force compresses the suspension, or, as they say in the motorcycle world, it makes the suspension dive.

In the literature, this sort of response is referred to as **pro-dive.**

In the second case (case **b**), the trajectory of the point of contact with the ground P is orthogonal to the ground; the suspension will not be affected by the horizontal braking forces, that is, it will have a neutral response.

In the last case (case **c**) illustrated here, the trajectory of P is such that the suspension tends to extend; the application of a braking force, therefore, limits the dive response of the suspension.

In the literature, this sort of response is referred to as **anti-dive**.

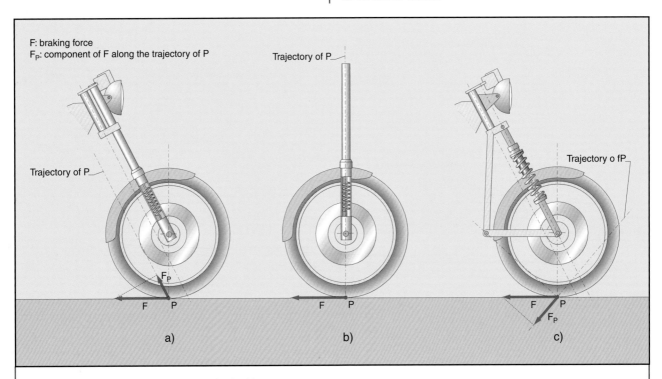

Fig. 6.17: behavior of front suspension during braking:
a) pro-dive behavior: the effect of the braking force compresses the fork;
b) neutral behavior: application of braking force has no effect on the fork;
c) anti-dive behavior: the effect of the braking force extends the fork.

In Chapter 5 we focused on the reactions between road surface and tires, taking the motorcycle as a rigid body without suspension, traveling upright in a straight line.

With this set of provisions, we analyzed the conditions that maintain the vehicle in a state of equilibrium during acceleration and deceleration, imagining a blocked suspension system.

In the chapter that followed, Chapter 6, we saw how horizontal traction and braking forces are transferred from the ground to the frame by means of the suspension and transmission systems.

As promised, in this chapter we will go on to examine the overall attitude assumed by the vehicle under various conditions.

In other terms, *we will determine how the effects (on the suspension) of weight transfer and transmission of the horizontal traction and braking forces are formed.*

When introducing suspension action into the dynamics of a motorcycle traveling upright in a straight line, the chassis will be subjected to two types of movements on the plane of travel:

• *A vertical movement* (lifting or lowering).
• *A rotational movement* (pitch).

The combination of these movements determines the so-called "attitude" of the motorcycle.

HOW TO DETERMINE ATTITUDE OF THE MOTORCYCLE UNDER ACCELERATION
Rear suspension

We have seen that the traction force under acceleration creates a surprising rebound effect on the rear suspension, according to the size of the chain pull angle. The behavior of the rear suspension and rear transmission when a force is being transmitted to the ground has already been illustrated in chapter 6, where we discussed how to determine the "Pole of the Moments" (**PofM**) and the angle σ of the "chain pull" effect.

We must now also consider the effect of the *weight transfer*, which *tends, instead, to compress the suspension.*

It follows, then, that the traction force generates two opposing effects on the rear suspension:

• An **extension** or **rebound** effect due to the

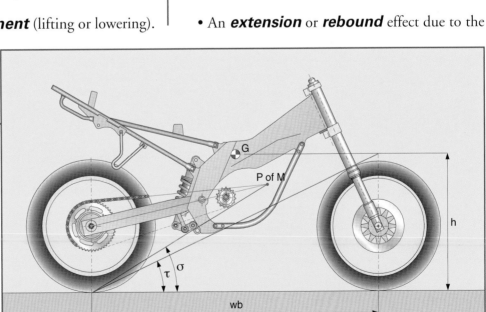

Fig. 7.1: chain pull angle is grater than weight transfer angle.
G: center of gravity
P of M: pole of moments
τ: weight transfer angle
σ: chain pull angle
h: center of gravity height
wb: wheelbase

chain pull effect, in function of angle σ;
• A **compression** effect due to the weight transfer, in function of angle τ.

To give a general idea, we could say that:
*when a traction force **T** is applied to the rear wheel, the suspension compresses or extends according to whether the prevailing effect comes from weight transfer or from chain pull effect.*
A quick calculation can be easily made by comparing the values of the two angles involved, σ and τ.
The following figure is an excellent aid for understanding this:

it represents a streetbike whose chain pull angle σ is slightly wider than angle τ, so under acceleration the rear suspension will tend to rebound and lift the rear end of the motorcycle.
With the exception of some old-style, shaft-driven transmissions and the case of scooters, the situation illustrated in Figure 7.1 is quite common for streetbikes, since the design of the vehicle generally assures that the two angles will be quite similar when traveling upright in a straight line with one rider mounted.

Naturally, during street use:
• The center of gravity of the total motorcycle-rider system varies according to the weight of the rider and the position assumed on the seat, the amount of gas there is in the tank as well as the possible presence of a passenger or luggage;
• The chain pull angle varies with the travel of the rear suspension.

Consequently, during the design process it is not possible to precisely identify what the relation will be between the two angles of configuration that the motorcycle may assume during use.
For this reason motorcycles are usually designed to have similar values for σ and τ when traveling upright in a straight line with one rider mounted.
During the development phase of the working prototype, the bike is tried out on the road and the choice of angles is put to the test; if changes are needed to create different handling responses, the values of the angles are modified.

Front suspension

Under acceleration, the front suspension only receives the force coming from the weight transfer.
No matter what the geometrical characteristics of the front suspension, when it is relieved of part of the load, it will rebound, lifting the front end of the vehicle.

Overall effect on attitude of the motorcycle

Under acceleration, the fork tends to lengthen, thus contributing to front end lift.
The rear suspension may behave, instead, in three different ways, giving rise to three possible types of attitude:

Case a) $\sigma = \tau$ in which the chain pull angle is equal to the weight transfer.

• The rear suspension remains **unchanged** (the shock absorber keeps the same initial length).

• Because of the rebound effect on the front suspension the **center of gravity of the whole vehicle rises** and the motorcycle experiences a **rotation** around the point of contact ground-to-rear wheel (the tires are taken as rigid).

The effect of the rising center of gravity is called **jacking**, to use a popular term in the automotive world.
Observe the trace left by the moving center of gravity of a motorcycle with this layout, described onto a plane parallel to the vehicle: we can see that with every increase in power, after shifting, for example, the line of the trajectory rises.
This means work is done to no purpose to raise the center of gravity (a loss of energy, substantially), work that is taken from the forward movment, not to mention that the course described by the center of gravity is longer (Figure 7.3).
This configuration makes it quite easy to pull the bike up into a wheelie.

Case b) σ < τ **in which the chain pull angle is smaller than the weight transfer angle.**

• The rear suspension **is compressed.**

• When the front end of the motorcycle lifts, there is a corresponding squatting of the rear end.

Consequently, the **vertical movement of the center of gravity will be limited**, while there may be an appreciable **rotation** of the vehicle (Figure 7.4).

When the attitude of the accelerating motorcycle is such that the chassis rotates appreciably, there is a concommitant variation in the geometrical parameters of the steering: since the chassis is rotating, the rake angle increases and consequently (see Chapter 3 for the mathematical formulas), by maintaining the turn angle while accelerating out of a corner, for example, **the vehicle tends to widen or open up its trajectory.**

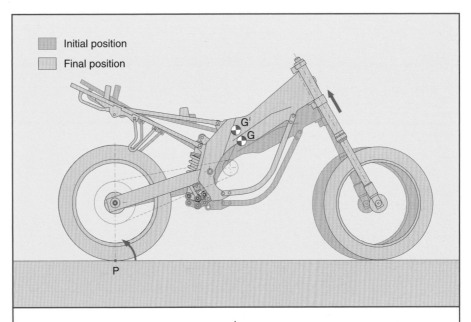

Fig. 7.2: the center of gravity rises from G to G^l and the motorcycle rotates around P.

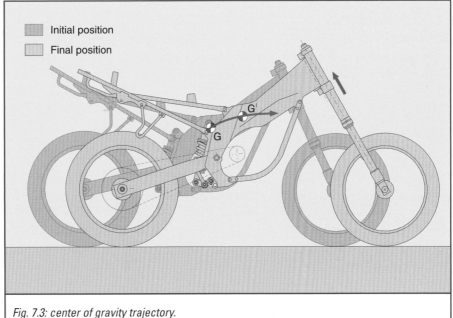

Fig. 7.3: center of gravity trajectory.

Moreover, because the rear end is squatting, it will tend to load the rear wheel, **aiding traction**, but at the same time making the vehicle understeer.

The consequences of this are described in the chapter regarding tires (Chapter 8).

So the tendency of a motorcycle to squat appreciably at the rear end can constitute a limit to its use as a sportbike.

We can imagine a particular case in which there is zero jacking; this would only come about when the front end extension is exactly equal to the rear end compression, or rather, to state this in scientific terms, when the two axes have equal vertical stiffness in opposition to the force of traction.

This would give rise to a rotation of the motorcycle around its center of gravity without any variation in center of gravity height.

The course described by the center of gravity when the motorcycle is under acceleration will be practically horizontal in this case, which means minimum waste of energy.

Once the motorcycle has completed the rotation, all the available power will be used to move the vehicle forward.

This sort of handling response is well-suited to large touring bikes, since the rider has the perception of a less "sensitive" vehicle: the fact that the shifting of the center of gravity is limited makes it easy to master the tendency of even high-powered bikes to rear up.

Case c) σ > τ, in which the chain pull angle is bigger than the weight transfer angle.

• The rear suspension **rebounds** under acceleration.

The chain pull angle will be bigger than the weight transfer angle.

In this situation, the center of gravity rises due to the action of the front suspension, and the rise is added to by that of the rear suspension.

The course of the trace left by the center of gravity during acceleration shows an even greater movement than in case a).

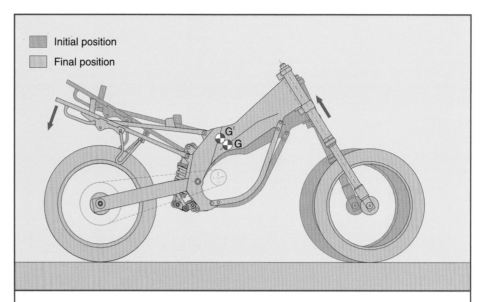

Fig. 7.4: • front suspension extends, rear suspension compresses:
 • center of gravity shifts a short distance, from G to G';
 • frame rotation appreciable.

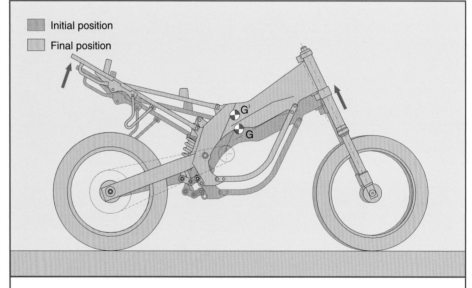

Fig. 7.5: • both front and rear suspension are extended:
 • center of gravity rises from G to G';
 • limited frame rotation.

The rise of the center of gravity will be very noticeable, while the rotation of the vehicle will remain quite limited (Figure 7.5).

Obviously, a vehicle with a rear suspension of

this kind lifts easily off its front end when accelerating. In fact, because of the rise in center of gravity from chain pull, there is a corresponding increase in the weight transfer as well.

In compensation, however, since the chassis rotation and, thus, the variation in the rake angle, are moderate, the "wide cornering" phenomenon while accelerating in a curve is kept to a minimum.

This sort of handling response is characteristic of sport and road-racing bikes.

HOW TO DETERMINE ATTITUDE OF THE MOTORCYCLE DURING BRAKING

Just as in the case of acceleration, the chassis will perform a complex movement combining two types of actions:
- the first, a vertical shift of the center of gravity.
- the second, a rotation.

Rear suspension

Let us suppose, for simplicity's sake, that *braking takes place only with the front brake*, as is common practice in road racing; the *load transfer* will therefore come off the rear wheel and, lightening the rear end, will allow the shock absorber to rebound.

The rear end of the motorcycle, then, will lift during braking, until the rear suspension hits its maximum extension.

This response is independent of the type of suspension.

Front suspension

A similar response, based on what we have seen during acceleration for the rear suspension, will occur with two effects placed on the suspension:

- The weight transfer will tend to compress the front suspension, since as we have seen, the front load is increased;

- The effect of the horizontal braking force will provoke a different response on the part of the suspension according to its geometrical configuration and, especially, according to the trajectory described by the wheel.

Overall effect of the attitude on the vehicle

Keeping in mind what we have discussed in the preceding chapter on the response of the front suspension during braking, the possible scenarios would be the following:

Case a)
Pro-dive response on the part of the front suspension.

Let us begin with the most commonly used kind of suspension, that is, a pro-dive telescopic fork.

The effect of the braking force tends to compress the fork; the dive due to this effect will be added onto that of the weight transfer.

The fork dives noticeably and may do so even violently when it bottoms out. Good fork settings are essential in these circumstances in order to maintain control over the motorcycle, as we shall see in the next section on overlap.

The lift of the rear end, limited by its suspension extension, is generally shorter than the front dive travel, so that the final result when braking is that the total center of gravity of the motorcycle will not only rotate, it will also lower.

During braking, then, we will have negative jacking and the final attitude of the vehicle will be characterized by a rotated and lowered chassis.

The trace of the line left by the shifting of the bike's center of gravity during braking will curve down towards the ground. With the sinking of the motorcycle, the height of the center of gravity from the ground will also diminish, helping to create *a greater braking capacity, because the tumble effect is reduced* (remember that the weight transfer depends on the height of the center of gravity).

The rake angle noticeably diminishes and this brings on a consequent reduction in the righting moment, partly compensated, however, by the load increase on the front wheel, which, as we have seen, tends to increase it.

Sportbikes, which have a small rake angle, have less stability during braking, so that even though the vehicle is always controllable, the rider should be cautious and alert under these conditions (Figure 7.6).

A pro-dive front suspension, then, is better adapted to sportbikes, which are designed more for high performance results than for smooth riding comfort.

Case b)
Neutral response on the part of the front suspension.

This state of affairs occurs when the trajectory of the front wheel contact patch is perpendicular to the ground and, therefore, to the braking force.

The dive effect depends solely on the weight transfer and, thus, turns out to be weaker than in the previous case.

This helps to dampen the hard hitting response of the fork when it bottoms out and allows the adoption of softer springs and an overall less rigid fork.

Given the limited front dive action, the motorcycle will be mainly characterized by a *rotational movement* and a small or zero vertical sinking.

If the front and rear suspension have equal vertical stiffness and the center of gravity is positioned at the halfway point of the wheelbase, the only response would be a rotation of the chassis; the center of gravity would remain at the same height from the ground.

The line traced by the center of gravity, described on a plane parallel to the motorcycle, would have a straight-line course during braking, something that would certainly contribute to solid control over the vehicle.

We might also note that since a neutral response from the suspension is completely independent of the braking force, the optimum suspension settings for straight-

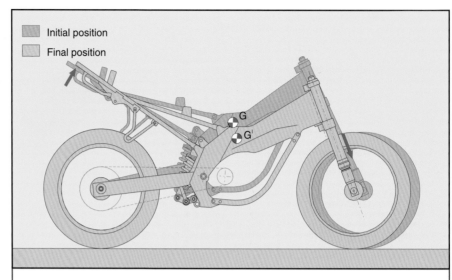

Fig. 7.6: center of gravity lowers from G to G'. The motorcycle rotates forward.

line travel are equally good during braking.

Case c)
Anti-dive response on the part of the front suspension.

This happens when the trajectory of the wheel-to-ground contact point (P) passes in front of the center of the wheel.

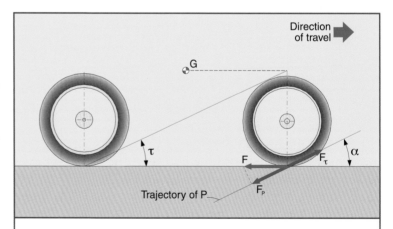

Figura 7.7: $\alpha = \tau$: the suspension neither extends nor compresses.
F: braking force;
F_p : component of F in the direction of the trajectory of P;
F_τ : components of the weight transfer in the direction of the trajectory of P;
α: angle of the trajectory of P;
τ: weight transfer angle;
G: center of gravity.

In this case the weight transfer and braking effects will be taken away, meaning minimal or even zero dive.

When the trajectory of point P forms an angle that is equal to that of the weight transfer, the front suspension will neither extend nor compress.

Finally, if the angle α of the trajectory of P is less than the load transfer angle **τ** , the suspension will **extend** under braking action.

A motorcycle with this type of front suspension will, therefore, have a minimal tendency to dive, or none at all, or even a lifting of the front along with the usual lifting of the rear.

This results, then, in **positive jacking** and a **minimal rotation of the frame.**

Raising the center of gravity brings on increased weight transfer and, thus, the vehicle may have more propensity to tumble backwards.

This can only be a drawback for a sportbike, because it limits its take-off acceleration potential.

By damping the pro-dive action of the front suspension, then, we add to the riding comfort of both the pilot and the passenger.

Without the rotational effect on the chassis, the passenger will no longer end up wrapped around the pilot's shoulders, and the pilot will no longer feel the dead weight of the passenger every time the motorcycle takes off in acceleration.

Furthermore, since the rake angle remains practically constant, the motorcycle is guaranteed stability during braking.

Anti-dive suspension is perhaps most suited to touring bikes or cruisers.

Overlap phenomenon

Braking action can at times be a quite violent, sudden impact, for example:

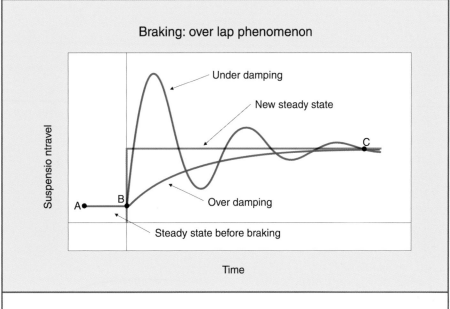

Fig. 7.8: braking: overlap phenomenon.

• A sudden deceleration in order to avoid an obstruction.

• In sport mode, when the braking action is delayed until the last possible moment.

In these situations, thanks to the power of modern braking systems, the fork compression action is very quick, and the movement of rotation of the entire vehicle will be just as rapid.

There will be heavy demands made on the suspension action, which must be efficiently dampened so that the fork does not bottom or top out, making the vehicle difficult to handle.

Let us explain the following diagram, Figure 7.8, which shows fork movements over time during a hard, sudden slam on the brakes.

In straight-line performance, during the segment A-B, the fork will be compressed, 30 mm for example.

At point B, the braking begins and because of the load transfer, once we achieve a steady state (point C) there will be a marked dive of 95 mm, for example.

The behavior of the fork from point B to point C may vary greatly, depending on its damping.

The figure shows two extreme cases.

Let us first look at the behavior of a fork with

little hydraulic braking, in theoretical terms called underdamping.

The peak point of maximum dive is considerably greater than the dive given by the load that should exist when the braked motorcycle is in a steady state.

This difference is called **overlap** and it is attributable to the overload imposed by the motorcycle's inertia of rotation. Significant amounts of overlap can lead to annoying problems, especially during sportbike riding.

If the overlap is very large, it may cause anniying responses, especially when sportbiking.

Equally annoying are the ensuing rocking movements, caused by rebound, which must be immediately *dampened.*

Remember, in fact, that until the rocking is dampened, the rider will hardly be able to lay the bike into a corner. This is because of the vertical fluctuations provoked by variations in the rake angle, and consequently, in the trail; these conditions make the parameters for controlling corner entry difficult to manage.

• In the second case shown in Figure 7.8 the cornering takes place in quite different dive conditions by making use of overdamped shock absorbers, that is, with an hydraulic brake with very strong compression and rebound.

This set-up is more likely to be applied to roadracers, which only have to go over small holes in the surface, and making it possible to use rather high settings.

For road use, damping strong enough to reduce the problem of overlap could cause an uncomfortable ride and create handling difficulties when having to pass over a series of bumps at high speed, even if they are not especially big ones.

Fine tuning for the correct fork settings is not an easy problem to solve: softer forks mean good absorption over potholes, but, on the other hand, bring on a steep dive and sudden attitude variations, with the possible consequence of bottoming out.

Remember: when the fork bottoms out, the rotation and sinking of the motorcycle are almost instantaneously blocked; the consequent overload brings on a sudden, big load transfer and this provokes an abrupt reaction of the vehicle, making it likely that the rear wheel will lift up.

Think of a bicycle, which doesn't have any suspension, and how easy it is to make the rear wheel jump up with an abrupt squeeze of the front brake: in effect*, in this case, the load transfer is immediate.*

The design, development and tuning of the fork settings turns out to be perhaps more problematic than those of the rear suspension because there is no effect analogous to the chain pull effect to hold up the suspension in the most critical phase, during braking.

Both in offroad use and roadracing, the biggest problems for tuning the vehicle settings are often related to the front end.

Fortunately, front fork manufacturers have gathered enough know-how over the years to be able to greatly minimize these sorts of problems.

The importance of having this kind of vast, solid experience is why new front fork builders have a hard time establishing themselves in the market.

The number of high-quality front fork producers remains quite small.

ATTITUDE OF THE MOTORCYCLE WHEN CORNERING

Let us now try to give a series of snapshots of the attitude of the motorcycle, which we will assume to be fitted with a telescopic fork, *during the different cornering phases.*

Let us begin by assuming **a constant straight-line travel speed**.

The attitude of the motorcycle will be determined by the vertical stiffness of the suspension and the chain pull angle.

When entering the corner, braking will take place with the vehicle still traveling in a straight line; the motorcycle will lower and pitch forward, loading the front end and thus improving deceleration potential. This is the phenomenon described in the previous section.

Having reached a state of equilibrium for the front suspension, the braking will proceed until we reach the desired speed for corner entry.

The rake angle under braking generally diminishes around 3 to 5 degrees (depending on the type of bike) and, consequently, **the trail also diminishes**, but surprisingly enough, this fact could be helpful for the next cornering maneuver.

Since a large part of the load bears on the front wheel when braking, the trail values that make the bike stable in straight-line motion would make it difficult to lay it into a corner because of the opposing force of the righting moment (described in Chapter 3) (Figure 7.9).

A **smaller rake angle and, therefore, a smaller trail value** mean not much force is needed to be applied to the steering in order to initiate cornering.

This is one of the reasons why the infamous telescopic fork suspension, which has been considered so outmoded and old-fashioned for some time now, at least in this phase of cornering, gives a "favorable" response (it reacts most favorably to contingent situations).

When **entering the corner**, the fork will be compressed and the rear suspension will be extended; the motorcycle will thus begin turning and leaning, creating a centrifugal force that will compress the suspension, while the brakes are gradually released.

Rear suspension: when entering the corner there will be a marked movement of the rear suspension, which will pass from a state of complete extension to a state of compression when going around a corner.

Front suspension: there will be an off-load owing to the decline of braking force, which will be partially compensated for, however, by the compression effect due to the centrifugal force. The fork travel, therefore, is quite limited in this phase.

Having set the bike in the corner, we go on to the *cornering* phase *in a steady state with closed-down*

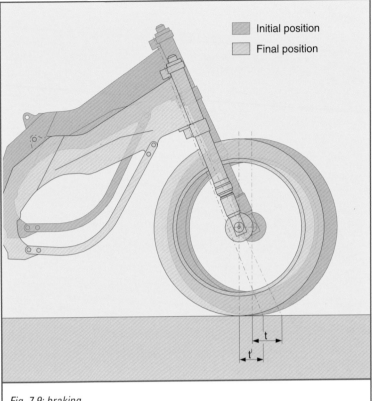

Initial position
Final position

Fig. 7.9: braking.

throttle; the attitude of the motorcycle will be determined by the vertical stiffness of the suspension systems.

With one g of lateral acceleration, that is, a lean angle of 45 degrees, the suspension will be compressed by a *load that is 40% bigger* than the static load that bears on the motorcycle in a stopped position.

This is why the stiffness of the suspension has such an influence on the attitude of the cornering bike.

For example, a rear suspension with very progressive springs, therefore stiff during the cornering phase, will keep the bike higher in the rear and will therefore give a reduced rake angle, with the previously discussed consequences.

Remember, in any case, that such high stiffness must be compatible with the need to provide satisfying absorption of surface irregularities, leading to the usual search for the right compromise.

The combined downward pressing effect on the suspension, the tires, and the lean angle noticeably reduces the cornering clearance.

For this reason sportbikes may end up touching the ground in a curve with a part of the fairing or the muffler.

In a corner, the rider is inclined more or less at the same angle as the motorcycle, and thus, feels the same acceleration forces and the same downward pressure onto the bike of a force equal to 40% of his or her weight.

In compensation, thanks to this state of equilibrium, the rider will not feel any effect from the centrifugal force, which tends to push the rider outwards from the curve!

The situation is quite different for car drivers who, following the same circular path at the same speed, with therefore one g of side acceleration, will have to fight against a sizable centrifugal force and will have to resort to their grip on the steering wheel, to the support given by the seats, and to their safety belt in order to maintain their position.

This is one of the reasons why racing car seats wrap around the driver.

On the motorcycle, instead, imagining constant motion in a curve, that is, with zero acceleration and braking, theoretically one could place a full glass on top of the gas tank without spilling any of the water.

Coming back to our motocyclist who is about **to exit the corner**, as soon as he or she accelerates, there will be an effect from the traction force (as described in previous section) but starting out from an initially compressed suspension.

The front suspension extends, and this provokes an attitude and a geometry variation of the bike; the rake angle opens up and consequently *the motorcycle will tend to open up the corner.*

The rider will have to turn the handlebars to keep the bike on line.

In this situation, a geometry of the suspension-transmission system that makes the rear suspension slightly extend can aid in limiting the bike's pitching response and keeping a more horizontal attitude.

HIGHSIDING

When the vehicle is leaning and accelerating, a quite common situation in track racing known as *highsiding* can occur. This indicates an oscillating, bucking movement of the rear end that pushes it up and tends to catapult the rider forward, just like a rodeo cowboy on a bucking wild horse.

This phenomenon is more likely to occur with high-powered bikes, since just a tiny exaggeration on the throttle can provoke loss of adhesion.

As we said, the initial conditions are the following:

- The motorcycle is in mid-phase of the corner, leaning to its maximum transversal grip of the rear tire, suspension pressed down.

- The rider accelerates rapidly; part of the transversal grip is used to transmit the longitudinal acceleration force, provoking tire slippage.

At this point there occurs a series of chain effects that are intimately connected to each other:

- The chain pull effect that varies between maximum friction and zero friction provokes fluctuations of the rear suspension;
- Being in a curve, every variation in attitude provokes a variation in the trajectory (and therefore in the radius of curvature) since the rake angle is changing; hence the centrifugal force will be discontinuous;
- The tire, subjected to steep load variations, will consequently alter its slip and drift angle values.

All these effects combined together provoke sharp bucking movements, that is, big oscillations of the rear suspension. Seen from the outside, this phenomenon appears as a large, violent rear end oscillating movement that puts to the test the balancing abilities of the rider, who is often left glued to the handlbars, while the bike does its best to throw the rider from the seat.

As the motorcycle gradually exits the corner and self-centers, reducing the centrifugal force and the possibility of sliding sideways, the oscillation dies down.

Various ways of reducing the problem or eliminating the reaction from the outset include:

• Damping of the rear suspension oscillations by means of greater hydraulic damping; this lowers the frequency of the system and allows the rider more time to intervene and get the bike under control by slowing the acceleration or correcting the trajectory.

• The use of higher-performance tires, characterized by very flat slip curves. In fact, high-siding is most evident towards the end of races, when the tires have deteriorated.

• Introduction of advanced suspension systems:

We have seen that front suspension **extension** *during acceleration is tied to the chain pull angle which may vary between two limits:*

• *Maximum friction conditions (hence, with power transmitted to the ground);*
• *Zero friction conditions (hence, with no transmission of power to the ground).*

Front suspension **compression** *depends instead on the angle of load transfer:*

We will thus find that if the chain pull angle in the two extreme conditions (and, hence, in the intermediary conditions as well) and that of the load transfer are equal, the behavior of the rear suspension becomes independent of the acceleration. This practically eliminates the high-siding *problem.*

This sort of suspension, called **track-lever** has already been designed. We give a diagram of it in Figure 7.9.

This sort of construction system for the rear suspension turns out to be quite complex and, at least for the moment, is not applicable to large-scale production.

To come closer to this type of setup using a traditional design scheme, the positioning between engine sprocket and swingarm is closely studied.

THE JUMP

Another spectacular development, performed with apparent ease by motocross and dirt bike racers, is the **jump.**

The trajectory of the motorcycle in the air is a good approximation of a parabola. Its analytical calculation is identical to any other body launched into the air. In other words, a rock or a motorcycle having the same mass and the same aerodynamic drag, when launched in the same direction and with the same velocity, will describe an identical trajectory, since neither has propulsion ability once they are in the air.

The size and height of the jump achieved thus depend solely on the following parameters:

• Velocity and angle of the initial trajectory;
• The aerodynamics of the motorcycle-plus-rider unit;
• Total mass.

The aerodynamic drag of the motorcycle-plus-rider unit is actually difficult to estimate with accuracy since riders generally tend to stand up out of their seat during a jump, either to land better, or to adjust their position in relation to the vehicle for the best control.

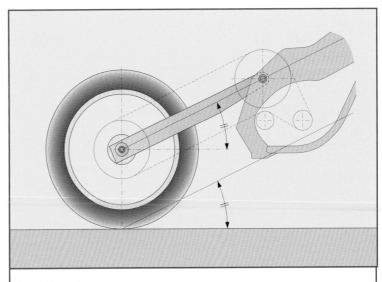

Fig. 7.10: tracklever.

The relation that links maximum jump length to velocity, ignoring aerodynamic drag for the moment, is the following one, obtained for an initial launch angle of 45 degrees:

Equation 7.1

$$L = \frac{V^2}{g}$$

Where:

L is the length of jump
V is the velocity of the vehicle
g is the force of gravity

Clearly, when in the air, *the righting moment due to trail ceases to exist*, given the lack of friction onto the ground, and in theory the motion of the vehicle tends to become directionally uncontrollable.

Fortunately, the time taken to perform a jump is normally short enough to avoid the appearance of unwanted rotational phenomena.

This sort of response can appear, instead, in extreme cases when it is a matter of making excep-

Fig. 7.11: jump.

tionally large jumps of over one kilometer, for example, during canyon crossings.

These enormously long jumps are accomplished, in any case, with very unusual bikes, propelled with reactor engines and equipped with flight stabilizing systems, making them very different from normal-use motorcycles.

Control of the motorcycle when in flight

Since the length and height of a jump are precisely set by the laws of physics and amply described in the literature, in the following section we prefer to describe how professional riders are able to perform acrobatic maneuvers while they are in flight.

Lateral shifts

The center of gravity trajectory, as we have said, is unequivocally determined; it is, however, always possible to exchange forces between rider and vehicle. In other words, due to the conservation of momentum principle, the rider can shift sideways making the motorcycle move in the opposite direction. The sideways movements that result will be inversely proportional to the value of the relative masses, so as to always maintain the center of gravity on its "theoretical" trajectory.

These sorts of maneuvers are made possible not only by the indispensable skill of the rider, but also by the necessary use of **very lightweight bikes:** the lighter the motorcycle, the easier it will be for the rider to make corrections to the vehicle's attitude.

For this reason, too, the structure of motocross bikes is reduced to the absolutely minimal necessities, with the goal of achieving the lowest possible weight acceptable for motocross competitions.

Lateral inclinations

Using the same technique just described, it is possible to tilt the motorcycle sideways, by shifting the body sideways.

Pull ups or nose dives

Shifting the weight of the body longitudinally (forward or backwards), the rider is able to bring about rotations around the transversal axis of the motorcycle, that is, he or she is able to make the front wheel lift (pull up) or lower (nose dive).

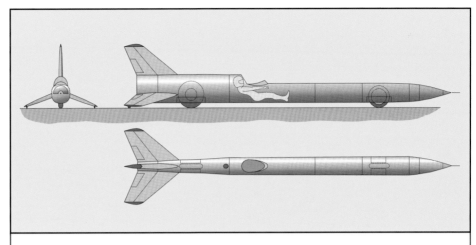

Fig. 7.12: unusual machines.

In order to facilitate these maneuvers the vehicle must have **very small inertia** with respect to this axis, allowing easy rotation around its center of gravity.

Since there is no contact with the ground, the only factor to take into account is the *inertia around the motorcycle's center of gravity*. The inertia of momentum with respect to the ground is no longer important (remember that it does not only depend on the distribution of the masses with respect to the center of gravity; it is also strongly influenced by a term proportional to the square of h). The rule that will be valid, then, is: the smaller the inertia of the bike, the easier it will be for the rider to maneuver it.

This explains why motocross bikes have all their masses largely concentrated around their center of gravity, with technical solutions that partially impede maximum engine power potential. The shock absorber, to give an obvious example, is positioned so close to the carburetor in order to stay within proximity of the center of gravity, that normal structural shape of the air ducts is hindered.

The maneuvers we have described until now can all be compared to those of a diver, who while dropping towards the water is able to perform somersaults and turns.

There is no doubt that were we to place a heavy backpack on the diver's shoulders, in addition to a swimsuit, the acrobatic moves would be slower and simpler.

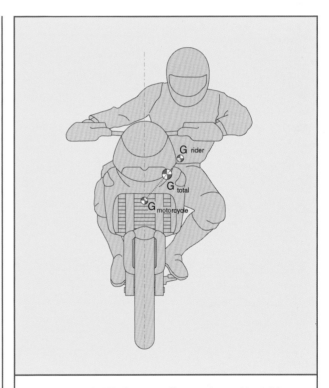

Fig. 7.13: lateral shifts have no effect on the position of the overall center of gravity of the rider-motorcycle unit.

Easy handling in the air is a fundamental factor for motocross bikes, given that they frequently make jumps, and that the terrain is a continual series of bumps and dips, making contact between wheel and ground often very intermittent.

The behavior of a motocross bike will therefore

Fig. 7.14: motorcycle inertia • angular acceleration of the motorcycle = wheel inertia • angular acceleration of the rear wheel.

be a compromise between the situation illustrated in the rest of the text, that is, normal road travel, and that of jumping.

It is therefore very difficult to optimize the chassis performance of these vehicles, inasmuch as the entire bike must provide optimum response in two completely different situations.

Other *important factors* that facilitate maneuverability of the motorcycle in flight are, instead, a familiar friend: **the gyroscopic effects of the wheels.**

Remember that when the *rotating parts* are *turning at a high speed* they *tend to maintain an unchanged axis of rotation,* so that even when the bike is in the air, the inertial effects of the wheels and the engine tend to keep the trajectory on line.

This means that there a relatively unconstrained, easy *method for maneuvering* the bike when it is in flight; a method that is, by the way, absolutely counter-intuitive, even if many riders apply it without consciously realizing it: it involves taking advantage of the rotational inertia of the wheels and the engine.

Pull ups with the aid of the engine

Let us suppose we are in flight; **by accelerating the rear wheel, the motorcycle will pull up.**

Let us try to explain why this happens: when the

rear wheel accelerates, its quantity of motion is increased (remember that this is a product of inertia multiplied by angular velocity). This creates an equal and opposite quantity of motion on the motorcycle, as a reaction, that makes the vehicle pull up (since the motorcycle system is isolated from the terrain).

The resulting rotations will depend on the relation between the inertias, as illustrated in Figure 7.14.

This technique has been developed by stunt-men who perform spectacular jumps over twenty or thirty lined-up cars and who are able to correct the attitude of the motorcycle during flight in order to optimize their landing.

In practice, motocross racers also use this technique a lot; when they are coming out of a jump, they accelerate, deriving a number of benefits from this, such as:

• A pulling up of the front wheel, as we have just seen, which thus improves the attitude of the motorcycle during its landing impact with the ground

• A quick, ready acceleration response when the tire touches down onto the ground.

• An aid to the rear suspension, since when the chain is tight, it opposes the sinking movement of the suspension, by running against a roller placed there for that purpose.

Nose dive with the aid of the rear brake

By applying the rear brakes while in the air *a nose dive effect will result* on the front wheel; this technique is rarely used.

Lateral inclination with gyroscopic effect

The **gyroscopic effect** offers the potential for a new form of controlling the vehicle: as we have seen in the chapter on stabilizing effects, when you turn the steering head to the right, a precession force is created that tends to lean the bike towards the left of the direction of travel, or rather, we should say, of flight.

This means, then, **it is possible to tilt the bike sideways by turning the steering head as well**, or, more realistically speaking, it is possible to adjust for an incorrect inclination of the motorcycle by making a rapid pull on the handlebar.

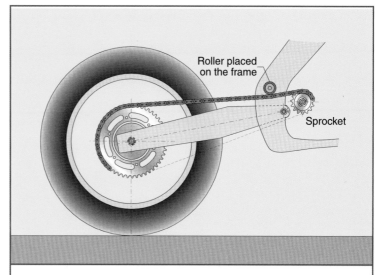

Fig. 7.15: principle of action-reaction roller to frame that forces the taut chain to oppose the sinking motion of the suspension.

CONCLUSIONS

We have therefore seen that there are a number of ways to maneuver the motorcycle when in flight and that by controlling the vehicle it is possible to have the attitude you want when the bike touches down.

Furthermore, sophisticated suspension systems on today's models make it possible to offer well-cushioned, damped landings, preventing abrupt jolts when bottoming out and at the same time helping to quickly dampen rebound reactions.

Combining with courage and mastery, then:

• body movement,

• the advantages offered by the inertial and gyroscopic effects of the wheels,

and facilitated by a motorcycle with:

• reduced weight,
• limited inertia,

it is possible, while maintaining control over the motorcycle, to accomplish those spectacular acrobatic jumps we have all enjoyed watching in motocross competitions or in indoor trials.

CHAPTER 8
INTERACTION BETWEEN GROUND AND MOTORCYCLE THROUGH THE TIRES

The functions of the tires are:

• To allow forces to be transmitted from the ground to the vehicle;
• To help create a comfortable ride for the rider and passenger.

Transmission of ground forces takes place in the area of the contact patch by means of:

• Friction between the tire and the road surface;
• Coupling between the rubber in the tires and the grain of the road surface.

Let us not forget that motorcycle tires, especially those on big displacement bikes and sportbikes, are subject to much more stress than those on automobiles.

In fact, a 750-to-1000 cc motorcycle with at least 73.5 kW (100 Hp) will normally be equipped with a rear tire having a width of 160 to 190 mm; the tires on a medium-powered car (1600 to 1800 cc), with the same 73.5 kW of power, will be equipped with tires having the same width. The essential difference between the two cases lies in the impression on the ground: the motorcycle tire leaves a much smaller one than that of the car, which has a pratically flat tire profile.

Nothing could be more obvious if you simply compare the tracks left by car and motorcycle tires on the road after crossing over a puddle.

Moreover, the motorcycle's driving force is discharged onto the single rear wheel, while a car always has at least two-wheel drive.

These simple considerations partly explain why motorcycle tires wear down faster than car tires.

Even today, a theoretical reckoning of the forces that interact between the tire and the road constitutes one of the most complex aspects of motorcycle dynamics.

Understandably so, considering the fact that the tire is a body whose mechanical properties are difficult to calculate, since it is usually composed of composite materials and anisotropes.

This means that its response will vary according to the direction of the stress that it is subject to.

In any case, even making do without sophisticated calculation models capable of measuring these forces, in the following sections we will try to illustrate how important the role of the tire is in motorcycle dynamics.

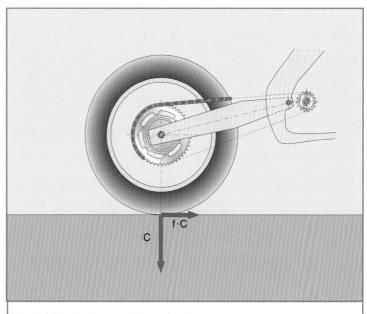

Fig. 8.1: friction force on the road surface.

FRICTION COEFFICIENT

The value of the friction coefficient between tire and ground is determined by the road surface characteristics, the type of tire used, and the presence of other elements between the contact surfaces (for example, water, oil, or other substances).

The maximum friction force available on the road surface is given by the relation:

$$\boldsymbol{F}_{friction} = \boldsymbol{f} \cdot \boldsymbol{C}$$

where:

f represents the coefficient of friction whose maximum theoretical value is 1,

C represents the vertical load bearing on the wheel.

In order to understand how the total force available to be used in the direction of the motorcycle's travel (Y axis) and in the direction that goes transversally to it (axis X), we turn to the theory of the friction circle.

We have said that the maximum value of the friction force is equal to **f · C** and, therefore, for any given load and friction conditions, the maximum value is constant.

We can therefore imagine the vector of the maximum available force as an arrow pointed at the point of contact wheel-to-ground, around which it rotates and describes a circle.

The maximum force that the ground may exert is, in other words, oriented in any direction within the circle of radius **f · C**.

If, for example, when braking *you use all of the force* **f · C** *in a longitudinal direction, you will not be able to turn the steering,* since there is no component of transverse force available in the direction of travel.

It is as if the ground provided an exact amount of force, a sort of bonus force; but when that amount is used up, it is unable to deliver any more. So, only by using less longitudinal force will you be able to begin turning the steering.

In other words, for the motorcycle to stay

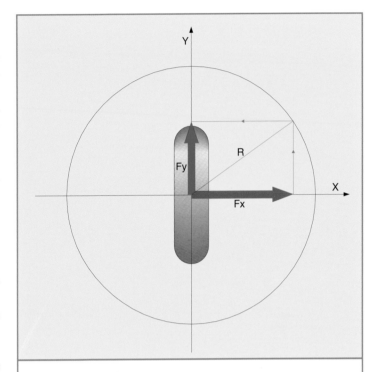

Fig. 8.2: friction circle.
Breakdown of the available friction force into its components Fx (side force) and Fy (longitudinal force): note that when cornering the side force Fx increases, through the radius, to the amount of available force obtained at acceleration Fy.

balanced, the reactions required of the tires must be limited to within the circle of friction.

In practice, because of manufacturing reasons, the tire performs differently when used longitudinally or transversally; and the theoretical circle of friction transforms into a ellipse, specific to each tire type.

For simplicity's sake, in any case, we will continue to refer to the theoretical model.

Racing tires for circuit use, which reach and go beyond the maximum theoretical friction coefficient equal to 1, hit values of even 1.2 to 1.3.

This sort of exceptional tire performance allows today's Grand Prix racers to lean their bikes into corners at as much as 50 degrees!

This level of performance is achieved by making use of a behavior of the tire under use that makes it similar to chewing gum; we can even talk about

77

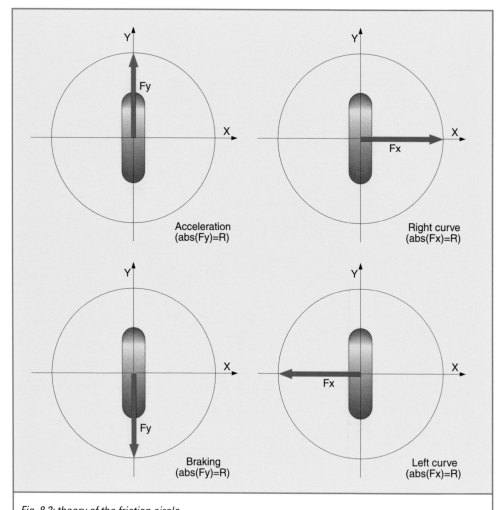

Acceleration
(abs(Fy)=R)

Right curve
(abs(Fx)=R)

Braking
(abs(Fy)=R)

Left curve
(abs(Fx)=R)

Fig. 8.3: theory of the friction circle.

influence on the optimum temperature of the tire.

The tire temperature problem can lead to the following riding problems. When we lean the bike into a corner, the contact patch rolls round to the side of the tire; since the tire must transmit acceleration torque as well as oppose the centrifugal force, it heats up considerably.

On some circuits in which almost all the turns are to the right, the optimum temperature will only be reached by the most heavily used side of the tire. Racers have to be careful when taking the few left-hand corners because their tires will offer less grip.

the tire actually "gripping" the ground. With this, we leave behind the traditional Newtonian model of friction described above.

Only under certain tire use conditions is it possible to create such high friction coefficients.

For one thing, the interval of temperature within which it can be obtained is quite small: with cold tires the coefficient of friction remains low, while when the temperature gets too high, friction once again drops while, at the same time, there is rapid onset of tire wear.

In the racing world, in order to always be able to work with the best use conditions for each type of tire, the racer has a number of different types available, differing according to construction and mix, each one suited to specific tarmac and temperature conditions.

Obviously, the type of tarmac and track have an

Even today's sport/streetbike tires, although much less sensitive to temperature, need at least a short warm-up time to obtain their optimum performance.

When it rains, the need for water removal requires the treads to be more or less deeply grooved.

Tires for offroad bikes represent a special case since they are designed to guarantee maximum traction on surfaces with a low coefficient of friction.

These tires are characterized by very pronounced grooves and by low inflation pressure.

When used improperly for street use, this leads to:

- High noise
- High drift angles (easy skidding)
- Severe wear on the tread.

For use on dug-up, loose ground, though, you can take advantage of the full potential offered by tires with these characteristics; **since the grooves penetrate into the earth,** the term "coefficient of friction" cannot be precisely applied here.

In this case, we can talk about a true geometric coupling, or, of a wheel-ground **form**, so the type of tread pattern, the height of the grooves and the distance between the rows take on importance in determining the tire's performance.

Each type of terrain (for example, rocky, muddy, sandy) requires an appropriate tread pattern geometry.

Completely **smooth** tires for racetrack use only are called "slicks."

AQUAPLANING

This term describes the phenomenon that takes place whenever a layer of water is introduced between the tire and the road, reducing the surface contact.

Similar to what happens with hydrodynamic lubrification, when you increase your speed, the contact patch area is progressively reduced until there is complete separation between the wheel and the road surface.

The coefficient of friction may become extremely low and handling of the motorcycle becomes problematic.

In order to avoid a complete lifting action, or to delay it, the water in the contact area must be removed.

The tire must therefore be provided with appropriate grooves on its surface to expel the water sideways, while the permeable qualities of tarmac can contribute to help avoid creating aquaplaning conditions.

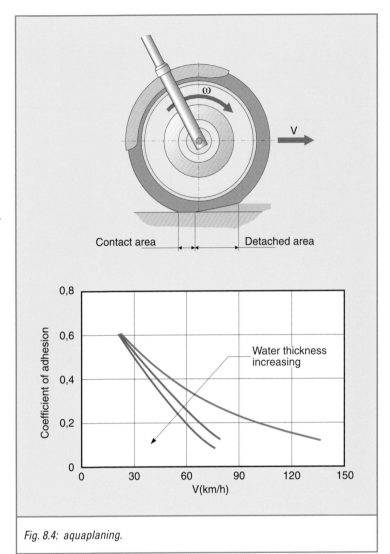

Contact area   Detached area

Fig. 8.4: aquaplaning.

Recent research on the part of major tire manufacturers has permitted the development of tires that perform well even under wet driving conditions, making aquaplaning something that happens only when the layer of fluid is very thick.

Remember, then, that tread wear leads to a drastic drop in water removal efficiency.

The wide tires on supersport bikes, especially, when worn down and flattened, can become dangerous even at low speeds and under light precipitation.

Rolling resistance is mostly due to the **hysterisis of the material** that the tire is made of, and

79

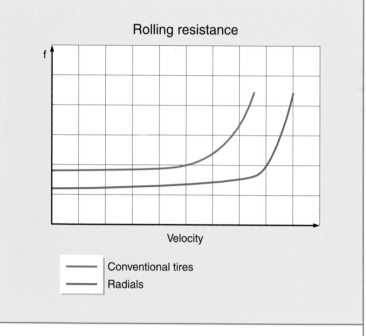

only partially due to the resistance that takes place between wheel and terrain, the friction on the wheel spindle, and the aerodynamic drag located at the wheel.

For practical ends, rolling resistance can be expressed in a relation of the following type:

Equation 8.1

$$R_{roll} = f_{roll} \cdot N$$

Where **N** represents, once again, the vertical load on the wheel, and f_{roll} indicates a value analogous to the coefficient of friction which depends on a number of parameters: such as, inflation pressure, wheel dimensions, the structure and material of the tire, the load bearing on the wheel, temperature, road surface, and especially **velocity**.

Fig. 8.5: rolling resistance.

The rolling resistence increases considerably depending on variations in velocity, just as the other parameters do.

The design of the tires plays a big role: so-called radial tires, for example, having a *more rigid* circumference, are less affected by an increase in speed.

In any case, all tires present a critical speed beyond which the resistance to travel increases drastically and there begin to be structural vibration phenomena.

Beyond this speed, which must never be exceeded, there is considerable overheating of the tires, in all cases mostly attributable to the material's hysterisis, which can lead rapidly to tire wear.

That is why tires are subdivided into speed classes:

> **V:** for tires over 210 km/h
> **H:** for tires up to 210 km/h
> **U:** for tires up to 190 km/h
> and so on.

For safety reasons, then, when you replace a worn-out tire on your motorcycle, it is advisable not to change the speed class by using a lower category, even if this would allow you to save some money.

The distribution of pressures on the tire at the contact patch is quite unusual and its center of gravity is generally shifted with respect to the projection of the wheel axis onto the ground (see the diagram in Fig. 8.6). This brings on a **positive or negative natural tire trail,** that creates its own **righting effect.**

This geometric measure, specific to each tire, is added onto or subtracted from the trail value given by the geometry of the motorcycle's steering.

Even if it is much smaller than the vehicle's trail value, it is still advisable to take it into account.

Clearly, every tire is characterized by different deformation patterns, and, therefore, different pressure distribution patterns.

This signifies possible **variations in the vehicle's performance when you change the kind of tire.**

COMPARISON BETWEEN TUBELESS AND INNER TUBE TIRES

Tubeless tires are mounted directly onto the rim without the installation of an inner tube between the rim and the wheel.

Tubeless tires offer the following **benefits**, making them an ever more popular choice:

• *Light weight,* thanks to the absence of an inner tube, and therefore less unsprung mass;

• *Less heat produced* because of the lack of rubbing friction between inner tube and tire;

• *Better discharge of heat* which, in order to pass out of the inner tube, must pass through two layers of rubber and also across the air channel formed between the outer casing and the inner tube, which acts as an insulator;

• *Better safety:* when the tire is punctured, pressure drops more slowly and the rider has the time to notice the problem and stop before the pressure is completely lost.

In some cases, if the puncture is caused by a sharp object that remains embedded in the tire, it is possible to ride for a while longer before having to repair it;

• The problem of the inner tube nozzle being pulled off because of the tire spinning on the rim is eliminated.

Drawback:

• *Higher cost* for the construction of the rim sealing.

The following consideration is fundamentally important: **there can be no transmission of torque without slippage,** both in the case of braking and acceleration.

The expression that defines slippage is the following:

Equation 8.2

$$\sigma = \frac{\omega}{\omega_0} - 1$$

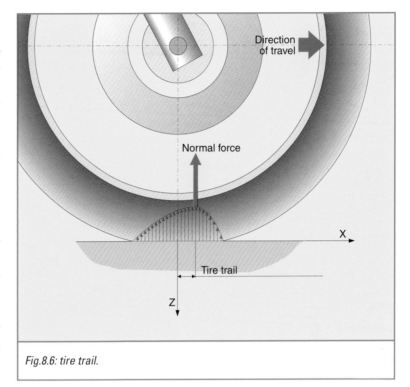

Fig.8.6: tire trail.

where ω represents the wheel rotation velocity, and, with reference to the figure,

Equation 8.3

$$\omega_0 = \frac{V}{h}$$

represents the angular velocity of pure rotation of a stiff tire going at a speed of travel V and having a radius equal to h, height of the center of gravity of the rear wheel from the ground.

The value of slippage is positive under acceleration, and negative under braking.

An illustration of what we have just stated is shown below, referring to Genta *"Automobile mechanics."*

Consider a wheel with a *braking couple* applied to it.

Let R be the wheel radius, V the velocity of the wheel center (in this case, the speed of travel of the braking wheel),

81

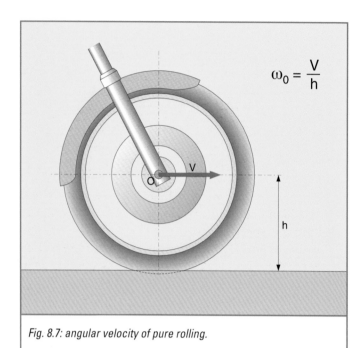

$$\omega_0 = \frac{V}{h}$$

Fig. 8.7: angular velocity of pure rolling.

ω *the angular velocity of the wheel and h, the height of the center of the wheel from the ground. Let us define:*

Equation 8.4

$$R_0 = \frac{V}{\omega}$$

rolling radius of the wheel, and keep in mind that:

Equation 8.5

$$\omega_0 = \frac{V}{h}$$

corresponds to the angular velocity of pure rolling of a wheel with no deformation, with radius h.

The brake caliper slows (and at its limit, locks completely) the rotation of the wheels, while, because of inertia, the speed of travel tends to change more slowly. Consequently, while when **braking** ω diminishes abruptly, **V** and, therefore, $\frac{V}{h}$ diminish more gradually.

This means that, using the notation that we have just introduced,

$$\omega_0 > \omega$$

Figure 8.8 may be helpful in visually summarizing these concepts: **C** represents the center of instantaneous rotation of the wheel, therefore, the length of the segment **OC** is equal to **R_0**; the point **C** in this case (that is, *when braking*) lowers below the level of the ground, and, defining this measure as *slip,* as we have seen above:

Equation 8.6

$$\sigma = \frac{\omega}{\omega_0} - 1$$

This value will be **negative when braking.**

On the contrary, **under acceleration,** the center of instantaneous rotation shifts above the ground level (the wheel rotation speed increases more rapidly than the speed of travel) and the **slip is positive.**

In the literature, graphs showing force on the tire under various load and friction conditions are calculated as a function of slippage.

Figure 8.10 shows typical slip curves, with the x-coordinate indicating the slippage percentage value and the y-coordinate indicating the friction coefficient. As we can see, the coefficient varies greatly depending on whether the road surface is wet or dry.

Of course, this data is hardly comprehensive and does not include all types of driving conditions, starting with a barely damp surface and going all the way to a torrential downpour.

In any case, the graphs clearly suggest that with the first appearance of dampness on the ground it is better to ride with caution.

The "dramatic" conditions brought on by snow or

Tire trail

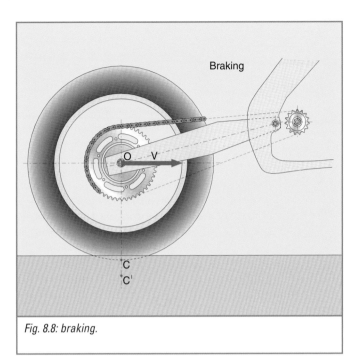

Fig. 8.8: braking.

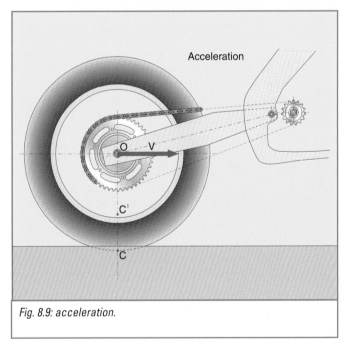

Fig. 8.9: acceleration.

Hints on race track powerslides

After having seen how the wheel-to-ground friction coefficient can change, it seems appropriate to make a few comments about powerslides, when the rear wheel is made to slide while accelerating out of a corner.

The virtuoso maneuver we are about to describe is actually a handling technique that is being consciously adopted by the best racers on the speed circuit.

First of all, a premise: slick racing tires, with no grooves, have been carefully studied by manufacturers, resulting in some surprising achievements over the past decade of research and development.

Their improved characteristics, as we have already mentioned, are due to a *higher friction coefficient value.*

That is, *the variations in friction are less sensitive to increases in slippage* and the curve that the friction describes on the graph, after it reaches its highest point, becomes quite attenuated and falls more slowly than in the zone preceding point X (please refer to figure 8.11).

For optimum efficiency in corners, the rider should make use of the most friction possible, or in other words, make use of slip in order to stay constantly at the apex of the curve in figure 8.11 (point X).

This ideal situation, though, would make for difficult, cautious handling, since, at the highest point, whether the force transmitted by the tire is increasing or diminishing, the coefficient of friction considerably diminishes along with the possibility to efficiently accelerate or decelerate. When accelerating out of a corner the rider may prefer instead to give a good slide to his rear wheel, making it work between the area of the slip curve between X and Y.

This way, sudden sharp tire slippage in the case of a fast, hard burst of acceleration, or of a slight loss of road holding because of a bump, causes a

ice are more than evident and explain the difficulty of maintaining control over the motorcycle.

Figure 8.11 shows how the cofficient of friction increases, and therefore, is able to transmit more torque, from the point where slip increases up to its maximum value, and then lowers once again when slip becomes very high.

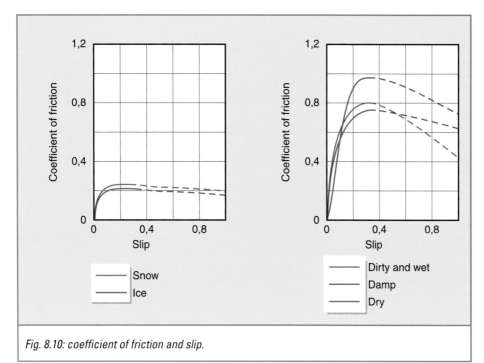

Fig. 8.10: coefficient of friction and slip.

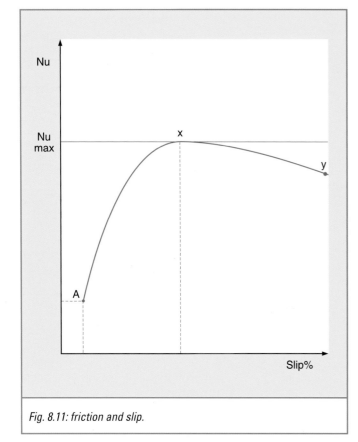

Fig. 8.11: friction and slip.

much smaller variation in friction and, therefore, in the torque being transmitted.

Moreover, when the rear end is in a controlled powerslide, the motorcycle tends to rotate and put itself in the direction of the corner exit, thus allowing you to come out of the curve more quickly than usual.

In practice, it is the same type of move that a racing car with rear-wheel drive performs to come out of a turn by oversteering (or sliding) the rear end.

On the racetrack, this powerslide technique is being adopted by more and more motorcycle racers thanks to developments in tire technology, biking characteristics, and the fact that the suspension is increasingly suited to these kinds of maneuvers.

Please note, however, that the handling response during slides is limited to a rather slim slip interval, so that *while it may be evident to the racer, it may not be obvious to spectators.*

The only way that the spectator may see the move is if the racer exaggerates throttle use, making a noticeable rear wheel slide visible.

Even if in theoretical terms the mechanics of the slide seem simple and recommendable, it remains an **extreme** maneuver, and as such, brings on high risks; seeing as it requires experience and skill, the slide maneuver should be considered out of the question for street bikes and tires, and never to be performed on roads open to traffic.

INTERACTION BETWEEN GROUND AND
MOTORCYCLE THROUGH THE TIRES

TIRE DRIFT

Cornering creates side forces on the tires, too, and, since they are not infinitely rigid, under the action of these forces, they twist, so that the direction of the tire track will no longer coincide with the direction of the wheel. The effect of tire drift is such that the direction of travel of the wheel does not coincide with the average plane that the tire is on. This effect is call **tire drift** and it is similar to the well-documented phenomenon in the car world.

Figure 8.12 shows the effect of drift in corners, *taking the motorcycle as perfectly vertical;* this makes the radius of curvature and, thus, the actual direction of the motorcycle, slightly different than those determined by the wheel axis.

α_1 **represents the angle lying between the direction of the front wheel and the average plane it travels on;**

α_2 **represents the angle lying between the direction of the rear wheel and the average plane it travels on.**

R is determined by the straight line formed at the intersection of the two perpendiculars of the velocities and the center of gravity.

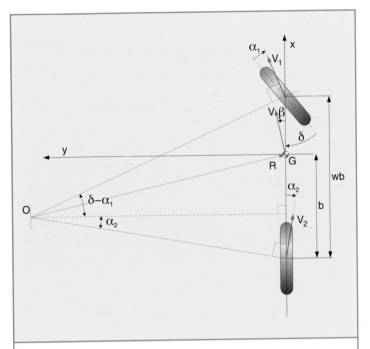

Fig. 8.12: drift in corners:
O: center of instantaneous rotation of the vehicle
G: vehicle center of gravity
wb: wheelbase
b: distance between CG and rear wheel contact patch
α_1: front drift
α_2: rear drift
V_1: front wheel speed of travel
V_2: rear wheel speed of travel
δ: steering angle of front wheel
β: angle of forward travel of the vehicle's center of gravity axis.

The effect of drift is determined by a number of parameters:

• **Load:** *the greater the load on the wheel, the greater the drift effect will be;*
• **Tire pressure:** *with a rise in pressure during use, drift diminishes;* (the pressure value cannot, however, go beyond the values determined by the tire characteristics).

This may seem surprising, given that one generally assumes that low pressure tires "hold" the road better.

To demonstrate what we have just stated, you might want to try an experiment in your car, rather than on your motorcycle.

Let out the front end tire pressure to its lowest recommended level (to go beyond the suggested limit could be dangerous) and do the opposite on the rear end tires, bringing tire pressure up to their maximum: you will notice that the car tends to understeer. Reversing the process, high pressure in front and low at the rear, you will find that the car tends to oversteer.

• **Use of longitudinal traction and braking forces:** *when a traction or braking force is applied, tire drift increases.* In other words, when you accelerate in a corner, as well as when you brake, tire drift increases. This is a response that you will notice in everyday handling of the motorcycle. The same thing happens during braking.

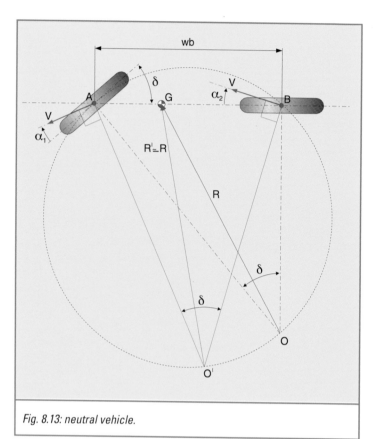

Fig. 8.13: neutral vehicle.

1. Front drift angle equal to rear drift angle (α_1 and α_2 equal)

At **very low velocity, drift is practically nil** and the steering will be kinematically correct; the center of the curve will be O and the radius of curvature will be delineated between the point O and the center of gravity of the motorcycle.

The angle **δ,** created from the perpendiculars to the trajectories of the wheels, will be approximately equal to its tangent (we are discussing a very small angle), or:

Equation 8.7

$$\delta \approx tan\left(\delta\right) \quad \frac{I}{R}$$

• **The type and construction** of the tire, for example, radial or conventional, sport or touring, tread pattern for expelling water (a tire with deep groves and a lot of treads versus a slick tire).

Neutral vehicle, oversteering or understeering

Let us see what the *drift effects are on a motorcycle that is cornering at a constant speed.*

Figure 8.13 gives a good idea of what happens from a "geometrical" point of view:

were:
wb represents the wheelbase;
A the front wheel center;
B the rear wheel center
α_1 the front wheel drift angle;
α_2 the rear wheel drift angle.

The vehicle may create the following conditions:

When the velocity increases, the drift angle of each tire will no longer be zero.

When front and rear drift angles are equal, the angle RO'A, created from the perpendiculars of the wheel velocities, continues to have the same value δ as for zero drift, and therefore the new center O' of the curve is found on a circumference passing through A, R, and O.

Since R is generally much larger than the wheelbase of the motorcycle, in this case we may consider R' equal to R.

The radius of curvature thus remains unchanged with respect to the kinematic steering and the **vehicle may be called 'neutral'.**

Assuming equal stiffness in both front and rear wheels, a neutral motorcycle, which would give the best handling response on the trajectory, would have *50%* of its weight distributed on the wheel axles, making front and rear drift coincide.

(In practice, as we have seen, the stiffness and dimensions of the front and rear wheels are quite different, not to mention other variables that have an influence on the angle of drift).

In any case, as experienced riders will have noticed, the time you spend cornering with the throttle closed and at a constant speed is very brief; so, while it is important to optimize your speed at this point, it is not vital in order to better the total time needed to traverse a certain distance or lap around the track.

2. Front drift angle greater than rear drift angle (α_1 is greater than α_2)

The motorcycle becomes understeering, inasmuch as it tends to open up its cornering path, thus placing itself on a wider radius of curvature; the effect is that of a motorcycle which tends to go straight.

The center of curvature moves to O" and the radius R" becomes bigger than R.

3. Rear drift angle greater than front drift angle (α_2 is greater than α_1)

The center of curvature becomes O", which is smaller than R.

The motorcycle oversteers, that is, it tends to carve a tighter cornering path, with consequent increase in the centrifugal force, tending to make the rear end slide outwards, radially, from the curve.

COMPARISON BETWEEN UNDERSTEERING AND OVERSTEERING IN CARS AND MOTORCYCLES

The same remarks just illustrated can be applied just as well to **automobiles**, and, in fact, "all-in-front" models are an increasingly popular choice.

Cars with front engine and front-wheel

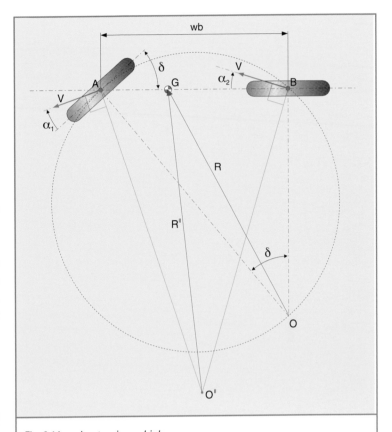

Fig. 8.14: understeering vehicle.

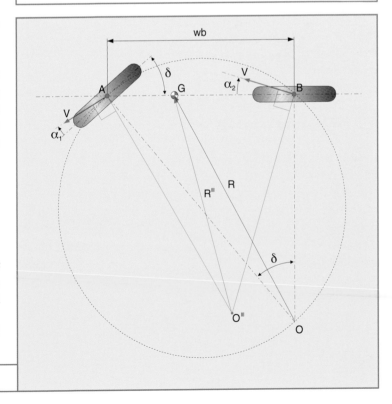

Fig. 8.15: oversteering vehicle.

drive are characterized by high drift on their tires because of the fact that the front axis:

- Bears more of the vehicle's carriage weight;

- The force of traction and a great part of the braking force are applied to it.

When taking a turn at too high a speed or with excessive acceleration, "all-in-front" cars tend to open up their trajectory because of the drift effect, making a wider turn.

The problem is easily resolved by slowing down **and by relying on your steering instincts**, that is by turning into the curve. Moreover, by taking your foot off the accelerator, and therefore, reducing the traction force, you also cut down on tire drift, helping even more to keep the vehicle in line.

This is why **understeering automobiles are considered safer, in that they are intuitively easy to control.**

Automobiles with primarily rear loading and/or rear-wheel drive will be oversteering, because of the high amount of rear end drift.

To go back to the situation of entering into a turn at high speed or with excessive acceleration, this time it will be the rear end that tends widen its turning path, putting the vehicle into a tail spin.

This would require the driver to turn the steering wheel in the opposite direction to the curve **(countersteering),** while continuing to accelerate, *which is hardly a simple, spontaneous maneuver.*

That makes it a favorite with professional drivers since it is such a spectacular maneuver, especially doable on race tracks where the margin for error is bigger.

Oversteering cars can be considered efficient, but only if there is an expert driver at the wheel, and only in particular situations.

Car designers can intervene on other parameters, in any case, in order to control or correct drift effects; for example, they may alter the geometry of the suspension, the suspension settings, and so forth.

For the **motorcycle sector** the situation is a

little different:

Above all, a few considerations:

- Practically all motorcycles with a rider mounted are slightly more rear loaded;

- Traction is always applied at the rear end;

- Under braking, as we have already discussed, because of the huge weight transfer, the reaction of the rear wheel will be the greatest.

On a motorcycle, then:

- **When entering a corner,** because of the weight transfer effect, a large part of the load is brought to the front; and because the application of the braking force may cause *high front drift,* this will tend to result in **understeering;**

- **In the middle of the corner,** with the throttle down, the drift angle is determined by the simple distribution of weight onto the bike, but making it, as we said before, slightly oversteering;

- **When exiting the corner** under acceleration, the weight transfer and traction provoke bigger rear drift, with a resulting oversteering response.

In the case of understeering (that is, greater front drift):

A *truly dangerous* situation is created, since the rider tends to continue steering into the direction of the corner, with the almost automatic consequence that the steering head "locks" and the rear wheel ends up being pushed towards the outside of the curve by a centrifugal force.

As we have seen in the first chapters, *rear tire grip is fundamental for maintaining balance* and for handling the vehicle.

When there is less adhesion on the front wheel, the righting moment due to trail instantly

INTERACTION BETWEEN GROUND AND MOTORCYCLE THROUGH THE TIRES

diminishes, making it, therefore, quite likely that loss of front grip will end up in a slide.

Very few riders can say that they did any understeering without being frightened or finding themselves on the ground!

In any case, as is easily witnessed on the racing circuit, loss of front tire grip fortunately generates only mildly damaging slides.

In the case of oversteering (that is, greater rear drift):

This, too, is a dangerous phenomenon. In practice, however, it turns out to be a rather easy slide to get under control: an expert rider is able to get the bike back into balance by shifting his or her body to the inside and forward, while centering the steering head.

This sort of situation arises quite often, especially during bursts of acceleration: the weight transfers to the rear end even more and tire drift increases, which actually makes for a "satisfying" experience.

Exaggerated oversteering is commonly used in offroad riding, and, in many cases, helps the rider to come faster out of a corner.

We have seen earlier that the rider's weight plays a fundamental role in the motorcycle's weight distribuition; the above considerations help to show once again how important the rider's handling ability and experience are.

By shifting your weight forwards or backwards on the seat, you are able to influence not only the vehicle's attitude, but also the tire drift angles, thus making a big difference to the bike's behavior.

INFLUENCE OF TIRE PROFILE ON THE RIGHTING MOMENT
Front tire

In Chapter 3 we analyzed the effect of trail on the stabilizing moment, which determines the bike's stability and maneuverability.

In this chapter we would like to show how tire characteristics affect the trail value and, consequently, the bike's handling, both in straight-line motion and when cornering.

• Straight-line motion

Tire deformation in the contact patch zone, as we have seen, creates a change in the theoretical straight-line trail that varies depending on speed and weight.

This explains why when the load on the front end increases significantly (for example, when entering a corner), tires with different stiffness will bring on different responses in terms of stability and safety.

• Cornering

Let us analyze, instead, how the value of the righting moment changes when we make the bike lean into a curve, first considering the influence of the tire profile.

For simplicity's sake, let us refer to a tire with a circular section.

In this case, as shown by the rear view proposed in figure 8.17, the point of contact wheel-to-ground will be situated closer to the axis of the motorcycle compared to the theoretical case of a tire with negligible thickness considered in Chapter 3. *This depends on the radius and, therefore, the profile of the tire section.*

The righting moment, then, in reality, has a value that depends greatly on the front tire **profile.**

Moreover, *the track* left by the contact point tire-to-ground will not be at one point, but *will depend on the stiffness of the tire.* By varying the stiffness, then, you may also vary the position of the point of exertion of the force.

Knowing that the righting moment has an enormous influence on all the motorcycle's handling responses, we may thus assert that:

both the profile and the stiffness of the tire can profoundly modify the motorcycle's handling response, both in straight-line motion and in corners.

In general, we may say that very wide tires with a flat profile tend to make the motorcycle more directionally unstable in straight-line motion but allow a more fluid response in a series of curves.

Tires with a narrower section and a more sharply pointed "V" profile will give more stability in straight-line motion, approaching the theoretical

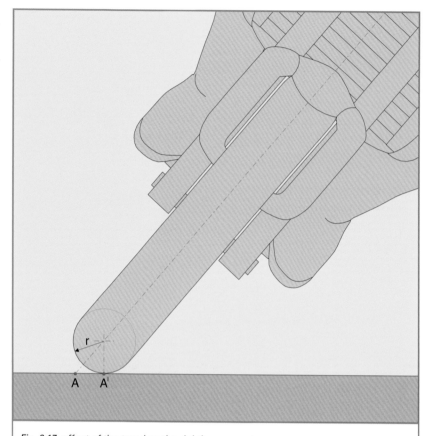

situation of a perfectly slim, lense-shaped tire with a single point of contact with the ground, and a more solid response in corners.

On the other hand, the characteristics of a tire combine with the characteristics of the vehicle in such a complex way that a tire that behaves perfectly on one bike may not give as good performance results when it is mounted on another model, even one of similar construction.

So, it may be misleading to only look at the type of profile of the tires you are choosing for your motorcycle, since their stiffness, which is determined by their internal structure, is not clearly visible from the outside.

As shown in figure 8.17, the steering axis does not pass through the center of tire pressure; consequently, when a couple is exerted on the tire, it will tend to twist. This, too, has an influence on the drift angle of the tire. Tire profile and stiffness, then, have a big influence on creating oscillating wobble or weave phenomena.

Fig. 8.17: effect of tire tread on the righting moment.

Rear tire

The rear tire does not directly generate any big variations in the righting moment, but a few remarks are in order.

First of all, the rear tire on a motorcycle has a bigger cross section than the front tire, for the following reasons:

• Because it is subject to a **heavier load** than the front tire (especially with a passenger and luggage on board);

• Because it allows the use of softer compounds without leading to unduly fast tire wear; in practice, a bigger section means more material to wear down (the use of softer compounds guarantees a better grip).

• A wider tread offers a bigger area to "grab"

onto the micro irregularities presented by the ground surface.

In effect, when the tire heats up, it has the so-called "chewing gum" effect, making it adhere to the asphalt grain; hence, the more contact surface, the better the grip.

It would not be possible to mount an equally wide tire onto the front wheel because of the big variations in trail it would cause, along with an obvious loss of maneuverability due to the increased weight and inertia.

The width of the rear tire determines the following aspects of the vehicle's behavior:

• *When the width is increased, there is an increase in the radius of curvature.*

When we lean the bike over, the contact patch shifts to the inside of the curve. As we can see

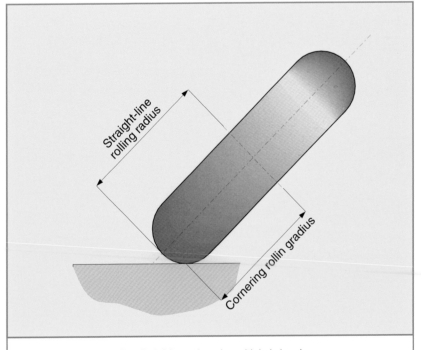

from the drawing, this fact, along with the difference in the two wheel sections, makes the direction of the bike opposite to the one it needs to go around the corner, requiring you to turn the steering more in order to keep the bike on the proper cornering path.

This is another reason why a bigger tire width leads to less maneuverability.

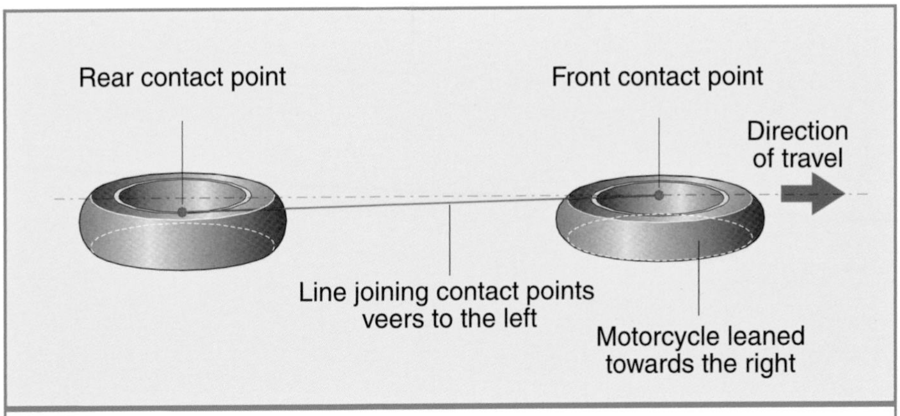

Rear contact point

Front contact point

Direction of travel

Line joining contact points veers to the left

Motorcycle leaned towards the right

Fig. 8.18: banking towards the right in order to corner to the right: the line joining the two contact points between wheel and ground actually veers off towards the left!

• *Greater widths mean greater sensitivity to the road surface.*

This may seem strange, but, as we can see from figure 8.18, if the tire width is big, with a less than perfectly flat surface, the actual point of contact shifts considerably sideways, giving rise to a sudden change of direction to the vehicle's axis.

In order to correct this deviation, the rider must turn the handlebar, which can cause annoying oscillations on the steering head.

The phenomenon we have just described is made worse by a tire worn flat, or with lower than recommended pressure.

VARIATIONS IN THE ROLLING RADIUS WITH THE ANGLE OF LEAN

At this point, remember an odd effect connected with the fact that the tire is not lens-shaped, but is actually characterized by a certain profile and a definite width.

Let us now consider a tire with a circular section: *when the motorcycle is leaning into a corner,* **the rolling radius diminishes,** as shown in figure 8.19.

This phenomenon takes place, for example, when going around a

long, wide corner: with the same horsepower used in a straight line, when entering the corner and leaning the bike, you will feel the engine revving up; on the contrary, when you straighten the bike up exiting the corner, you will notice that the rev speed decreases.

Let us remember at this point that *the tire radius,* not only varies according to tire inflation

Straight-line rolling radius

Cornering rollin gradius

Fig. 8.19: the rolling radius diminishes when the vehicle is leaning.

INTERACTION BETWEEN GROUND AND MOTORCYCLE THROUGH THE TIRES

91

pressure and load (and, thus, also according to deformation brought on by interacting with the ground), it *also varies according to the speed, which will tend to have a centrifugal effect on it.*

RIDING COMFORT

The tire is also equipped with **damping characteristics.** However, they are difficult to calculate and depend on the structure, whether cross-ply or radial, on the pressure, on the height of the walls and on the type of compound used.

In any case, the tire can be thought of as a shock absorber placed between the rim and the ground. Hence, it is no surprise that when you change the kind of tire, the level of comfort can also be affected.

VIBRATION MODES: A QUICK LOOK AT VIBRATION MECHANICS

Let us consider a mass M suspended from a ceiling by a spring. When undisturbed, the system will assume a certain position in equilibrium (position O in figure 9.1); when it is deflected a distance equal to Δx from its resting position the system will start to oscillate around position O with an amplitude of Δx and with a crossing frequency equal to f times a minute.

Repeating the experiment and deflecting the system now by a distance $\Delta x'$, the amplitude of the oscillations will be equal to $\Delta x'$ while, surprisingly, the frequency will remain the same; that is, the equilibrium point will still be crossed f times a minute (see Figure 9.2).

The pulsation that corresponds to this frequency is indicated in the literature as ω_n, and it is characteristic of the system; that is, it depends on the mass and stiffness values of the spring and is referred to as the system's natural frequency.

This means that in the absence of external forces, an elastic system oscillates around its resting position at a frequency ω_n whenever it is deflected from its position of equilibrium.

Vibration mechanics teach us that when a force is applied to a mass varying in time between minimum and maximum frequency values equal to those of the system's natural frequency, the amplitude of the resulting oscillations could theoretically increase to infinity (resonance).

In order to prevent the oscillations of a mechanical system from becoming too big (with easily-imaginable, disastrous consequences), dampers are introduced into the system along with the elastic elements in order to dissipate the energy (see Figure 9.4).

The free vibrations of a mechanical system like the one described in the previous example will behave as shown in Figure 9.5); that is, they will subside over time.

In any case, to make sure that the oscillations remain contained, the frequencies with which the elements of a mechanical system are made to oscillate must never coincide with their natural frequencies.

Let us turn now to the motorcycle: we are obviously talking about an unquestionably complex mechanical system, in which a number of parts are able to move relative to each other.

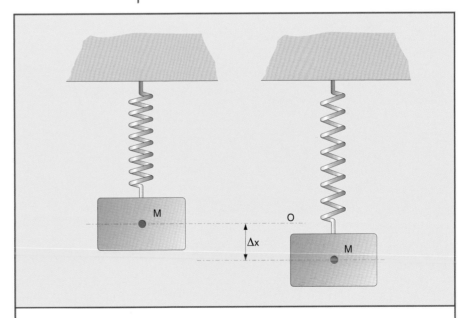

Fig. 9.1: a sprung mass on a coil spring when deflected Δx from its resting position will oscillate around it.

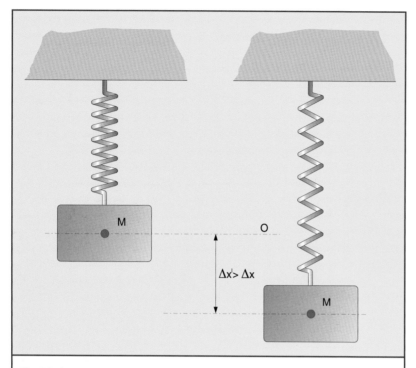

Fig. 9.2: the greater the angle of deflection from resting position, the larger the amplitude of the oscillations.

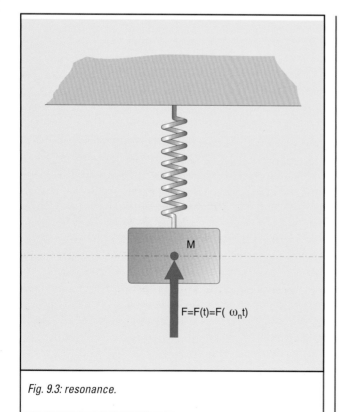

Fig. 9.3: resonance.

Since every movement of the different parts in relation to each other is associated with a specific frequency and, thus, a different way of vibrating, the motorcycle system is characterized by various, different vibration modes.

As far as a study of frame movement on the vertical plane is concerned, with the frame considered as a mass suspended between the front and rear suspension, it will be briefly examined in the chapter on suspension.

These dynamic aspects are completely analogous to a car's and they are studied in depth in the automobile sector.

What we will examine in the next section are a few vibration modes that are completely peculiar to and characteristic of the motorcycle.

As far as movement *in space* is concerned, the simplified model that can be used to study vibration modes is the following:

• Imagining the wheels to be rigid and the suspension blocked, we can think of the motorcycle mechanism as being essentially composed of two bodies, the front and rear ends, which are able to rotate in relation to each other around the steering axis.

The elastic functioning of the springs described in the previous examples is substituted by a rebound action brought about by the reactions on the tires.

The vehicle's rotation axes, as we can see from Figure 9.7, are thus:

• The axis of the ground around which the motorcycle can roll, and, hence, called the **roll axis**;

• The axis of vertical rotation of the motorcycle, or the **yaw axis**;

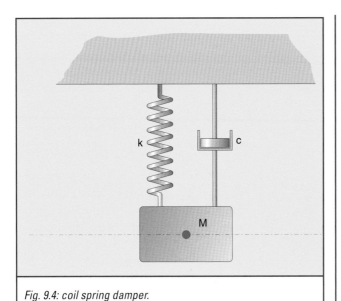

Fig. 9.4: coil spring damper.

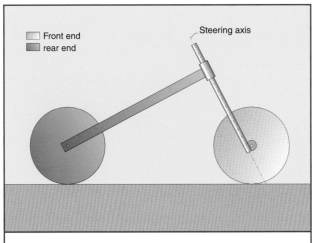

Fig. 9.6: front and rear ends rotate relative to each other around the steering axis.

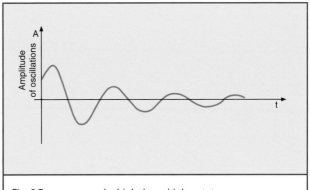

Fig. 9.7: axes around which the vehicle rotates.

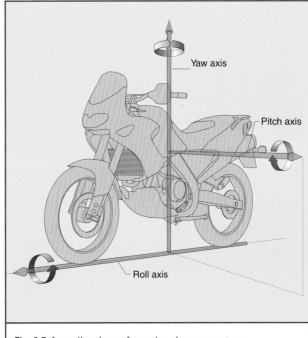

Fig. 9.5: free vibrations of a spring-damper system.

• The **pitch axis**, due to the lowering of the steering head when it is turned.

Riding experience has allowed us to identify the main vibrational modes which have also been studied recently in mathematical terms, using the same models and calculation strategies developed for studying vibrational modes of other mechanisms (Figure 9.6).

The results obtained from this approach are not only of scientific value, they are also important for practical purposes. In fact:

A motorcycle's type of response to different vibration modes constitutes an extremely important indicator of the vehicle's ease of handling .

We will look at the three main vibration modes, referring to mathematical descriptions, but making an effort not to lose sight of everyday experience.

The oscillation modes that have been identified are:

• Wobble
• Weave
• Sideways falling motion at low speeds

WOBBLE

When you push a dessert tray or a shopping cart with front turning wheels, you will probably notice that one of the wheels will suddenly start to oscillate with a twitching movement around its steering axis when it reaches a certain speed or when it passes over irregularities in the ground surface.

This is called *shimmy* in the literature.

Interestingly enough, this term comes from an American dance style that was popular in the 1920s, similar to a fox-trot and characterized by a rhythm of beats that is perfectly evocative of the phenomenon we are about to describe.

Anybody who follows road racing competitions will be aware of a similar phenomenon that occurs with racing bikes.

The attentive spectator will certainly have noticed that when a racing bike is placed under certain conditions, such as accelerating out of a corner or after contact with a curb, the handlebar and the whole front end suddenly start to oscillate furiously for a brief but spectacular instant.

This steering oscillation is an unpleasant sensation that many riders will have experienced during everyday sportbike use, when speeding over train tracks or across a series of potholes.

The steering suddenly seems to come alive and starts to oscillate violently for a few seconds, while the motorcycle continues on its path and the rider is unable to intervene in any way at all.

Fortunately, the phenomenon quickly dies down and it becomes possible to regain control of the motorcycle before the vehicle is completely destabilized. Most likely, though, the event will shake up the rider enough to take the tracks or the potholes at a slower, more cautious speed when passing that way the next time.

Unlike a slow-speed falling motion (as we shall see), a wobble is more likely to occur at higher speeds, that is, at over 60 to 70 km/h.

This phenomenon is characterized by a *high frequency,* from 4 to 10 Hz (which means 4 to 10 oscillations per second) and by *forces and amplitudes that may be quite big,* having steering effects of even 8 to 14 degrees; that is, much bigger rotations of the steering than those typical of street use over 50 km/h.

These sorts of amplitude values help to explain why the steering is absolutely uncontrollable under these conditions.

Wobble is a *periodic phenomenon,* closely studied both from an experimental and theoretical point of view, since it also occurs on car wheels and especially on airplane landing wheels.

Mathematical explanation

There are various approaches to a mathematical description of the phenomenon.
We will refer to the simplest approach:

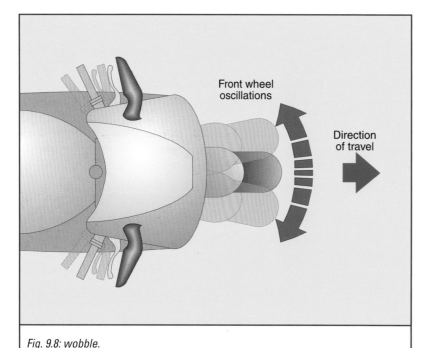

Fig. 9.8: wobble.

Front wheel oscillations

Direction of travel

I_a: = moment of inertia of all the steering masses around the steering axis (front end inertia)

δ: = angle of rotation around the steering or handlebar turning angle

δ': = angular acceleration of the steering

k_d: = (lateral) drift stiffness of the tire

t: = trail

ε: = rake angle

k_m: = stiffness of tire moment

The equation that represents the state of equilibrium of the moments acting around the steering axis is a second degree linear differential equation, with coefficient constants given by the expression:

Equation 9.1

$$I_a \cdot \delta^1 = \left(k_d \cdot t \cdot sin\varepsilon + k_m \cdot sin\varepsilon \right)\delta$$

from which we derive the frequency of the destabilizing oscillation that affects the steering shimmy.

Equation 9.2

$$\omega_{wobble} = \sqrt{\left(\frac{sin\varepsilon}{I_a} \right) \left(k_d \cdot t \cdot k_m \right)}$$

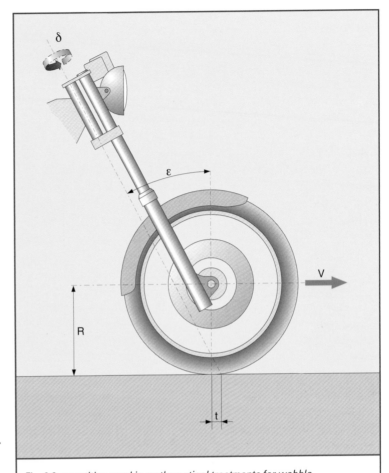

Fig. 9.9: quantities used in mathematical treatments for wobble.

Phenomena that generate wobble:

Front wheel shimmy is usually generated by external stressors such as, for example, a small pothole or any other type of unevenness in the road surface which "pushes" against the tire, including lateral pressures.

Wheel imbalance, and eccentricities due to tire or rim deformation, repeated, obviously, with the same frequency that the wheel rotates, can also provoke dynamic imbalance that generates wobble. The oscillation is likely to appear when you travel, for example, with tires "smoothed down" by braking or with a rim that has static imbalance or is deformed by collision impact.

These conditions will give rise to a wheel vibration phenomenon that can generate an oscillatory movement around the steering axis.

We have come upon yet another surprising aspect of the motorcycle!

Main parameters that influence wobble:

• *Trail:* motorcycles with high rake angle and trail will certainly be stable up to high speeds, but when headshake phenomenon occurs it will be decidedly violent and thus difficult to control;

97

• *Front end inertia around the steering axis:* high moments of inertia around the steering axis, instead, reduce the frequency, giving rise to slower, milder oscillations;

• *Front tire:* by varying the type of tire, that is, its stiffness and damping characteristics, the behavior of the motorcycle can be substantially altered.

The latest generation of tire products make use of recent developments in this field, offering improved riding safety;

• *Lateral flexibility of the fork:* In the presence of external shocks, such as a series of hollows or wheel imbalance, the high rigidity of the latest generation of forks makes it harder to dampen the wobble than with more elastic and shock absorbing forks.

A steering damper is very effective for damping wobble movements: it dissipates the energy around the steering axis, making the motorcycle more stable.

Racing bikes with very stiff forks, low moments of inertia around the steering, and very small trail and rake angles, must almost always be designed with a steering damper system; even so, as we have said, when these bikes exit a corner they still exhibit very visible steering head shaking.

The above mathematical treatment above does not take into account *elasticity* or *play* in the steering system.

These parameters *play an important role in generating wobble,* and in fact, even structures with no suspension at all, like the shopping cart we referred to earlier, can present oscillatory phenomena thanks to the presence of play or elasticity in the steering system.

This should serve as a reminder of how important it is to check periodically to see that the steering bearings are clamped tight.

WEAVE

Weave is the most complex of the vibration modes, because the vehicle oscillates in a rolling motion around the axis of the ground, in addition to a rotating motion around the vertical axis (yaw).

Technically speaking, this is a different vibration from wobble, even if, in practice, it is easy to confuse with head shimmy just from the feel of it.

In fact, given the much smaller inertia of the steering part compared to the non-steering part, it makes sense that the oscillation of the latter would be smaller and less obvious.

The mathematical descriptions available from the literature confirm that this vibration mode does not oscillate at low speeds and its natural frequency is nil, as it is when the motorcycle is stopped. As speed picks up, though, the oscillation frequency can rise to 2 to 3 Hz, with little damping, making it potentially dangerous. At high speeds the weave frequency can become so high that the rider is unable to intervene effectively, causing practical difficulties in controlling the bike.

The main parameters that cause weave mode to occur are the same as those we examined for wobble and which we will return to when we look at falling motion, although, there, with differing importance.

Let us see how some of these parameters qualitatively influence weave mode:

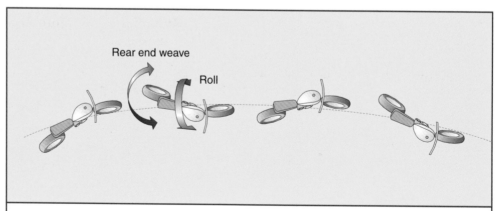

Fig. 9.10: weave.

• *Center of gravity height:* Tends to stabilize this oscillatory mode; by raising the cg with respect to the ground, when the motorcycle rolls, the inertia increases, and thus, the oscillations will be slower.

• *Wheelbase of the vehicle:* The longer the center-to-center distance, the stabler the oscillatory mode.

• *Rear tires* that are very wide and possibly slightly deflated and flattened significantly facilitate the occurrence of weave.

• *Heavy weights* that rebound onto the rear, like luggage, for example, noticeably modify the rear end inertia, amplifying the oscillating weave effect, especially if the loads are not rigidly attached to the body of the bike.

• *Bodywork:* Motorcycles with correct bodywork diminish front end lift owing to the rider's sail effect, and are stable up to higher speeds.
A classic example is an enduro bike with a rider traveling in a straight-up sitting position, producing a noticeable sail effect, which lifts the front end and makes it easier for a weave response to occur.

Simply by crouching down lower, modifying the aerodynamic drag, the rider can significantly reduce this phenomenon. In order to eliminate the problem in some modern enduro bikes that have high-speed potential, small but efficient dome-shaped windscreens are adopted.

Many motorcycles have geometrical characteristics that, at speeds over 60 km/h, should bring on weave mode oscillations, and yet very few riders have this problem.

Why there is such a big difference between theory and practice?

In most cases an oscillatory phenomenon occurs at frequencies a little higher than 1 Hz and with moderate amplitudes, so the rider remains unaware of it and automatically adjusts the handling of the bike.

Furthermore, the oscillatory phenomenon described above continues to repeat over time only if the surrounding circumstances remain unchanged.

But in reality, during normal use, the road surface is never perfectly straight and even, with no hollows and no side winds that change the inclination of the motorcycle.

Because the road surface is generally irregular and always characterized by slight variations in sideways slope (like the center hump of the roadway), the oscillatory phenomenon is quickly dampened by variations in the road surface characteristics, making its appearance less likely to occur.

Remember, too, that the human body is more sensitive to some frequencies than to others.

For example, frequencies in the range of 1 Hz, which correspond to normal walking frequency, are almost automatically controlled by our brain, making them less pronounced to our perception.

SIDE FALL MOTION

Unlike the preceding modes, this one is not vibrational; that is, *it does not repeat over time.*

This aspect makes it the most unusual of the three, and one can essentially see it in the image of the motorcycle simply falling over, without any control on the part of the rider.

In more practical riding terms, *this falling motion can be perceived as an effect of "falling into the corner"* that all motorcycles have to some degree at low or very low speeds when going around a tight corner like a switchback road or a U-turn.

As we have seen in the chapter on straight-line motion, each motorcycle is characterized by a minimum speed below which the bike becomes unstable and only the rider, by continuing to adjust steering and posture, is able to keep the vehicle balanced.

In any case, this falling mode becomes stable when the speed is increased, or at least, it becomes "almost stable," allowing the rider to pass into automatic pilot and unconsciously control the bike.

The parameters that influence stability in falling mode, although in different ways and with differing importance, are:

- Speed of travel;
- Wheel inertia;
- Inertia of the vehicle with respect to the axis of the ground (or roll);
- Mass of the vehicle;
- Position of the center of gravity;
- Rake angle;
- Trail;
- Tire dimensions.

Given the multiplicity of parameters that influence sideways fall, it is difficult to provide a simplified numerical explanation.

In any case, it may be interesting to note that this phenomenon is described according to the falling time: *the shorter the duration, the more unstable the mode.*

This instability does not necessarily have to be interpreted as a drawback; consider the sort of a situation that exists when setting the bike into a corner: clearly, in fact, the agility required of a racing bike to complete a circuit with rapid changes in direction will benefit from a constant, short falling time; a bike that essentially "enters" or "falls" effortlessly by itself into corners.

Skilled racers with quick responses are able to efficiently exploit this characteristic of the, technically, almost unstable vehicle, obtaining optimum results on their circuit times.

At the same time, this built-in, quick falling time explains why even these champions end up in a fall or making errors when their concentration fades for an instant. How many times have we heard, even from expert riders: "I was going slowly and then suddenly I found myself on the ground!"

As far as touring bikes are concerned, instead, the user will certainly prefer to have a more solid, slow, and manageable control over the bike when leaning into a corner, so touring bikes are designed to have longer falling time constants.

CONCLUSIONS

Daily use of the motorcycle is conditioned by the presence of the oscillatory motions described above.

A mathematical analysis thus becomes important in order to adequately tackle these problems.

If we want to make a gross generalization that is mathematically incorrect, the three vibration modes can be associated with three fundamental requirements of the vehicle:
1) ease of entry into corners - falling motion;
2) steering (handling) stability - wobble;
3) rear end (handling) stability - weave.

Moreover, the two oscillatory modes, weave and wobble, which we have treated formally as two completely separate phenomena, in reality often occur together or are not always disassociated.

Whenever there is an occurrence of weave there is almost always a steering oscillation, that is, a component of wobble that makes it difficult to say whether the problem is due to one or the other.

By letting the motorcycle slowly decelerate on a slight slope, with throttle closed, and coming down from high speeds with no hands on the handlebar, some very perceptive test riders have found from experience that there is a speed interval at which the motorcycle "comes alive" because of the vibration modes we have discussed, and begins to slowly oscillate around the steering axis and/or the roll axis.

In any case, recent developments in tires and suspension systems make modern motorcycles subject to such minor occurrences of these phenomena that they have become more an object of curiosity than a real source of dangerous instability.

An accurate and close analysis of vibration modes requires the use of very complex calculating instruments, while the creation of mathematical models takes place *ad hoc* during the manufacturer's development of a model, making them unavailable to the public.

For those of you who would like to explore the matter more fully, there are some mathematical approaches in the literature suggested by Sharp and, more recently, by Professor Cossalter.

FUNCTIONS OF THE BODYWORK

Originally, the motorcycle evolved out of the bicycle, so it did not incorporate any kind of protection from the wind. Only later were different types of bodywork developed, with different purposes in mind.

The first, most simple type of bodywork was created for city bikes with low performance expectations. It is composed of a front windscreen, varying in height and positioned to protect the passenger from atmospheric agents, such as rain and cold, or, considering today's cities, from polluting agents such as the clouds of exhaust fumes that are put out by big transport vehicles.

The second type, for sportbikes, was created both to improve aerodynamic characteristics and the handling response of the vehicle, as well as to limit air pressure on the rider at high speeds.
This is a much more complex kind of bodywork that may involve the entire structure of the motorcycle.

Finally, the last type, developed for cruisers and big touring bikes, addresses both the needs that inspired the first two types. The idea, in fact, is to simultaneously provide riding comfort, even when riding in a straight-up sitting position, and protection from external agents, while at the same time allowing the bike to reach high speeds, without, moreover, compromising ease of handling.

This allows the rider to push the motorcycle to its limit without overtiring and without having to grip tightly onto the handlebars.
Given the rapid evolution of today's motorcycle performance levels, the use of an aerodynamic protection is becoming ever more widely-adopted, even for medium-powered bikes.

AERODYNAMICS

A motorcycle's resistance to motion depends, as we have seen in the chapter on keeping balance in straight-line motion, on the rolling resistance of the tires and on aerodynamic drag, whose influence increases according to speed of travel.

The aerodynamic force absorbed as a function of the velocity is given by the following relation:

Equation 10.1

$$P_A = V \cdot \frac{(p_o \cdot v^2 c_x \cdot s)}{2}$$

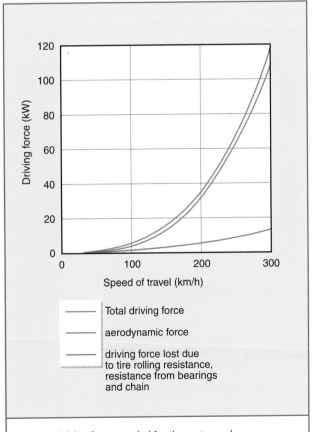

Fig. 10.1: driving force needed for the motorcycle.

Legend:
— Total driving force
— aerodynamic force
— driving force lost due to tire rolling resistance, resistance from bearings and chain

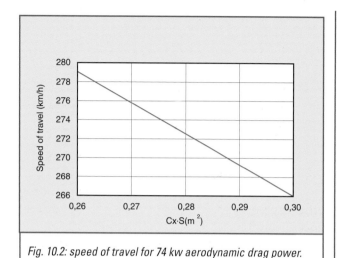

Fig. 10.2: speed of travel for 74 kw aerodynamic drag power.

Where:

ρ_0 = air density
V = speed of travel
S = frontal area of the vehicle
C_X = aerodynamic drag coefficient

As we can see, *looking at the graph that shows overall driving force needed to travel at a certain speed, the contribution of the driving force necessary to overcome aerodynamic drag is considerable,* especially as the speed gets higher.

But even low-speed vehicles are heavily effected by drag: think of the aerodynamically efficient positions that today's bicycle racers assume on their record-breaking bikes, designed especially to minimize the frontal area and to streamline their form.

Looking now at the motorcycle considered in Figure 10.2, we can calculate that a vehicle with 74 kW driving force (about 100 hp) will have quite different top speeds when the aerodynamic drag ($S \cdot C_X$) varies between 0.30 and 0.26: *The difference is over 12 km/h, hardly a negligible amount!*

These results make it easy to appreciate why accurate aerodynamic studies are so important for racing bikes and why the overall design of the vehicle must seriously take into account aerodynamic aspects. The performance of a powerful engine can be impaired by inadequate attention to aerodynamic forces.

It becomes increasingly evident that high-performance levels can only be obtained by hitting on the correct mix of ingredients, a "cocktail" made up of a number of parameters that are intimately related to each other.

Frontal area

The projected frontal area is equal to the area contained within the motorcycle-plus-rider profile, viewed from the front.

The frontal surface of a motorcycle is generally much smaller than a car's.

Because of the enormous differences between bike models, however, aerodynamic drag values vary considerably.

To begin with, the position of the rider is fundamental: with rider crouching flat, the surface exposed to airflow is much less than in a sitting position or when standing up on the footrests, as in offroad riding.

Secondly, the frontal area of a road racing bike will be much smaller than a super tourer in which the fairing must be high and wide in order to protect the rider from wind pressure and other atmospheric agents.

This value can vary between 0.4 and 0.9 square meters, depending on the model of the bike.

Let us analyze in detail the different factors that influence the measurement of the frontal area.

The shape of the rider's body is important: since it is exposed to the airflow, the projected area will vary depending on:

• Height of rider (there is a big difference between how someone 1.7 meters tall is able to fit into the form of the fairing and someone who is 2 meters tall);

• Build (more or less bulky).

The same motorcycle, then, when mounted by different riders, will obviously reach different top speeds.

Furthermore, to optimize aerodynamic aspects, the rider's posture and position are crucial.

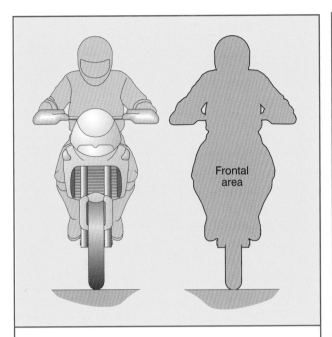

Fig. 10.3: frontal area includes the rider-plus-motorcycle unit.

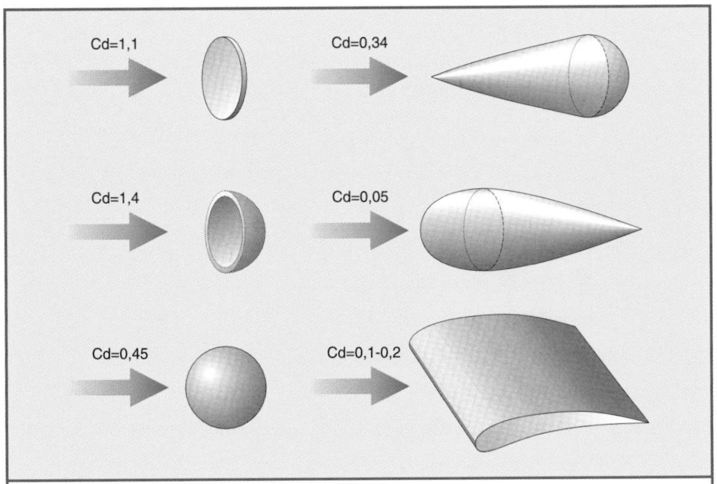

Cd=1,1   Cd=0,34

Cd=1,4   Cd=0,05

Cd=0,45   Cd=0,1-0,2

Fig. 10.4: aerodynamic drag coefficient for various bodies in motion.

For optimum aerodynamics, especially in racing, riders must pay attention to a few small adjustments that can help reduce their projected area.

It is important to keep your elbows in front of your knees, and not splaying out to the sides; keep the balls of your feet on the pegs to make sure that your boots do not become wings; and keep your helmet pressed to the fuel tank, sheltered under the dome of the windscreen.

These measures will minimize the amount that the rider protrudes out from the bodywork profile.

Furthermore, it is important to form the most continuous surface possible in order to avoid sharp indentations which, as we shall soon see, can create harmful turbulence.

Wind tunnel testing has brought to light the fact that the rider has a big influence not only on the projected area, but also on the C_x value.

A racer's ability to assume an aerodynamically efficient position can make a significant difference, from 3 to 4 km/h on a Grand Prix bike.

Clothing, too, has a big influence: to demonstrate this fact, we do not have to flog our horse power to the max down the straight-away.

Simply try sitting on a bicycle, without pedalling, and go down a gentle slope while wearing:

- The first time, your leathers;
- The second time, winter rain gear.

The perceptible difference will be convincing enough to help understand what happens when riding at speeds over 200 km/h.

Aerodynamic drag coefficient (C_x)

The C_x, **or aerodynamic drag coefficient,** is a dimensionless value which, in the speed ranges typical of cars and motorcycles, is specific to every object; that is, it can be considered a constant.

Figure 10.4 shows C_x values characteristic of several bodies moving through air.

It is immediately evident that these values vary significantly from object to object, and it is interesting to note that the tear-drop shape has the best C_x value: it is no accident, then, that the form assumed by falling water is the naturally best design.

The tear-drop shape is obviously the best silhouette for a motorcycle (see Figure 10.5) both from a side view and from above.

In practice, however, there are some serious difficulties in constructing a motorcycle with this sort of profile.

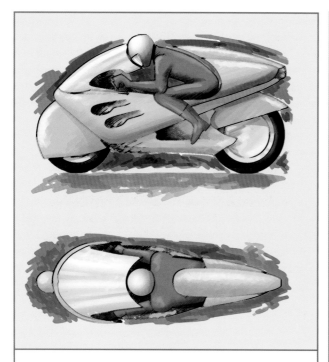

Fig. 10.5: the motorcycle's teardrop silhouette.

COMPONENTS OF RESISTANCE TO FORWARD MOTION

A body's resistance to aerodynamic motion is due to three components:

- *Friction resistance*
- *Induced drag*
- *Form drag*

Let us analyze these factors separately.

Friction resistance

Friction resistance is the part of resistance solely attributable to *viscous action* which acts in the boundary layer of the fluid that the body is moving through.

Just remember that the boundary layer is the contact area within which the fluid (air, in this case) makes a transition between the velocity of the moving object and its undisturbed velocity (zero, in the ideal case of no wind).

This boundary layer is characterized by two types of airflow:

- *Laminar*, when the motion is vortex-less and the airstreams do not mix.
- *Turbulent*, when the motion is a vortex and is characterized by mixing airstreams inside the boundary layer itself, even if the vortex motions are microscopically small.

Induced drag

The resultant force of fluid-to-vehicle friction plus the unbalanced pressures that act on the vehicle moving through air, has one component going in the motorcycle's direction of travel, but it also contains a component perpendicular to the direction of travel.

This is the *lift and downforce (negative lift) effect* which is at the basis of design criteria for airplane wings, for example.

In order to create suspension lift, the wings must generate a loss of energy in the induced drag.

In the case of a symmetrical wind profile whose axis is oriented along the direction of airflow, the induced drag is clearly zero.

Motorcyrcles almost always have a lift effect; in fact, one could think of the lateral profile of a motorbike as a wing with a more curved top part.

Form drag

Form drag is responsible for *most of the motorcycle's aerodynamic drag* and is due to the presence of a wake.

Sudden separations in the streamlines can be provoked by sharp variations in the form of the bodywork, or from any surface detail that impedes regular airflow in the boundary layer, such as a spike or a sharp indentation.

A wake is more likely to occur especially in areas where the fluid slows down, hence, generally, around the rear end of the vehicle.

Wake formation in both cars and motorcycles is easy to observe on the highway when it is raining: watch the behavior of the water clouds that passing, high-speed vehicles leave behind them.

Ignore, of course, the fine dust clouds kicked up by the wheels and you will clearly see the wakes and their different shapes and intensities, depending on the profiling of the body contours.

The aerodynamic characteristics of a motorcycle are not particularly good: its *surface is anything but continuous* and this generates a series of local rising and lowering pressures that are not favorable from the point of view of aerodynamic streamlining.

Aerodynamic analysis can be divided into two parts:
- **External airflow analysis**
- **Internal airflow analysis**

EXTERNAL AERODYNAMICS

Let us begin our aerodynamic analysis of the various zones of the vehicle starting with the front end:

- The *front wheel* is not protected by a fairing. In order to eliminate losses due to ventilation generated by the rotation of the spokes, studies have shown that fully lense-shaped tires (like bicycle tires) give some improvement to the C_x. This is a serious detriment to stability, however, because the whole bike becomes highly sensitive to side winds.

Furthermore, the disc brakes must remain open to the wind for cooling purposes. Car disc brakes are, effectively, completely enclosed inside the wheel (as well as being located within the carriage itself) and little exposed to airflow, but they are made thicker in order to better absorb heat, and in some cases they are even self-ventilating.

This sort of solution applied to a motorcycle would add a lot of weight and would heighten the gyroscopic effect.

Fortunately, the drag coefficient of the front wheel is quite modest, since motorcycle tires have smaller widths and their profile is rounded; in other words, they have a moderately aerodynamic shape.

The lift component due to Magnus effect is of secondary importance.

For interest's sake, we show the flow field around an automobile-type tire (hence, with quite a large section and flat profile) that generates a Magnus effect (Figure 10.8).

Case a: wheel distant from ground;
Case b: wheel in contact with the ground.

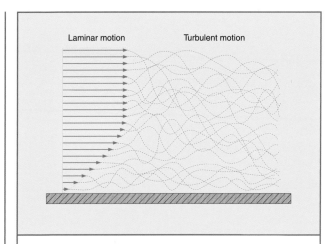

Fig. 10.6: laminar and turbulent motion in a fluid.

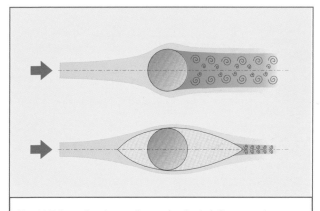

Fig. 10.7: how the shape of a moving body influences drag.

The function of the mudguard is important since it must offer minimal frontal area while still guaranteeing protection, and it must not disturb the airflow that goes towards the radiator.

- The *frontal part:* is clearly the area that receives the most air stress. There is a total force of several tens of kilos on the windscreen at speeds over 230 km/h. A well-designed and constructed fairing is the only answer for preventing harmful deformations and vibrations.

The *windscreen* dome has the important function of protecting the rider's shoulders and helmet as well as creating a certain aerodynamic downforce which, as we shall see, is fundamental for handling the vehicle.

The tilt and the form of the outer edge of the windscreen are crucial for achieving good aerodynamic form: even variations of a few centimeters can give rise to big differences in terms of resistance to motion and, especially, riding comfort.

To form an idea of the importance of even small details, anybody can try this simple experiment:

place a strip of adhesive sponge, about 10 mm thick and 10mm wide, across the whole upper profile of the fairing, that is, from the lower edge of the handguards to the top of the windscreen, at a distance of 10 to 15 mm from the end of the fairing profile. Setting off at medium-high speed, you will notice a considerable change in the airflow, and generally, a reduction in the wind force on your body. This sensation is especially easy to notice in cold weather.

The radiator is generally placed behind the front wheel, in the lower part of the fairing. Clearly, there must be enough airflow passing through here in order to guarantee proper engine cooling.

In order to ensure air feed to the radiator, the entrance duct into the fairing must be big, even if this is obviously to the detriment of a streamlined bodywork profile.

This explains why a motorcycle with a super-powerful engine, but requiring a big-sized radiator or a big entrance duct in the fairing, may be at a disadvantage in terms of maximum speeds.

• The *side flanks:* are substantially "clean" zones whose influence on total aerodynamic efficiency is quite small. Generally, the side flanks must serve as exit areas for the radiator airflow, which must be located in such a way as to not disturb the external airflow. The fairings should be prolonged as far as possible towards the rear in order to prevent the formation of vortices and wakes due to openings and cavities.

• The *mid-zone:* is largely covered by the rider. Big aerodynamic losses are especially localized in this area: between the edges of the handguards and the rider's hands, and also between the edges of the windscreen and the helmet.

The pressure inside the windscreen dome is familiar to all motorcyclists, as is the turbulence that, in some cases, can become a strain on the neck muscles over time.

• The *tail end:* must be optimized in order to close off the airflow in such a way as to minimize wake resistance. To obtain good aerodynamics, the rear part of the seat, which acts as a support under acceleration, must be high enough to fit well against the rider's back.

In reality, however, because of safety reasons, this cannot be done: in the case of a fall, this back support could block the rider and create difficulty in getting clear of the motorcycle.

Aerodynamic development is limited by the rider's need to move about freely on the motorcycle. So if we could "seal" all the openings between rider and motorcycle, thus creating *a continuous surface, the C_x would greatly improve* but, other than the fact the different physiques and sizes of the users would make it necessary to customize the bodywork, it would make it impossible for the rider to move around and, thus, to be able to handle the bike in perfect freedom.

In racing bikes, the limits imposed on the dimensions of the bodywork are quite restrictive; there is a particular regulation that states that the racer can never be covered on the sides, and thus be confined by the fairings.

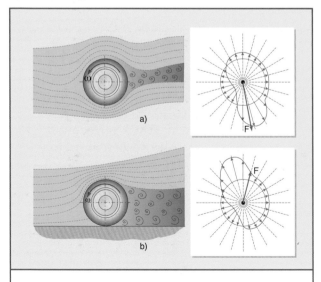

Fig. 10.8: fluid motions around a wheel.

• The *rear wheel:* due to the fact that it is located in the area of the wake, the rear wheel contributes a negligible effect to the total aerodynamic drag.

Elements that contribute to poor aerodynamics are anything that sticks out of the bodywork, like turn signals, rearview mirrors, mufflers that are out of line with the fairing, the rear license plate and splashguard; each of these parts, but especially rearview mirrors, increases the frontal area and creates vortexes.

Figure 10.9 gives a few typical values.

INTERNAL AERODYNAMICS

The optimum aerodynamic form for a motorcycle would be a tear-drop shape, characterized by a fairing *with no internal openings,* which inevitably create airstream disturbances both at their entrances and exits.

However, a number of requirements necessitate a series of internal airflow ducts and passages, for the following purposes:
• Engine cooling;
• Engine air feed and exhaust;
• Engine heat discharge and exhaust tubes located so as not to bother the rider;
• Accessibility for servicing and maintenance.

Cooling:

As far as cooling is concerned, the **housing of the radiator** inside the fairing must be carefully designed. In order to optimize heat exchange and at the same time reduce aerodynamic losses, the radiator must be placed as shown in the Figure 10.10

The airstream is slowed when it passes through the diffuser, whose sides should open at an angle no bigger than 7 degrees, thus allowing the pressure to pick up again; the airstream is then guided once again towards the exit, having passed through the radiator.

The perfect layout would then discharge the hot air into the rear wake, thus reducing the length of the wake itself and, theoretically, *contributing a push* to the motorcycle.

Obviously, because of the presence of many other mechanical bodies, this sort of layout is diffi-

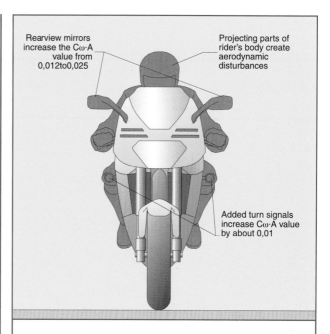

Fig. 10.9: elements that contribute to poor aerodynamics.

cult to achieve on a motorcycle. The air is made to exit out of the side flanks, trying to minimize disturbance to the external airflow.

The same sorts of considerations hold true for all the other air passages. The optimum airflow design for very individual model has to take into account the structure and bulk of the set-up.

The resultant C_x value for sportbikes ranges between 0.30 and 0.60. This is higher than the latest generation of automobiles, whose "streamlined" aerodynamics are characterized by C_x values around 0.26 to 0.35.

The frontal area of a motorcycle, however, whose product $S \cdot C_x$ is minimal, is almost always smaller than a car's.

The projected frontal area of a car, as we have said, is always much larger than a motorcycle's and generally varies between the following ranges:
• *1.7 to 1.9* square meters for a compact;
• *2.0 to 2.2* square meters for a mid-range;
• *1.6 to 1.8* square meters for a sportscar.

For further confirmation of this data, we reproduce the chart from chapter five, with the addition of maximum speeds for each vehicle.

Note that the higher power of the cars is, for the most part, compensated by lower $S \cdot C_x$ values for the motorcycles.

The bodywork on a motorcycle also has an important esthetic function.

That is why for high-performance sportbikes, more study is put into the aerodynamics than into its visual appeal, while for bikes that are not expected to perform at such high levels, there is more freedom in creating its appearance.

For models like enduro bikes, where high speed is not as important, a few areas are studied with particular attention, like the profile of the windscreen, which must both provide protection at speeds over 100 Km/h and diminish the lift effect, as illustrated below.

INFLUENCE OF AERODYNAMICS ON HANDLING
Aerodynamic lift

As we previously hinted, the lateral profile of a motorcycle can in some ways be compared to the profile of an aircraft wing.

In other words, when the velocity increases, **an aerodynamic force is generated that tends to lift the motorcycle**; this means that the loads on the wheels will no longer be static.

A motorcycle passing over a trip-chord connected to scales, shows a dynamic weight that is tens of kilos less than its static weight!

The component of load on the wheels owing to aerodynamic lift (positive or negative), which is vertical, will be called L_{front} and L_{rear} to indicate front and rear.

The position of the rider takes on great importance here: when sitting, like on an enduro bike, not only does the rider increase the frontal area, he or she also acts as a further airflow deflector, notice-

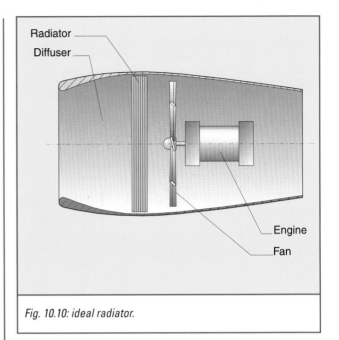

Fig. 10.10: ideal radiator.

ably lightening the motorcycle's weight.

Lift effect can be reduced by using specially designed profiles, with particular focus on the contour of the frontal part and, theoretically speaking, it can even be eliminated by adding spoilers or special wings.

Downforce (or negative lift)

Just as *for masses, there exists a point called the center of gravity* at which the resultant of weight forces may be imagined to act, in the same way, for aerodynamic forces, *the center of pressure is the point at which the resultant of aerodynamic forces may be imagined to act.*

Every type of bodywork and motorcycle is characterized by its *center of pressure* (to be referred to

MOTORCYCLE HIGH-POWERED SPORTSBIKES			CAR	
	$S \cdot C_x$ rider sitting	$S \cdot C_x$ rider prone		$S \cdot C_x$
mod 1	0,46	0,39	compact	0,55
mod 2	0,44	0,36	mid-range	0,64
mod 4	0,48	0,43	high-powered	0,73
500 cc racer		0,24		

as *CofP*), something that is difficult to locate, but which will certainly be positioned above the axis of the ground (given that the whole motorcycle lies above the ground).

The distance from the ground to the center of pressure is determined by an arm that, when multiplied by the value of aerodynamic drag, **gives rise to a downforce (or negative lift).**

Equation 10.2

$$Downforce = F_{drag} \cdot d$$

type of vehicle	displace ment cc	weight with rider kg	power kW (CV)	weight power/ratio kg/kW	top speed km/h
automobile					
compact	1200	980	53.7 (73)	18.25	170
medium-sized	2000	1415	97 (132)	14.2	190
high powered	2800	1570	142 (193)	11.1	230
sportscar	3200	1515	236 (321)	6.4	250
high-powered sp.	3500	1500	280 (380)	5.35	295
motorcyrcle					
low-powered	125	215	24.2 (33)	9	175
medium-powered	600	272	70 (95)	3.9	244
high-powered bike	1100	300	101(138)	3	275
superbike	900	270	98 (133)	2.7	270

This downforce, in order to be balanced, determines two vertical loads on te wheels given by the relation:

Equation 10.3

$$Lift = \frac{Downforce}{Wheelbase}$$

The higher the center of pressure is located, the greater the downforce will be on the motorcycle.

When in motion, the sum of the vertical aerodynamic forces on the wheels is given, then, by the aerodynamic lift effect and by the downforce.
In particular, on the front wheel:

Equation 10.4

$$L_{net} = L_{stat} - Downforce - L_{front}$$

From this we understand that the weight on the front wheel is reduced by two effects: one contribution to the reduction comes from the lift force and another from the downforce.

This **front end weight reduction provokes a drop in the righting moment**, giving rise to that light weight sensation characteristic of all motorcycles traveling at a high speed, and by that we mean, at speeds higher than 200 km/h.

Fig. 10.11: a) profile of windshield offering poor protection.
b) profile of windshield offering good protection.

For the rear wheel, we have the following relation:

Equation 10.5

$$L_{net} = L_{stat} + \textbf{\textit{Downforce}} - L_{rear}$$

On the rear end, the weight reduction due to lift is opposed, at least partially, by the overload due to the downforce.

This allows an adequate load on the rear end at all times, otherwise, at very high speeds, we might end up with the paradox of a slipping rear wheel.

In theory, even with access to infinite driving force, because of these aerodynamic effects, **there exists a standard speed limit for every motorcycle.**

This limit could be reached by:

• Elimination of front wheel load:
In this case, the speed limit would be hit when

the lift effect of the downforce eliminates the load bearing on the front wheel, thus impeding directional control of the motorcycle.

• Inability to transmit the driving force to the ground:
The limit in this case derives from the lack of rear wheel adhesion which, if the lift effect is very great, can be made worse by insufficient weight, making transmission to the ground of the driving force unable to move the vehicle forward.

In both these cases, the phenomenon can be reduced by adding aerodynamic wings or appropriate contours to the bodywork in order to minimize lift.

The latest generation of high-performance streetbikes have windshields designed to create a certain downthrust *(anti-lift)* to counterbalance front end weight reduction at high speeds.

For example, especially in the case of high-powered 500 cc of Grand Prix bikes, you may observe that over the years they have taken on a configuration that places a certain aerodynamic load onto the front.

Evidently, the peak speed of a long, straight-line run can be slightly sacrificed in the interest of better handling performance during the rest of the course.

STRAIGHT-LINE STABILITY

The *longitudinal position of the center of pressure* is also important.

If the **CofP** is ahead of the motorcycle's center of gravity, a gust of side wind or a corner can make the resultant aerodynamic effect yaw the bike in the direction of the wind.

This is clearly a dangerous, destabilizing effect.

On the contrary, if the *CofP* is behind the center of gravity, the motorcycle will tend to maintain its rectilinear motion; the aerodynamic effects will counter directional changes.

A good example of this is given by **machines designed for very high-speed records** which have to maintain a strictly upright, straight-line trajectory and remain stable at high speeds:

BODYWORK AND AERODYNAMICS

110

they are equipped with large, vertical tail fins.

Even though these bikes look completely different from the regular bikes we see around town, these record-breakers are able to reach *top speeds of over 500 km/h.*

To limit front end lifting tendencies, they are made very long and ballasted in the front area, often even overhanging.

Furthermore, they are very low to the ground and the pilot is positioned "lying down", for two reasons:

• To reduce the frontal area;
• To keep the height of the *CofP* low, and thus, reduce front end lift.

TAIL FINS AND GROUND EFFECT ON AUTOMOBILES

In recent years, automobiles have surprisingly increased the speed at which they can go around corners by using the vertical downthrust effect, called anti-lift, generated by aerodynamic fins or by the ground effect. The ground effect is generated by making use of the pressure drop between the bottom of the car body and the ground, and of specially designed lower carriage profiles.

In Figure 10.14 we can see how airflow changes around a body that is placed near the ground.

In particular, we can see that aerodynamic drag increases and the streamlines are closer together above the axle, indicating greater speeds, which, then, cause an anti-lift effect.

As we have already seen, the creation of lift or anti-lift forces cannot be obtained without causing some detriment to net motion resistance.

In fact, current Formula One racing cars powered with about 700 hp "only" reach a top speed of 330 km/h.

Evidently, in order to obtain the best lap times, top speed has been sacrificed in favor of higher cornering speeds.

In effect, Formula One cars reach lateral acceleration values of 3 to 4 g (***g*** indicates *acceleration of gravity* equal, on average, to 9.81 m/s^2), while we

have seen that with a uniform coefficient of friction, motorcycles that lean at 45 degrees reach centrifugal forces equal to 1 g.

The speed at which a Formula One racing car can go around a corner is therefore much higher than a motorcycle's.

It is natural to wonder why motorcycles do not make use of the same sort of aerodynamic wings in order to increase their cornering speeds.

Initially, wings were even added directly into the wheels of Formula One racing cars, but they were later prohibited by racing regulations.

INCREASED VERTICAL LOADS ON MOTORCYCLES
Making use of aerodynamic wings

By appending one or more wings onto an aerodynamically clean area of the motorcycle, you are able to create an excellent vertical anti-lift force, with the added advantage of being able to increase wheel weights as much as you want without increasing the sprung masses, all of which is to the benefit of traction and holding.

In a corner, the wings incline along with the motorcycle, and their vertical load will always be

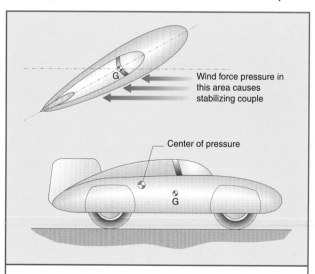

Wind force pressure in this area causes stabilizing couple

Center of pressure

Fig. 10.13: record machine with center of pressure to the rear of its center of gravity.

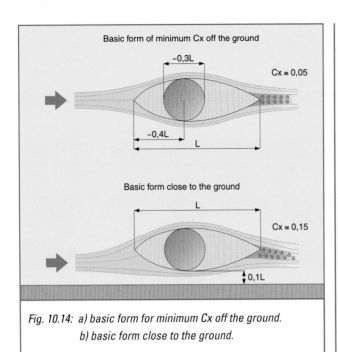

Fig. 10.14: a) basic form for minimum Cx off the ground.
b) basic form close to the ground.

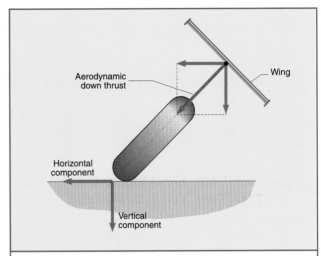

Fig. 10.15: increased vertical loads on the motorcycle by means of aerodynamic wings.

orthogonal to the wing profile.

What happens, then, is *a response equivalent to a weight increase,* but this *does not permit an increase in cornering speed, although, as in straight-line motion, it does improve road holding adhesion.*

The benefits are therefore minimal, and furthermore, there would be all the problems associated with the changing attitude of the motorcycle in different riding situations, which would also affect the critical angle and efficiency of the wings.

Moreover, any aerodynamic fins that project out of the contour of the motorcycle are prohibited in the racing sector and this has discouraged their development.

Consequently, even all the streetbikes that are direct discendants of racing bikes are currently free of aerodynamic additions.

It would be more useful, instead, to attach *the wings directly onto the wheels.* The increase in vertical load given by the wings would go directly to the ground, without having to pass through the suspension; this would mean that the suspension would not be compressed at high speeds, with obvious gains for the attitude.

Making use of the ground effect

The bottom of the motorcycle's bodywork is always very narrow and, therefore, it cannot be made use of for its ground effect, as an automobile's can; in any case, greater straight-line adhesion is not that important to us.

When cornering, instead, during races, the whole side of the fairing brushes the tarmac; with the right kind of modifications, it could provide a large enough surface to create a good ground effect.

The result, however, would be tremendous: the motorcycle would tend to lean more and more, making it difficult to pull upright.

CHAPTER 11
THE ENGINE

We will limit our discussion on the engine to aspects that directly or indirectly influence the motorcycle's handling response. As far as the analysis of the functioning and performance of the motorcycle propulsion system is concerned, we prefer to refer the reader to other authors on the subject.

COMPARISON BETWEEN CAR AND MOTORCYCLE ENGINES

Motorcycle engines are characterized by high specific power, generally higher than that of automobiles.

Let us refer once again to the chart first shown in Chapter 5, adding a column for power/displacement ratio, or rather the **specific power**.

This is, in fact, a powerful indicator of the difference between motorcycle and automobile engines.

It can easily be seen that the specific power is extremely high for low-powered 2-stroke engines.

This engine configuration is ideal to reach high performance levels with a small, light, economically designed construction that makes it easy to service.

We can see that a 125 cc, 2-stroke streetbike engine has a specific power comparable to a sophisticated, expensive Formula One engine, designed, moreover, to last through only one race.

Even 4-stroke, medium-and high-powered motorcycle engines generally deliver more specific power than car engines.

This is made possible by much higher revolution speeds that deliver a power curve that peaks at a very high rev speed.

Except for a few cases, we can state that a car engine delivers its maximum torque at around 2,500 to 3,000 rpm, and is characterized by a maximum rpm of 6,000 to 7,000 rpm; a motorcycle engine with the same specific power reaches its maximum torque around 5,000 to 6,500 rpm and is characterized by maximum speeds that can be over 10,000 rpm.

If you replaced a mid-range car engine with 1,800 cc and 73 kW of power with a 600 cc motorcycle engine with the same maximum power delivery, even after having substantially modified the velocity ratio it would be necessary to rev the engine up and let the clutch "slip" for a good while before getting the vehicle to move!

Moreover, car engines are designed for a lifespan of 200,000 to 250,000 kilometers, and minimal maintenance needs; generally, then, the specific wear associated with use is limited as much as possible in order to keep the daily costs of the vehicle down. In essence, the design philosophy of the automobile is dedicated to improving its long-term costs and reliability rather than concentrating on high performance results.

With the exception of scooters, perhaps, in most industrialized nations motorcycles are not perceived simply as a substitute means of transport for the car; while they are perfect for getting round traffic jams in the city, at the same time they are viewed as an ideal recreational vehicle.

Motorcycles, therefore, must be fun to ride and offer high performance, too.

A motorcycle's lifespan is, actually, quite short compared in terms of kilometers to a car, and this

automobile	displacement (cc)	weight with rider (kg)	power kW (CV)	power/displacement ratio kW/dm³
compact	1200	900	53.7(73)	**45**
medium-size	2000	1415	97(132)	**48**
high-powered	2800	1570	141(193)	**50**
sportscar	3200	1515	236(321)	**73**
high-powered sp.	3500	1500	280(380)	**80**
formula 1	3000	......	551(750)	**183**

motorcycle	displacement (cc)	weight with rider (kg)	power kW (CV)	power/displacement ratio kW/dm^3
low-powered	125	215	24 (33)	**192**
medium-powered	600	272	70 (95)	**116**
high-powered	1100	300	100 (138)	**91**
superbike	900	265	98 (133)	**108**
500 Gp	**500**	**225**	**147 (200)**	**294**

allows the rider to push the engine to rpm speeds that are much much higher, obviously causing more rapid engine wear.

As we have seen previously, moreover, the total weight of the motorcycle must be as light as possible in order to:

- Enhance performance levels, both in terms of acceleration and braking force;

- Allow good handling response;

- Make stationary maneuvers easier.

To these ends, motorcycle engines are extremely light; each component is studied in depth to keep its weight and bulk down.

The whole structure of the motorcycle is constructed, in fact, in aluminum alloy (while, generally, car engines are in cast iron, a less expensive but heavier material) and some parts that receive less mechanical stress are even made of magnesium alloys.

The preceding chapters have explained the behavior of the motorcycle in various riding situations; we especially focused on a number of parameters that have an important influence on the bike's maneuverability, such as:

- The net weight of the vehicle;
- The distribution of weight onto the wheels;
- The height of the motorcycle's center of gravity;
- The vehicle's inertia, both around the roll axis and the center of gravity;

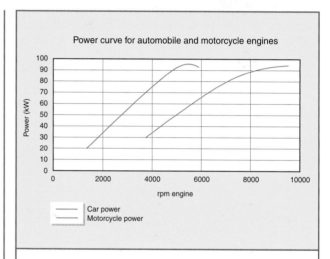

Fig. 11.1: power curve for automobile and motorcycle engines. Note that: with equal maximum power, the revolution speeds of car and motorcycle engines are quite different; to be specific, car engines rotate at significantly lower revolution speeds.

- The length of the swingarm and the position of the pickup point in order to create the desired "chain pull" angle.

We will soon see that a pleasureable riding experience also depends to a great extent on how the engine is designed and constructed.

INFLUENCE OF THE ENGINE ON WEIGHT DISTRIBUTION

Engine weight represents approximately 30 to 35% of the total weight of the motorcycle; and most of the other masses cannot be moved from their normal positions because of a number of construction requirements.

In fact, about 20 to 25% of the total weight is represented by the wheels and other unsprung parts like the brake discs, the brake calipers, the crown wheel, and small moving parts in the fork and the swingarm, which, for obvious reasons, cannot be moved to any degree from their conventional positions at the outer ends of the motorcycle.

Many auxiliaries like the front and rear lights, the turn signals, and the mirrors are equally location-bound by obvious factors determined by their functioning.

Even components like the display panel, the handlebar, the fuel tank, the rider-passenger seat and the footrests, which represent another 10% of the total weight, are bound by obvious ergonomic requirements.

The remaining weight of the motorcycle is almost uniformly distributed along the length of the bike, in the form of the fairing, the electrical system, the frame, and small auxiliaries.

It becomes clear that changing the position of the engine is the most effective parameter (in fact, we are talking about the heaviest component) for changing the location of the center of gravity to where it can provide the vehicle's best dynamic response.

By shifting the motor a few centimeters we can completely change the dynamic behavior of the vehicle.

The engine structure heavily influences the positioning of the engine within the frame: think of a hypothetical 6-cylinder engine placed in line with the drive shaft, parallel to the motorcycle's axis; this set-up would obviously necessitate a long wheelbase, or the adoption of problematic, unwelcome mechanical solutions.

For motorcycling, the best engine is the one that offers the best compromise between:

• Limited weight;
• Reduced bulk;
• High-performance levels, above all, in line with the bike's intended uses.

In reality, an engine layout always has its strong and weak points which must provide the best compromise for the bike's intended uses.

It is as hard to imagine an agile trial bike mounted with a 4-cylinder, inline arrangement, as it is unlikely that a luxury custom bike be mounted with 2-stroke engine.

Engine and *motorcycle* designs must, therefore, be developed together.

This is an obvious difference from the automobile sector, in which the same engine is mounted onto various types of bodies of the same make, or even onto cars made by different manufacturers.

In the following section, which gives an overview of the main types of motorcycle engines, we focus our attention on the bulk and vibration characteristics that heavily influence the structure of the frame, which we will analyse later on in this chapter.

VIBRATIONS

All motorcycle engines, because of their mechanical construction and type of functioning, generate vibrations; all riders will have certainly experienced some annoyance due to vibrations.

Without going into too much detail, let us examine where engine vibration comes from.

The parts of the engine that have alternating movements create imbalances that, ensuing from and depending on the rotation frequency, give rise to vibrations.

For non-experts, remember that the parts with alternating movement which must, therefore, be balanced, are:

• The piston;
• The piston pin;
• Part of the conrod (generally estimated as two-thirds of this component).

The heavier these parts are, the more unbalanced the whole motorcycle will be.

TWO-STROKE AND FOUR-STROKE ENGINES

A preliminary, general subdivision of the different motorcycle engines can be made on the basis of their working cycle; we can distinguish, then:

- Engines with four-stroke cycles; in these engines, one power cycle, that is, one combustion, corresponds to two turns of the crankshaft;

- Engines with two-stroke cycles; in this case, every power cycle corresponds to one turn of the crankshaft.

A two-stroke engine, when compared to a four-stroke engine with the same displacement, presents the following benefits:

- 20% less weight;

- 40% greater power;

- Fewer rotating parts; just think of the absence of the valvegear in the cylinder head.

Simple, light-weight, powerful—these adjectives summarize the great advantages offered by these propulsion systems.

On the downside, though, we must mention: high fuel consumption and, above all, big difficulties in maintaining emission standards, which are increasingly severe in order to control air pollution.

On the basis of what we have seen, it is understandable why two-stroke engines are widely used in racing, especially in small displacement classes.

Furthermore, its great simplicity makes it a favorite for small, light-weight vehicles intended for city use, like scooters.

Conversely, practically all medium- to high-powered motorcycles are equipped with four-stroke engines, with both single and multi-cylinder set-ups.

To conclude this very brief overview, we give some data regarding a few specifications of two classes of sportbikes, representative of the two types of engines:

- 500 cc, Grand Prix, 2-stroke, four cylinder engines reach 147 kW of power (200 hp), with a specific power of **294 kW/dm^3** (400 hp/liter)

- 750 cc, superbike, 4-stroke, four-cylinder engines have about 125 kW (about 170 hp) available, corresponding to a specific power of **166 kW/dm^3** (226 hp/liter).

In this case, the maximum power of the 2-stroke engine is superior by 70%!

A four-cylinder, 2-stroke engine, we must remember, has a smaller uniform displacement, while a 4-stroke engine, mounted on a superbike, is derived from a streetbike production model, so it has all the limitations that come along with mass production.

PRIMARY MOTORCYCLE ENGINE LAYOUTS
Single-cylinder engines

This is probably the most widely-diffused and earliest layout to be applied to motorcycling, given its simplicity, light weight, and lack of bulk.

It is used for very different applications: single-cylinder motors are mounted onto everything from simple scooters to sophisticated enduro bikes with 650 cc and more.

As far as the frame concerned, it is an excellent solution, given its:

- **Longitudinal bulk:** since its length is so short, it allows a free choice of wheelbase distance, with a good length for the swingarm, and makes it possible to concentrate all the masses around the center of gravity.

Because of this, motorcycles with single-cylinder engines can boast greatly reduced inertia;

- **Transversal bulk:** its smaller width allows this type of engine to be positioned at the desired height without having to worry about it easily grounding in turns; it does not impede the rider's space. At the same time, it is easier to position auxiliaries like the radiator, the carburetor, the exhaust system, and so forth.

By limiting weight and bulk it is possible to

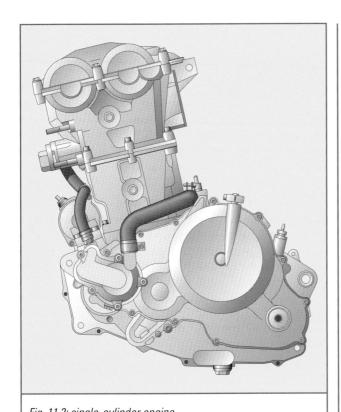

Fig. 11.2: single-cylinder engine.

create very agile bikes, so practically all offroad bikes are fitted with single-cylinder engines.

These engines are also excellent for high torque delivery at low rpm speeds, a characteristic that facilitates handling on rough, cross-country terrain.

As far as vibration aspects are concerned, however, these engines are clearly less balanced: the primary and secondary forces are not completely counter-balanced, giving rise to strong vibrations. The only way open to the designer is to choose a preferred direction along which most of the force will be transmitted.

This level of disturbance is tolerated for racing bike engines, for example, in which light weight, minimal bulk, and the search for maximum power is paramount; or for very simple, inexpensive bikes (such as scooters, in which, as we have already seen, very sophisticated elastic supports are added).

In order to reduce the vibration problem, a counter shaft, called a balance shaft, may be adopted.

This is a widely-used solution, both for many 4-stroke engines, especially those with big displace-ment in which the heavy weight of the piston would be too troublesome, and for 2-stroke, high-performance engines, characterized instead by light pistons, but with very high rpm speeds.

In this layout, primary forces are eliminated, while secondary forces are not.

It is also possible to achieve a completely balanced single-cylinder engine, which we show in Figure 11.3; as we can see, it is quite complex, so much so that it is not commonly used.

The cost, the bulk, and the ensuing complica-tions can be compared to a more fractional horse-power motor that, given the same displacement, would offer much better performance.

Twin-cylinder engines

There are a number of layouts for these motors: **inline; 60, 70, or 90 degree V- arrangements; boxer** (horizontally opposed) design, with and without balance shafts, with both 2-stroke and 4-stroke cycles.

What makes this type of propulsion system so popular is the excellent ratio between **power/bulk** and the possibililty it offers to design compact, elegant bikes.

In some construction layouts the transverse width is the same as a single-cylinder engine, which allows very narrow frames and bodywork with small frontal areas.

A confirmation of the popularity of twin-cylinder engines is given by the fact that it is used for a vast variety of models:

from the simple commuter bike used to go from home to office and back, to the sophisticated supersport for circuit or off-road use, from the big displacement bikes used for highway cruising, to the luxurious, super-accessorized custom bike.

Parallel twin-cylinder:

a simple engine, very similar to a single-cylinder in terms of length, with a slightly larger transversal width. Generally used for simple, low-cost and high-maneuverability bikes.

V-twin with transverse crankshaft:

a lot of different angles are used to set up the cylin-ders, using various layouts for this type of motor. Most arrangements use 90 degree or 60 degree angles.

These engines can deliver a narrow profile, as in the case of single-cylinder engines, while clearly offering bigger power delivery.

Broadly speaking, these propulsion systems offer greatly improved engine balance, and all engines with more than 750 cc displacement offer perfectly balanced primary forces, at times making use of a countershaft.

Twin-cylinder with longitudinal crankshaft:

there exist various versions, with 90 degree or 180 degree angles (boxer design). Since the cylinders project out directly out of the bike contour into the air, this layout offers exceptional cooling capacity. However, it does create some problems for longitudinal development of the bike because the boxer cylinders have to be positioned high up from the ground in order to protect them from scraping the ground when leant over in turns.

Both versions are excellently balanced.

Multi-cylinder engines (with 3 to 6 cylinders)

These are the kinds of high-performance engines we see on medium-to high-powered streetbikes, sportbikes and cruisers.

Appearing on the motorcycle scene during the 1970's, multi-cylinder engines soon became widely adopted thanks to their high-performance delivery and the attractiveness of being able to reach high rpm speeds.

Their other strong point is that they run very smoothly, giving a very comfortable ride.

3- or 4-cylinder inline engines

Longitudinally compact, they offer good weight distribution; their downside is the **bulky transverse width,** which makes for quite wide profiles.

Furthermore, when they are mounted in sportbikes able to lean at big angles, an incorrect location height may cause the side covers of the crankshaft to scrape the ground.

To eliminate this problem, some of the latest generation 4-cylinder, inline motors are designed to reduce transverse bulk.

For example, components like the ignition have been repositioned and driven by layshafts operated by the crankshaft, instead of being parallel to its axis.

Because of their bulk, they are rarely fitted to

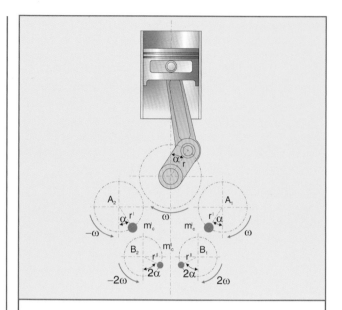

Fig. 11.3: perfectly balanced alternating forces in a single-cylinder engine.

enduro or offroad bikes.

They are well-balanced.

Primary forces are completely balanced, while secondary forces, in some particularly sophisticated engines, are eliminated by means of one or two countershafts rotating at twice the speed of the crankshaft.

If the engine's crankshaft is longitudinal, it is well-suited to shaft-drive transmission, perfect for the creation of splendid touring bikes.

4-cylinder V-engines

This is a good arrangement for motorcycle purposes, uniting bulk comparable to a twin-cylinder engine with the power delivery characteristics of a 4-cylinder engine.

The only drawback: the complexity of the mechanical construction.

6-cylinder inline engines

These are perfectly balanced, both for primary and secondary forces, and offer exceptionally smooth power delivery and, even if it cannot be considered a properly technical advantage, their exhaust sound is unmistakeable.

Clearly, because of their signficantly bulky transversal width and because of construction complexity, they are not often fitted to sportbikes.

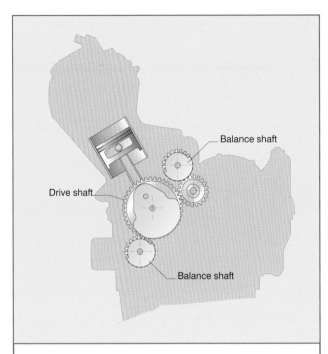

Fig. 11.4: multi-cylinder inline engine with balancing of secondary forces.

Balance shaft

Drive shaft

Balance shaft

FITTING THE ENGINE IN THE FRAME

There are two ways that the engine can be fitted in the frame.

    a) Rigid mounting;
    b) Flexible mounting.

a) Rigid mounting

In this case, the frame and the motor become a single entity and vibrations pass directly between one and the other.

The engine must be attached to the frame at at least two points: in old-style installations the rear engine attachment coincided with the swingarm-pickup point.

This system offers the undeniable advantage of allowing torque transmission directly from the engine to the swingarm, without having to pass through the frame.

In this case, there is less stress on the frame and the whole structure is simplified; only one other mounting point is necessary to anchor the engine.

This kind of solution is often used for motocross bikes, which require the simplest and lightest layouts possible.

Often, to increase the stiffness of the frame-engine unit and to reduce vibration, another anchoring point is added at the cylinder head, thus triangulating the frame and, as is intuitively easy to grasp, altering the vibration mode of the upper sections, given that the free deflection length is halved.

An ever more widely adopted solution is to double the rear engine attachment on the swingarm pivot, putting one mounting point above and one below the swingarm-pickup point, as far as possible away from each other in order to better distribute frame stresses (Figure 11.7).

This offers the advantage of freeing-up the positions of the gearbox sprocket and the swingarm relative to each other and allowing the desired chain pull angle to be created.

Given that the stiffness of the casings must be extremely high in order to impede flexure of the rotating shafts, the engine can be imagined as an infinitely rigid triangle that closes the open structure of the frame.

By adding to the number of mounting points between engine and frame, engine vibrations can be more efficiently dissipated.

Rigid engine mounting can double the stiffness of the frame; if it were not for the engine's contribution, most modern frames would likely experience deformation when placed under severe loading action.

Particular attention is given to constructing the engine-to-frame mounting lugs because the engine reaches temperatures of 70 to 80 degrees (Celsius) when in use, causing signficant transverse extension.

Steel mounting lugs have an expansion coefficient that is lower than the aluminum used for the engine, and the difference in extension all along the lug is in the order of tenths of milimeters.

The tensions on these lugs, then, become enormous when the engine is running, in addition to tensions due to clamping and those due to power transmission and vibrations.

In some cases, the mounting lug is divided into two parts so as to reduce weight and bulk and to eliminate the extension problems we have just discussed.

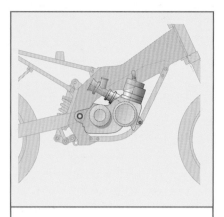

Fig. 11.5: rigid engine-frame mounting attached at 2 points.

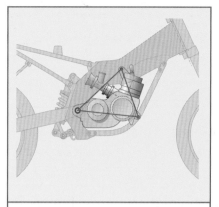

Fig. 11.6: engine-frame mounting with triangulated structure.

b) Flexible mounting

This system is used when the aim is to provide a high level of riding comfort with an engine that puts out strong vibrations. In practice, the engine is fitted with bonded-rubber bushes in the engine's attachment lugs that isolate it from the frame.

In this case, the engine only contributes a small part to frame stiffness, since the stiffness of the rubber mountings is less than the structure's.

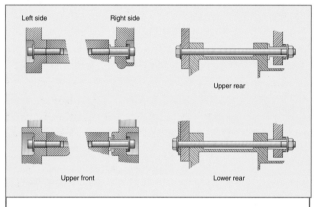

Fig. 11.8: engine mounting lugs.

Engine movements due to vibrations and forces on the chain are easily visible to the naked eye. They are so strong that they can cause fracture problems because of fatigue on the components that are attached both to the frame and the engine, like the exhaust tubes.

Clearly, it is difficult to provide flexible mountings for extremely heavy, powerful engines, since the rubber mountings are subject to such high loads that they would end up losing their isolating properties.

One example of rubber mounting is shown in Figure 11.9.

Mass-produced bikes often make use of **mixed solutions** in which the engine has at least two rigid attachments to the frame, and one or more flexible mountings.

These sorts of systems are adopted to solve local resonance problems on the frame.

The area of the frame around an engine attachment can, in fact, have a rigidity and a mass that makes it particularly sensitive to engine vibrations. These vibrations can cause failures in the area or propagate throughout the whole structure, causing annoyance to the rider.

In this case, the attachment is isolated with a rubber mounting.

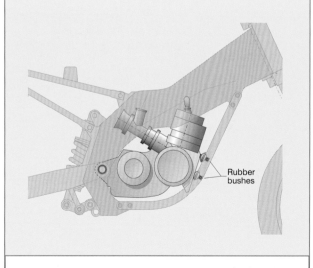

Fig. 11.9: example of flexible mounting.

THE FRAME

The **functions** of the frame include:

A structural function: which means guaranteeing a rigid, secure attachment between the front suspension, the steering head, the rear suspension and the rear fork, and, at the same time, holding in place:

• the engine (as we have seen, with rigid or flexible mounting);
• the rider, passengers, and any luggage;
• all the auxiliaries, such as: fuel tank, radiators, batteries, filter housing, fairing, lights, mirrors, etc.;

A geometrical function: that is, to satisfy all the requirements necessary for good biking performance.
It must allow the creation of appropriate steering head and trail angles, provide the desired stiffness, distribute the weight correctly, determine the fixed wheelbase distance, and finally, set the correct positioning of the engine sprocket and swingarm axis.

The structure of the frame must therefore provide a delicate compromise meant to satisfy a number of different requirements.
In reality, every type of motorcycle has a corresponding type of frame structure that may favor functionality or visual appeal, weight distribution or stiffness requirements, the cost or the sophistication of the particular model. *In other words, there is no ideal frame design; the choice depends on the purpose the vehicle is intended for.*

FRAME CONSTRUCTION MATERIALS

Before we get into the various kinds of frame layouts, let us take a look at a few properties of the materials used to construct them.

Steel

Its ability to be formed into tubes of all shapes and sizes, its great strength, the ease with which it can be bent and welded, and not least, its low cost, have made steel historically the first material to be utilized in the fabrication of motorcycle frames.

Even today, its benefits make it the most used construction material in frame fabrication.

Steel is used for fabricating both round and squared tubes, since, if they are properly designed, it makes round ones easier to bend and squared ones easier to prepare for mating and subsequent welding; these constuctions may be characterized by a high moment of inertia as well.

Steel is also used in the form of pressed sheets, joined together to create box-section tubing that offers benefits in terms of appearance and high stiffness.

Within the steel family there are materials with mechanical properties that vary across a wide spectrum:

• you can choose starting from non-alloyed structural steel with low stress values (with

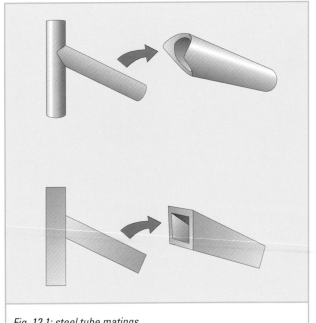

Fig. 12.1: steel tube matings.

breaking strength values of about 420 N/mm^2), going on to alloyed steel with good mechanical properties (with breaking strength values of about 1000 N/mm^2), to reach superalloys with breaking strength values of even 1600 N/mm^2.

The choice of material will obviously depend on its use, which determines the kinds of stresses the structure will subjected to.

Aluminum

Aluminum is a lightweight alloy that makes it an ever more popular choice for motorcycle frames, thanks to its mechanical properties. In particular, its specific weight (see Table 12.4) is approximately one third of iron's.

This property makes it particularly useful for keeping the overall weight of the motorcycle down.

Its drawbacks, in comparison to steel, include higher costs for the raw material and much more sophisticated welding techniques.

In order to stop the welding bath from oxidizing too rapidly, the procedure must take place in an inert gas controlled ambient: that is, it requires TIG (Heli-Arc) or MIG (CO_2) welding.

Another advantage of using aluminum is that it can be transformed using various technological processes into:

- **Cast and presurcast aluminums**: with quite complex shapes and thin wall thicknesses, given the metal's good casting properties;

- **Extrudates**: with thin thicknesses and complex forms, with the possibility of obtaining internal ribbing;

- **Laminates**: subsequently pressed and joined together to give box-section structures;

- **Forged**: with excellent results both from the point of view of appearance and mechanical properties.

By using the best technology for each part, depending on the type of stress and the demands that it is subject to, aluminum makes it possible to assemble the same material together in the form of various structures, which makes for excellent frame construction.

We have already said that the cost of aluminum construction is higher, but all this is made up for by the weight and/or stiffness advantages it offers.

Let us take the example of the side sheet of a sportbike frame that is fabricated using 2.5 mm thick aluminum sheets, bent and welded together. In order to maintain the same weight, box-section steel sheet would have to be 0.86 mm thick.

Clearly, a sheet structure that is only 0.86 mm thick would be highly unstable; that is, a slight side bump would be enough to cause deformation and would also make weldings difficult. Aluminum sheeting structures with 2.5 mm. thickness are much more stable.

To enhance the stability of the form, the sheets may be joined together with struts or they can be

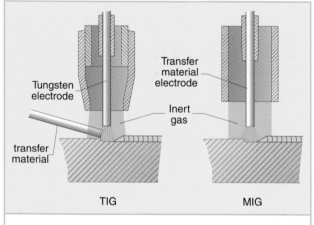

Fig. 12.2: TIG and MIG welding processes.

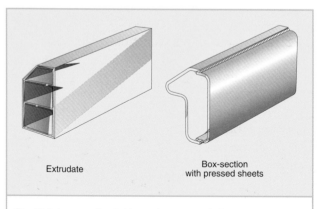

Fig. 12.3: box-section tubing using pressed sheets.

ribbed with appropriate ridges that add both visual appeal and stiffness.

Ideal stability is provided by extrudates with internal ribbing (see Figure 12.3), but they are clearly not moldable into curved forms and do not offer the properties that pressed sheets do.

Another advantage of aluminum is made possible by advanced technology castings that can produce complex forms out of alluminum alloys, with thicknesses of 4 to 5 mm.

To summarize, then, **when high stiffness/weight ratios are needed, aluminum structures are an excellent choice,** and thanks to the diffusion of ever faster and more reliable robotic welding techniques, these sorts of alloy frames are being used on more and more models.

Magnesium

This is a very lightweight material that could hypothetically become the natural substitute for aluminum in the near future; for the moment, though, it is not being used on production bikes because of the following drawbacks:

• Poor resistance to oxidation (which means rapid degeneration over time because of atmospheric agents), unless the surface receives complicated and expensive coating treatments;

• Decay of its mechanical properties with temperature rises; in some types of racing cars, magnesium engine casings are even prohibited because of the metal's low softening point and the fact that is highly flammable;

• High cost of the raw material;

• Poor welding properties.

In some specialized sectors, in any case, because of its properties, magnesium is a highly-prized alloy.

In the racetrack world, for example, where a short lifespan is not important, all wheel rims are made out of cast or forged magnesium, and when the regulations allow it even engine casings are constructed out of special heat-resistant magnesium alloys.

Titanium

This is a very expensive material that was in short supply until recently because of the fact that the biggest producers in the world are countries coming out of the former-Soviet Union.

Even if it is amenable to being shaped into tubes, at present it is not used for industrial applications for large series of titanium frames; and since its mechanical properties are very similar to those of steel, it is used to make special boltings for racebikes.

Composite materials

Composites used for a long time in warfare and aeronautic technologies are now starting to be introduced into motorcycling applications with a whole series of materials that are also referred to as "composites."

These materials are **anistropes,** that is, they behave differently depending on the direction of the applied stress.

This is a vast sector where advanced research is constantly coming up with innovations, especially with regard to improving their mechanical properties.

The design of a composite material is a very complex process because of the numerous factors that come into play.

Here are the main parameters:

• Type of material

These mainly include **carbon, kevlar, glass, boron, and other filaments** that are placed inside a resinous matrix, producing a sort of metallic fabric.

These filaments have high mechanical strength and, at the same time, can offer extremely varied properties, making them fine materials for every conceivable purpose.

Some materials are good for resisting bumps and abrasion (kevlar is even used for armored vests), while others are extremely stiff and strong, making them ideal for sophisticated structures with low weight/stiffness ratios (like today's Formula One carbon frames).

Using the right resinous matrix and combining different kinds of materials within the same metallic fabric makes it possible to create very low specific weights, generally lighter than for magnesium.

• Fiber orientation

The capacity to orient the fibers of the fabric in the direction that you want allows the fiber properties to be enhanced in that direction.

For example, with all the fibers aligned, you create a uni-directional metallic fabric that offers very good tensile properties along that direction, with low strength in the perpendicular direction.

The fabric can be woven across at 90, 60 or 45 degrees, giving different properties depending on the weave.

• Lamination

This indicates a panel of composite material that is generally composed of several layers of fabrics that vary according to the composition or orientation of the fibers.

The list of possibilities we have given in this very broad overview helps to explain why *composite materials are challenging to design.*

Apart from the technical design expertise that is needed to optimize the structure, to take into account all the existing possibilities requires computer support with fully-developed component programmes.

The construction techniques themselves are extremely sophisticated: laminates must be placed in specially designed molds and undergo a heat cycle in high pressure autoclaves.

In spite of the undeniable advantages offered by these materials, their industrial use *is limited by very high costs and production times,* much longer than the techniques used for conventional materials.

In the racing sector, where light weight combined with high stiffness is a priority over low costs and short production time, however, composite materials are widely employed.

Uses of composite materials can be subdivided into:

• Structural applications, replacing construction materials like steel, aluminum, magnesium;

• Bodywork applications or coverings that are subject to low stress, replacing plastic materials.

Structural applications: these include particularly important motorcycle parts that are subject to high stresses.

For example: the rear fork, the wheels, the brake discs, the seat mount, the fork tubes. All these parts require extremely sophisticated construction techniques and precise controls;

Bodywork applications: these are the most common, used for fairings, filter housings, collision bulkheads and conveyors or auxiliary supports.

These sorts of constructions require much simpler techniques and only visually-based, much less demanding controls.

Quality control for composite material production is very complex and is based almost exclusively on experimental verification of the item's stiffness.

For example, a swingarm that is created with 1000 Nm/degree stiffness must be put back on the testing machine after a collision, and to be passed, must give the same initial stiffness value.

Composite materials have only recently been made use of in the motorcycling world, so it is too early to form an accurate judgement of their worth.

We can certainly say, though, that they are extremely reliable, especially for their performance under fatigue: it would appear that the anisotropic structure of the material makes it less "sensitive" to stress cycles.

CONSTRUCTION MATERIALS: CONCLUDING REMARKS

The following **chart summarizes** some of the most important properties for the construction of motorcycle frames:

Where:

• Specific strength is the relation between breaking strength and specific weight;

• Specific rigidity is the relation between shear modulus of elasticity and specific weight.

The chart makes it clear that traditional construction materials have strength and rigidity values that are quite similar, while *composite materials differ widely amongst each other.*

This fact is very revealing: it shows their potential and ability to substantially reduce the weight of a structure while maintaining the same strength and stiffness.

Something that makes motorcycles so interesting is the extreme variety of models and solutions used for frame construction techniques.

In the automobile sector, the frame remains hidden by the body, and the laws of high production and high costs have made the technical solutions adopted for constructing the unitized body all very similar to each other.

In the motorcycle world, instead, there is a much greater variety of designs and structures.

In many cases, moreover, the frame is highly visible and is part and parcel of the bike's visual appeal, which leads to the necessity of sophisticated production techniques to satisfy esthetic demands.

A look at all the motorcycle frames produced since the Second World War til now reveals a huge variety of designs *depending on the various purposes the machine is intended for,* and the different engine sizes and configurations that are mounted into them.

One approach is to classify frames according to the **specific use** of the vehicle, which gives us different kinds of frames for:

- Trial bikes;
- Motocross bikes;
- Enduro bikes;
- Streetbikes;
- Touring bikes;
- Offroad bikes;
- Custom bikes.

another approach is based on the **type of engine** mounted into the frame, thus giving types of frames for:

- Single-cylinder;
- Twin-cylinder;
- Inline;
- "V";
- Boxer;
- 4-cylinder and multifractional engines;
- Engines with transversal drive shaft;
- Engines with longitudinal drive shaft.

On the basis of these kinds of categories we would come up with an extremely long list, and something would probably be missed out in the end.

Let us try, then, to summarize frame designs according to their **general construction layout,** without, however, expecting to be exhaustive about it.

Frame construction types

A motorcycle frame is generally **composed** of, from front to back:

- **Steering-head tube** containing the steering-axle bearings;
- **Linking tube or beams** from the head-tube to the rear fork pivot point;
- **Rear fork pivot point area**: the frame must necessarily bifurcate out to the sides in order to hold the rear fork;
- **Lower cradle** that passes under the engine and links the head-tube with the rear fork area.

material	name	breaking strength [N/mm²]	shear modulus [N/mm²]	specific weight • 10⁶ [N/mm³]	specific strength [mm]	specific rigidity • 10³ [mm]
steel	18 NiCrmo5	1250	210.000	78,6	15,9	2,672
aluminum alloy	Avional uni 3581	420	72.000	27,0	15,6	2,667
magnesium	az 91	260	45.000	18,0	14,4	2,500
titanium	6AL4V	800	112.000	45,0	17,8	2,533
high shear modulus carbon	1300	200.000	16,0	**81,3**	**12,500**	
kevlar		1200	85.000	14,0	**85,7**	**6,071**

Type A: with curved tubes

The most widely used kind of frame is made with steel tubes that alternate between straight and curved sections welded together.

The simplest of these sorts of structures is the so-called "Cradle" frame, made of a center tube that starts from the steering head tube, passes over the engine, bifurcates around the swingarm pivot area, then joins up with the cradle, wrapping around the lower part of the engine, to finally link up back with the head-tube.

This basic layout has a lot of variations, including:

- *Duplex cradle* frames with two tubes that start from the head-tube area, wrap around the engine, link up the swingarm and lead back to the head-tube;

- Frames that can be *disassembled,* for engine mounting purposes;

- *"Open"* cradle frames, only to one side;

- *Single tube cradle* frames which start out from the head-tube and bifurcate around the cylinder or the exhaust tubes.

These are very simple designs to fabricate and they are both practical and sturdy; in fact, they are used in most motorcycle production.

Type B: trellis or lattice-girder

The tubes may be round or squared, but not bent; instead, they are cut and welded together, giving rise to lattice structures variously configured in space.
|These are rigid, lightweight structures, very delicate to fabricate because of the precision necessary to create the weldings and joinings between the inclined tubes.

If the engine is used as an integral part in closing the trellis, we can speak about it having a **stressed** or **lifted engine,** since without the motor, the frame's stiffness would be diminished.

Type C: mixed layouts

Casted, box-section or extrudate sheets, or else straight or curved tubes welded together, are all used to fabricate these mixed structures.

They may be made out of *steel or aluminum,* with or without the presence of a lower cradle.

This is a very advanced construction design that is increasingly popular, in that it allows the use of materials produced according to the technological process most suited for each particular area, depending on the stresses it is subject to.

Take the head-tube: this is a very complex piece that is also placed under a lot of stress; it must be very rigid and requires a number of attachment points for the fuel tank, the radiator, the steering block, and so forth. The most sensible solution, without taking costs into account, would be to use aluminum casts.

The thickness of the cast would guarantee adequate stiffness in the structure, thus solving problems associated with complex forms. The various mountings can be made directly out of the castings without having to use gussets or plates, as shown below.

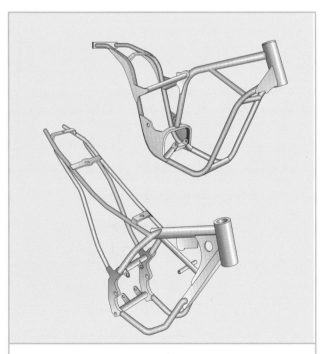

Fig. 12.4: bent multi-tubular frames.

Type D: monococque

These structures are inspired by automobile frames, in which the body also has a structural function.

Today's medium-to-high-powered bikes rarely use monococques because of their poor adaptibility.

In other words, products are evolving so fast these days that their lifespan only lasts a few years.

Such a brief period of time makes it difficult to get a return on high investments into equipment and machinery.

Small restyling changes or slight modifications for small problems can translate into additional time and money.

Box-section frames have been used in the road racing sector on occasion but have not lived up to expectations, perhaps because they were overly futuristic.

Certainly this line of research could prove to be very useful, especially if the body is made out of composite materials that are low-weight with strong mechanical properties.

In the automobile racing world, the most advanced car bodies have been made along these lines for some time now (not only Formula One cars but the latest generation of touring cars as well).

The main problem in the motorcycle sector, limiting the adoption of these kinds of solutions, is that monococque frames would have a much different form and esthetic appeal than production bikes.

In the motorcycle world, racing bikes often adopt technical solutions that are very similar to those later used for bikes that are available on the market; it even happens that racing bikes derive directly from models sold to the public.

This is another aspect in which the two-wheel world differs greatly from the four-wheel world: just think of how little one Formula One series car has in common with another.

OSCILLATING OR SWINGING REAR FORK

The main function of the rear fork is to link the rear wheel with the frame, providing a place to attach and house the suspension.

There are two main types of rear forks which, although providing the same geometrical function of keeping the wheel on the same path, have different structures:

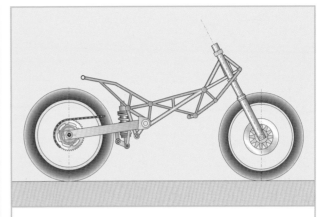

Fig. 12.5: trellis or lattice-girder frames.

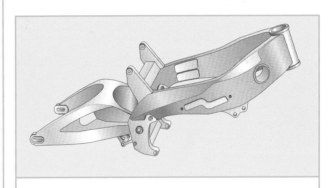

Fig.12. 6: frame 1000.

- With two arms (**Traditional**);
- With a single lateral arm (**Swingarm**).

Traditional rear fork

This is the set-up most commonly used since the earliest models, since it allows the construction of a symmetrical structure, easily fabricated out of round section iron tubes, either oval or rectangular.

Over time, this simple structure evolved on more sophisticated motorcycles, turning to the use of tubes or castings in aluminum, along with more complex forms.

To enhance stiffness, the form of the arms became triangular, with appropriate modifications to allow the chain to pass from one side and the exhaust tubes through the other.

The enlargement of the joining section between the two arms has enhanced the torsional rigidity of the structure.

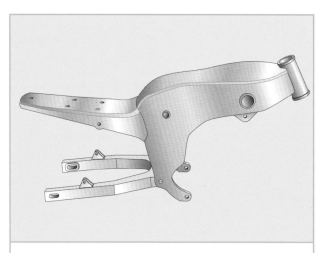

Fig. 12.4: bent multi-tubular frames.

Single swingarm

This is an asymmetrical structure, and as such, is always placed under a torque (a twisting moment), so to prevent unwanted shifting of the wheel, it must be extremely stiff.

Torsion is present even in a straight line and it gets stronger with increases in vertical load, for instance, when the vehicle is passing over a series of hollows.

The wheel must not, therefore, be tilted or it will cause variations in the trajectory and give rise to gyroscopic moments that have a negative effect on the bike's handling response.

The wheel lug is attached to an automobile-type hub and both are amply oversized to solve the rigidity problems just discussed.

The wheel rim must have a camber to fit the hub and brake disc.

The single beam that connects the wheel with the central part of the swingarm is a big piece made out of pressed steel or aluminum casts.

A few remarks about the single arm solution:

advantages:

• Quick rear wheel replacement time

• A smaller polar moment of inertia around the longitudinal axis.

disadvantages:

• As we have said, even with vertical loads and in a straight line, the rear fork is subject to twisting stresses, so to prevent harmful wheel inclinations, it must be extremely sturdy, adding on to the weight;

• Rear brake disc cooling may be a problem since the disc sits inside the rim and is poorly exposed to air.
The diameter cannot be made too large or it will create bulk for the calipers on the rim, and under high stress the disc could overheat, causing a loss in breaking efficiency;

• Since this is an asymmetrical structure, there could be problems caused by differing handling responses in left- or right-banked corners.

An interesting comparison can be made between the two types of rear fork in terms of their behavior under the effect of a side force exerted at the ground (what occurs in a corner).

The single arm twists more easily compared to the traditional design, giving a wider angle to the longitudinal axis of the vehicle; the wheel turns towards the direction of the corner being taken.

• This is a potentially negative response inasmuch as it modifes the radius of curvature of the path, making the motorcycle perform a wider curve;

• From another point of view, the self-steering effect of the wheel has a stabilizing effect.

This helps to create a considerable reduction in weave mode frequencies, making the ride much more stable.

Some rear car suspensions have been designed along the same line of thinking in order to bring on the same response, thus enhancing the car's stability.

FORCES ACTING ON THE FRAME AND SWINGARM
Longitudinal (braking) loads

During braking, as we have seen, some strong longitudinal forces are created, giving rise to a bending moment that gets stronger as it rises from the ground up to the steering head tube, then is transmitted to the whole frame.

The strongest moment is located at the steering head tube; since this is the point with the least depth of section, this is the major plane of stress.

In response to these considerations, careful research and study is given to the design dimensions of the whole steering tube.

Any flexure on its part during a big thrust of acceleration would cause a trail variation and, moreover, when the braking stress dies out, for example, when entering a corner, there would be an annoying elastic rebound action in response.

The rear fork, on the other hand, is not subject to much stress during braking.

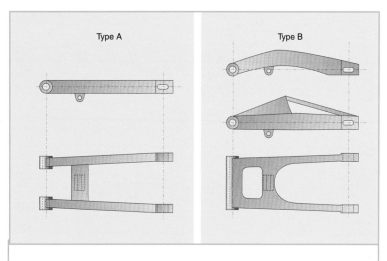

Fig. 12.8: traditional rear fork.

Vertical loads

When passing over deep dips in the ground or sudden bumps in the road surface, the vertical loads can reach very high values, so the frame structure has to be stiff enough to avoid excessive deformation; at the same time, it must have the capacity to absorb all the instantaneous bumps that occur whenever the suspension bottoms out.

In the front end, the area to receive the most stress is once again the steering head tube, while in the rear end, the shock mounting and the connecting rods come under the most stress.

The load values that appear during normal use are **2 to 3 times as big as static loads** normally acting on the wheels when the motorcycle is stationary. For a medium-powered streetbike, we are talking about hundreds of kilos of stress that may be exerted on the structure when taking a hole at high speed.

Maximum load values go up, too, when talking about offroad bikes, where jumps and crossing over obstacles are the norm.

At this point it might be helpful to offer some information used during the design process, regarding frame dimensions and weight:

for a motorcycle frame used to carry a passenger

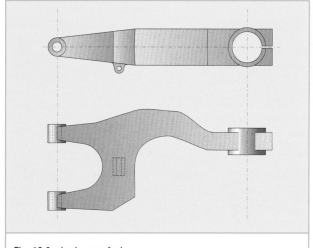

Fig. 12.9: single-arm fork.

and luggage, the size of the structure needed to provide good support for the vertical loads does not change much whether mounting a 125 cc engine or a super powerful 1100 cc engine.

In fact, the total weight of the rider, plus passenger, plus luggage will always amount to around 170 kg, generally subdivided between:
 • 75 kg for the rider and the same amount for the passenger;
 • 18 kg for the luggage.

A 125 cc streetbike weighs about 130 kg while a 1100 cc will weigh in at about 210 kg, so the net weight will be:

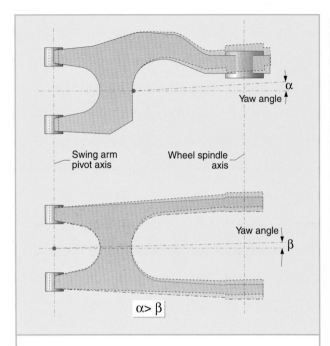

Fig. 12.10: comparison between the transversal flexibility of a traditional rear fork and a single arm.

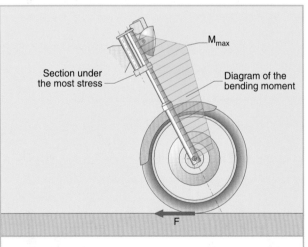

Fig. 12.11: stresses on the front fork due to longitudinal (braking) loads.

There is a **25%** *difference between the two vehicle weights,* not as much as one would expect.

The two types of frame must have similar dimensions in terms of their strength under vertical loads, even though the models that are being equipped with them are for such different purposes and at such different prices!

The loads acting on the **rear fork** are easily explainable in broad terms.

On the basis of the two types of linking systems used to connect the suspension to the rear fork, two situations are created:

- Rear fork with *two shock absorbers near the wheel axle:* the bending moment is very small and the rear fork comes under little stress;

- Rear fork with *monoshock spring:* the bending moment is high, especially in the area of the suspension mounting.

Twisting moment

As shown in Figure 12.13, because of the effect of the *width of the tire and the movements of the rider* towards the inside of the curve, the direction of the resultant of the body and centrifugal forces does not always lie along the motorcycle axis.

This brings on the creation of a twisting moment that acts both on the frame and on the rear fork.

Under the following conditions there is no occurence of a twisting moment:

- When *entering a corner and still decelerating:* the rider is braking and setting the bike into a corner; most of the weight bears on the front wheel, which, being turned, does not lie on the plane of the motorcycle; torsion will take place mainly on the front part of the motorcycle;

- *Mid-corner at a steady speed:* the load on the wheels is increased by 40%; if we imagine banking at 45 degrees, the width of the tires and the center of gravity of the rider shifted towards the inside of the curve create a significant twisting effect, both on the front and rear axles; this effect is greater the more the axle is loaded and the bigger the rim (remember that, generally, the back rim is bigger than the front rim);

- When *exiting a corner under acceleration:* the weight is distributed mainly onto the rear of the motorcycle, the bike is still banked and the rider is still leaning far into the inside of the curve.

Type of motorcyrcle	motorcyrcle weight [Kg]	gas weight [Kg]	rider weight [Kg]	passenger weight [Kg]	luggage weight [Kg]	total weight [Kg]
small cylinder	135	15	75	75	18	**318**
big cylinder	210	20	75	75	18	**398**

The twisting moment is at its greatest on the rear end.

Under acceleration, we have seen, racing bikes may get caught in some highsiding phenomena: if the rear part of the bike is not rigid enough, the situation can very visibly deteriorate.

In fact, along with the compression and rebound movements of the rear fork, there is also an elastic deformation that amplifies the movements, making them even more pronounced and intense.

This is one of the reasons that the rear fork has been developed to a high degree of complexity and stiffness.

In shop-talk, these structures are measured in terms of "stiffnesses": when placed under certain vertical loads and pre-set twisting moments they must offer minimal flexure. In the case of Grand Prix bikes, values of 500 Nm·degree torsional rigidity obtained in the 1980's have been developed to values of over 1000 Nm·degrees in the 1990's.

Since they are designed to be extremely rigid, the internal stress of these structures during street use is minimal.

The frames and rear forks on the latest generation of sport streetbikes can sustain bikes that weigh even twice as much as the ones they are presently mounted onto!

The same remarks we made about the rear end are valid for the front end, which is subject to major stresses, as we have seen, when braking.

These structures, too, are designed to be extremely rigid: just think how much fork leg diameters have been enlarged over the course of the Nineties.

The same thing holds true for today's most-advanced streetbike frames: they have values of over 3000 Nm·degree torsional rigidity.

The reason the frame is so much more rigid than the rear fork is because of the shape of each structure:

• the rear fork is an open structure, that is only connected at the rear by means of the wheel mounting lug. Over the past few years the mounting lug has growin in size, precisely to increase rigidity in the linking between the two arms of the fork.

In any case, the frame, as we have seen, is instead a closed structure, the depth of its section is generally much bigger and it benefits, moreover, from the contribution of the engine or the lower cradle.

INFLUENCE OF STIFFNESS ON THE MOTORCYCLE'S HANDLING RESPONSE

Experimental testing has shown that every form of frame elasticity, whether it is flexural or torsional, brings on a clear change in riding perception, so it is crucial that the stiffness be adequate to cope with changes in weight and performance of the vehicle.

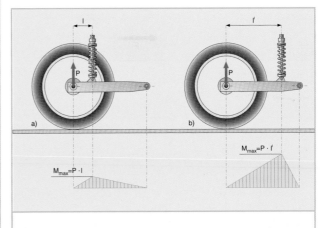

Fig. 12.12: stresses on the rear fork vary according to the positioning of the shock absorber.

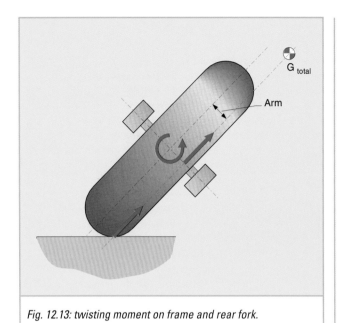

Fig. 12.13: twisting moment on frame and rear fork.

Above all, elasticity variations provoke changes in the geometrical characteristics of the chassis. Having seen in previous chapters the importance of the rake angle size, it is easy to understand how a motorcycle with changing angle sizes would inevitably lead to poor maneuverability.

Let us examine what would happen if the front end of the motorcycle were elastic:

in order to keep on a desired path, the rider turns the handlebar a certain angle; because of the low front rigidity of the bike, the handlebar angle will not exactly correspond to the angle transmitted to the wheel axle; the rider must therefore first wait to sense the amount the bike has moved in the desired direction before then going on to make the appropriate steering adjustment.

High flexability thus provokes a time delay; this means that until the elastic phase is concluded, the rider will probably not be able to initiate another maneuver.

Elastic deformation, in energetic terms, must be compensated for by the rider, in addition to the work that must be done to bank the motorcycle and rotate the steering.

The rider's perception of a *motorcycle with low rigidity values is quite particular,* making the bike seem "jelly-like", slow and heavy; the same bike with the same weight distribution and structure, but characterized by higher rigidity, offers the rider a greater sense of responsiveness and handling ability.

Naturally, as always, there is "another side of the coin" to increased stiffness.

Vibration modes, especially, wobble or front wheel shimmy, are amplified in size and intensity in stiff structures with little damping and they can be significantly reduced only by a complete, rigorous overhaul of the entire vehicle design.

That is why a sport-oriented bike has high rigidity values, while for a touring bike it may be preferable that it be characterized by less structural rigidity.

Another important consideration to keep in mind is the *twisting effect* on the motorcycle.

We have seen what phenomena determine torsional phenomena, while *the momentary reaction depends on the distribution of the masses* along the axis of the motorcycle.

During *braking,* the twisting moment will be greatest on the front end and nil on the rear wheel; it decreases from front to rear end depending on the distribution of the masses.

In *acceleration,* the twisting moment will be greatest at the rear axis and will decrease along its way toward the front, coming to zero at the front axis.

To get the best performance from the motorcycle and a satisfying response to commands, it is therefore necessary that the stiffness and weight distribution of the entire frame-rear fork system be well-correlated and homogenous. If only one element is made more rigid it could lead to only partial or even no improvement at all.

CHAPTER 13
THE SUSPENSION

The suspension system of the motorcycle allows wheel movement with respect to the chassis and is made up of:

• An elastic component (characterized by stiffness);
• A damper;
• A kinematic mechanism that regulates movement.

The following sections of this chapter will illustrate the first two parts, that is, the elastic component and the damper, while the geometrical aspect related to detailed kinmatic mechanisms making up the mechanical aspect of the suspension, and which are very different for the front and rear suspension systems, will be dealt with in separate chapters that follow.

The tires also significantly contribute to the functioning of the suspension by filtering high frequency, low amplitude vibrations. We can therefore say that the motorcycle's suspension system is characterized by two degrees of freedom and can be represented by the classic dynamic model illustrated in the Figure 13.1.
Remember that:

• The unsprung masses are those that are more or less *directly connected to the ground*, that is:

tires, rims, wheel spindles, brake discs, brake calipers, mudguards (if attached to the wheels), the whole part of the fork that moves along with the wheel, rear sprocket, and parts (the usual proportion that is given is equal to a third of the net weight) of the swingarm, the chain, the shock absorber and any connecting rods.

• The sprung masses, on the other hand, are the components situated above the suspension and rigidly attached to each other, that is: the frame, the fuel tank, the engine, radiator, fairings, and so forth.
Since the suspension system is necessarily located both on the front and rear axes, the complete model of the vehicle becomes even more

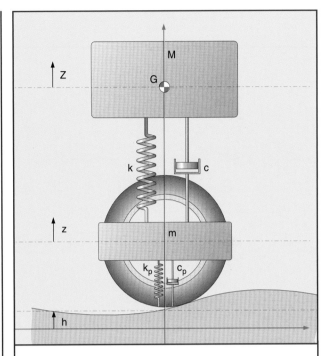

Fig. 13.1: where:
M = sprung mass of the motorcycle;
m = unsprung mass of the motorcycle;
k_p = tire stiffness;
c_p = tire damping;
k = suspension stiffness;
c = suspension damping;
G = center of gravity of the sprung mass;
Z = displacement of sprung mass;
z = displacement of unsprung mass;
h = road surface profile.

complex than the previous one, going from two to four degrees of freedom; Figure 13. 3 gives an illustration of this model.
A mathematical treatment of this system becomes somewhat forbidding at this point.
The main thing to remember is that the functioning of the front and rear suspension systems must be as uncoupled as possible, that is, their frequencies must be very different from one another.

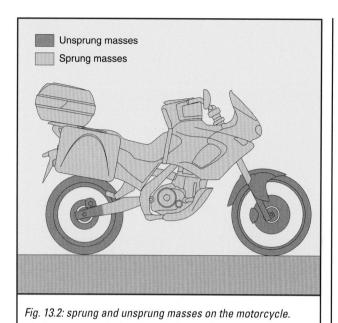

Fig. 13.2: sprung and unsprung masses on the motorcycle.

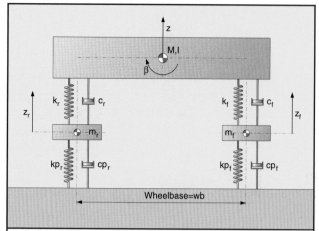

Fig. 13.3: suspension with 4 degrees of freedom.
The symbols indicate:
β = pitch of sprung mass motorcycle
M = sprung mass
I = inertial mass relative to center of gravity
m_r = unsprung rear masses
m_f = unsprung front masses
c_r = rear suspension damping
k_r = rear suspension stiffness
c_f = front suspension damping
k_f = front suspension stiffness
cp_r = rear tire damping
kp_r = rear tire stiffness
cp_f = front tire damping
kp_f = front tire stiffness
z_r = vertical position rear tire
z_f = vertical position front tire
z = vertical position frame.

In other words, it is necessary, for example, that when the front wheel passes over an obstacle, its movement should bring on a minimum reaction from the rear wheel, and vice versus.

In order to uncouple the suspension, the easiest solution is to apply a stiffness system on the front that is lower than the rear wheel system, thereby lowering its frequency.

This is quite easy to demonstrate: try pressing down on each axle one at a time; you will note that the front end offers less resistance to sinking than the rear end.

ELASTIC COMPONENT

The almost universally adopted kind of elastic component is a coil spring with round cross-sectioned wire.

This solution ensures the possibility of obtaining varying stiffness responses to varying demands, with moderate cost, limited bulk, and practically 100% reliability. With the kinds of materials and construction techniques presently employed in the industry, it is unlikely that the spring will ever "wear out" and give a changing spring elasticity modulus, except, perhaps, in the motocross sector, where the stresses are so severe that they inevitably leave some effect.

Coil spring manufacturing processes also guarantee the creation of very limited tolerances, that is to say, a particular model of springs will always present almost identical characteristics.

A good approximation of the force exerted by a compressed spring can be represented by the simple relation

Equation 13.1

$$F = k \cdot x$$

where:
k = spring stiffness;
x = working range of the spring.

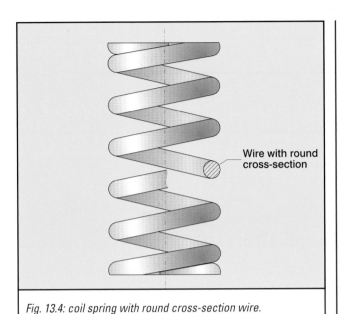

Fig. 13.4: coil spring with round cross-section wire.

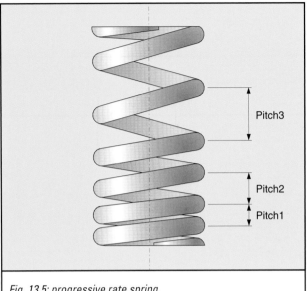

Fig. 13.5: progressive rate spring.

Coil springs can also have progressive rates, or in other words, the stiffness increases the more the spring is pressed down.

It is easy to tell if a spring is progressive or not: let us suppose that the diameter of the wire is constant, as it usually is; if the spacing between the coils (called the pitch) is constant, the spring will offer constant stiffness, while if the spacing varies, the stiffness will be variable.

The closer-spaced coils are the most elastic and will therefore be the first to compress.

So progressive rate springs can be created by placing springs with different stiffnesses end to end in series (see Figure 13.6).

With these kinds of layout we should note, *you cannot obtain springs with decreasing rates* (in fact, it is always the weak part of the chain that is the first to yield!)

Other elastic systems like torsion bars for automobiles or leaf springs are rarely applied to today's production bikes.

In any case, remember that *coil springs also work through torsion.*

Under normal load conditions, torsion is applied to the axis of the spring and acts as an arm r, with respect to the axis of the rod.

A twisting moment thus arises, given by:

Equation 13.2

$$M_t = P \cdot r$$

forcing the cross section of the rod to rotate on its plane.

The coil spring is subjected to torsional stress.

To go into more detail, the wire is also subject to flexure, to shearing stress, and to tensile stress, but these stresses are completely negligible, amounting to only 2 to 3% of the overall stress.

Something else about coil springs worth taking note of: The end part of the coil which comes into contact with the little plate must be properly levelled to allow uniform support and to prevent improper stresses on the spring.

Let us suppose that the spring ends have not been joined up very well: when the coil is compressed it will not be able to rotate properly on the little plate that it sits on. In theory we talk about springs blocked at their ends, and it is possible to demonstrate that a spring blocked at its end would give noticeable stiffness variations in comparison to its freely moving rate, especially if it has a short length.

To summarize: the load on the suspension depends on the amount the spring is compressed,

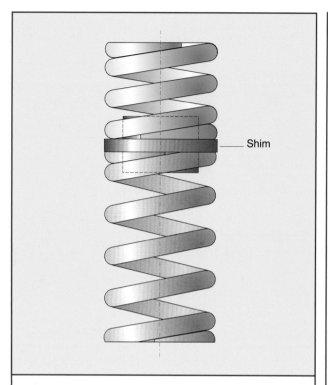

Fig. 13.6: progressive rate spring obtained from parts with different stiffnesses.

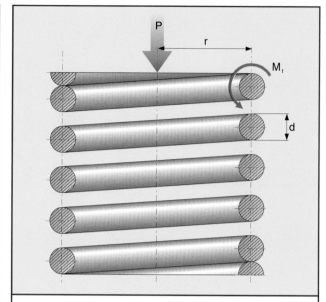

Fig. 13.7: twisting moment on the coil spring wire, where: P : load on spring r : arm.

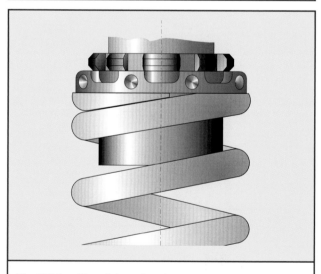

Fig. 13.8: levelling of the coil spring.

or in other words, on the relative displacement of its ends.

DAMPING COMPONENT

Suspension systems also require a damping system, that is, an element that dissipates energy to stop the mechanism from continuing to oscillate indefinitely once it has been set in motion by a bump.

In practice, the contribution of the damper is vital for a comfortable ride and good dynamics of the motorcycle.

Vintage bikes created damping by making use of the friction that develops between surfaces made to rub against one another; the energy was dissipated through the heat generated by the friction.

These systems had severe limitations in terms of even functioning and wear, and were replaced by oil-based dampers, which are now almost universally adopted.

The general comments that follow can be considered valid for both the front and rear suspension systems.

During the movement of the suspension, the oil, made of a special composition developed for optimum performance, is forced to flow through passages bored through the inside of the pistons that are located both in the shock absorber and the front fork.

Because of the effect of its viscosity, when the oil passes through these throats it dissipates energy in the form of heat, which is subsequently transmitted to the outside through the body of the shock absorber.

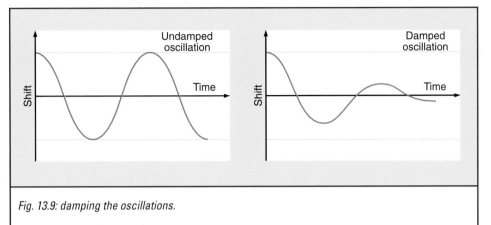

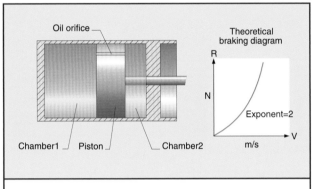

Fig. 13.9: damping the oscillations.

Fig. 13.10: hydraulic braking using calibrated holes.

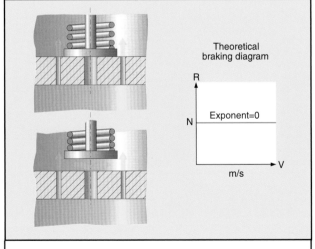

Fig. 13.11: hydraulic braking using open passages.

To have a practical demonstration of this, try touching the outside body of a motorcycle's shock absorber after passing over a dug-up terrain: it will, of course, be hot.

You can have the same demonstration from the front fork, although less striking. The front fork, in fact, is quite exposed to cooling airflow, and the mass through which the heat can be diffused is much bigger than the mass of the shock absorber.

The passages that regulate the flow of the oil and that act, then, as a hydraulic brake, may be of the following two types:
- Calibrated holes or bleed orifices;
- Open passages.

Calibrated holes: when the oil passes through these small-diameter (generally from 0.8 to 3.5 mm) holes, called bleed orifices, it creates a resistance (or pressure difference) that increases at the square of the velocity.

Figure 13.10 offers an illustrative diagram of this:

It is intuitively easy to grasp that small diameter holes exert greater braking force than bigger diameters; the faster the working speed, the more noticeable the effect is.

The quadratic form of the curve produced by hydraulic brakes is easily recognizable from the graph, along with the sudden rise that accompanies the increasing velocity (Figure 13.10).

Since these holes are always open, the oil starts its transit as soon as the piston begins to move.

A damper that only uses bleed orifices may not be adequate for proper functioning of the suspension.

On the one hand, tiny holes allow good braking at low speeds, but the damping effect could be overly effective, making for an uncomfortable ride when the wheel has to climb at high speeds.

For example, to pass over a small overlapping joining in the tarmac when traveling at low to medium speeds (40 to 60 Km/h), the speed that the wheel climbs at may make the opposing resistance value of the hydraulic damping action much bigger than the spring action, resulting in a bumpy ride.

With big holes, on the other hand, at low speeds the hydraulic damping may be inadequate,

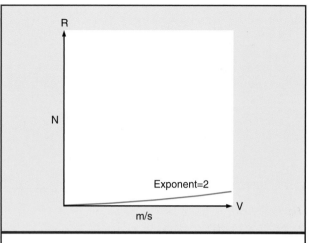

Fig. 13.12: braking diagram showing open passages in relation to opening pressure.

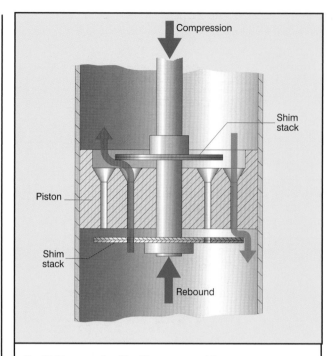

Fig. 13.14: example of braking system with open passages.

allowing the suspension to continue oscillating.

When passing over long rises on highway bridges, for example, you would find that if the low-speed damping is inadequate, the motorcycle would continue to slowly oscillate after having passed them.

Open passages:
Springs are positioned on the pistons, acting on special shims that close quite large passages (about 20 times as big as calibrated holes).

When the pressure on the lower piston wall, and therefore on the shims, reaches the right amount to move the springs, they lift off, opening big passages where the oil can easily pass from one part of the piston to the other.

The theoretical diagram for open passage braking is of the kind seen below, that of a classic *linear lifting* valve.

In reality, when the upward stroke of the piston (or the suspension) increases its velocity, even open passages start to behave like orifices with big cross sections, and therefore, with less loss of the load, as shown in Figure 13.12.

By properly combining the load losses coming from bleed orifices and spring-controlled openings *it is possible to obtain a damping curve that corresponds to the speeds demanded by the vehicle's layout.* (Figure 13.13).

A classic example of

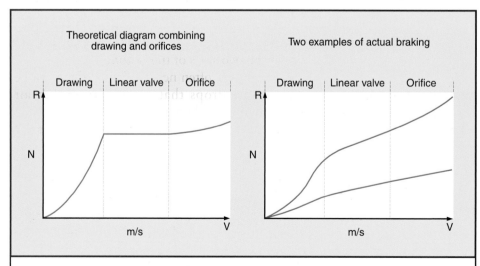

Fig. 13.13: damping curves obtained through various combinations of load loss using spring-controlled bleed orifices and open passages.

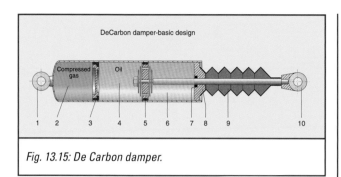

Fig. 13.15: De Carbon damper.

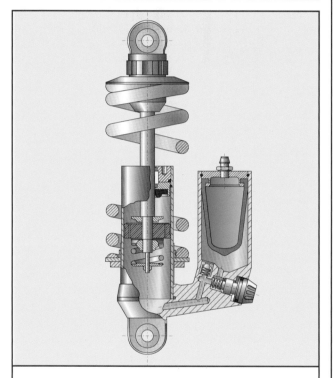

Fig. 13.16: example of damper with pressurized oil and air cannister out of line with the shock absorber unit.

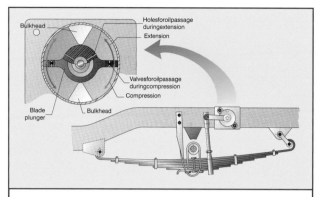

Fig. 13.17: from Lucchesi's "automobile construction techniques" Houdaille damper.

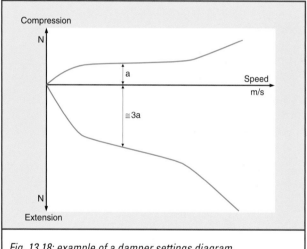

Fig. 13.18: example of a damper settings diagram.

open passage systems is illustrated in Figure 13.14 and is composed of a sophisticated structure of special elastic components called "leaf" springs made of shims that open the passage when the underlying pressure rises.

This sort of "valve" system is *unidirectional*, since it only opens from underlying pressure.

To create damping in both piston movement directions, a stack of shims is placed at each end of the piston.

Generally, we talk about compression settings, when the spring is "loaded" and rebound adjustments when they are extended; they may be calibrated differently.

The passing of the oil through the damping system piston creates a big pressure difference between the two sides of the piston.

In some zones, often near the holes, there can be local pressure drops that are so strong that air bubbles are created, known as cavitation.

What happens is similar to the more easily observable phenomenon around a motorboat propeller when it starts to turn and generates the creation of a whirl of bubbles, even though the engine is completely immersed in the water.

This, too, is generated by the difference in pressure between one side and the other of the propeller blade.

The presence of air bubbles can clearly give rise to a foam, impeding normal functioning of the damper.

Advanced dampers maintain the oil under such high pressure, with pressure values that range from 10 to 16 bars, that gas is unlikely to form.

In Figure 13.15 we show the layout of a De Carbon damper (a pioneer in damping system techniques for automobiles, who invented the still widely-used solution that bears his name).

In this application, the compensation chamber into which the high pressure gas is inserted creates a septum zone that makes it impossible for the oil and gas to mix and form a foam.

Another damper layout used on motorcycles is shown Figure 13.16.

This solution maintains gas and oil separation by means of a deformable rubber membrane.

The air is contained in a cannister that is not lined up with the main body of the damper, in order to reduce length and bulk; at the same time it dissipates the heat, making the system work at low temperatures.

We should note that the viscosity of the oil changes according to its temperature; consequently, the braking effect changes along with the temperature.

This explains why riding comfort feels different after a long stop, especially during cold weather, compared to after a long "cruise" on a bumpy street.

The suspension settings seem softer.

Advanced dampers make use of sophisticated solutions that for the most part are able to compensate for the different responses that come at different working temperatures.

In addition to the classical damper we have just described, which is almost universally adopted, there are many other damping systems.

Figure 13.17 shows a Houdaille rotary-type damper.

Generally, a motorcycle's damping system works both during extension and compression, but practical experience tells us that the damping must be much stronger during extension than when the suspension is coming back down. In any case, *the amount of hydraulic braking in extension must be approximately three times bigger* than the compression values.

A possible graph of the final calibration of the damping component of a motorcycle suspension is shown in Figure 13. 18.

Summary: hydraulic damping force depends on the compression and rebound speed.

SUSPENSION FUNCTIONS

The functions of the suspension are the following:

• To provide *riding comfort* for rider and passenger;
• To *control* the dynamics of the bike's motion, or, *attitude;*
• To guarantee wheel-to-ground contact, or *grip.*

Riding comfort

Road surface irregularities would provoke pronounced movement of the whole bike, with unacceptable consequences for the rider's comfort, were it not for the help of the suspension.

Motorcycles were first developed out of the bicycle frame, which of course is rigid; over the course of the years suspension systems were evolved to filter out ground disturbances in more efficient ways.

Remember, too, that the best indicator of riding comfort is the amount of movement that is transmitted to the rider.

The derivation of acceleration is also studied in quantifiable terms, and is called Jerk, although its practical meaning is somewhat difficult to explain.

Were we to obtain the best, ideal level of riding comfort, it would mean having created a chassis that remains perfectly stationary and with only the unsprung masses moving when it hits a bump. The acceleration forces on the rider in this case, clearly, would be nil.

Obviously, this is not possible. The most reasonable objective is to minimize the movement of the sprung weight, its speed, and, as we have already mentioned, its acceleration and derivative action.

So to enhance riding comfort it is advisable to provide:

• Low stiffness suspension;
• Limited compression damping;
• Very lightweight unsprung masses;
• Very large, or rather, very, very heavy sprung masses, even if these are certainly not conducive to easy handling.

Let us take a look at the ratio between sprung and unsprung masses for different kinds of motorcycles:

Take a light bike weighing 140 kg and a big touring cruiser weighing in at 230 kg: while the ratio between their sprung masses is about 2, the unsprung masses only comes to 1.3.

This explains why it is much easier to obtain high riding comfort from heavy cruisers than from light transport bikes.

No matter how much one tries to optimize the suspension settings, a heavy motorcycle will always have an advantage when it comes to comfort.

Solutions adopted to get the best level of comfort, however, may not be in line with the requirements of the other functions of the suspension.

Control of attitude

We have said that the attitude of the motorcycle under various conditions is determined by the suspension stiffness and, therefore, by the spring's modulus of elasticity and its initial preload.

A motorcycle with very soft suspension will sink just when you take it off the main stand; it will sink further when the rider gets on the saddle, and will press down even more when going around corners because of the effect of the centrifugal force.

Its attitude will vary, then, depending on the situation; what changes substantially with respect to its initial conditions and parameters are such factors as the center of gravity height from the ground and the rake angle.

These simple considerations explain why a sport-type bike must be equipped with quite stiff suspension so that the ride will not be subjected to overly significant variations in attitude.

If *a steady attitude is determined by stiffness, the time and means used to achieve it* depend on the *hydraulic settings.*

Strong damping is typical of sportbikes that have to minimize transitions between a series of differing attitudes, while touring bikes can get by with much softer settings.

As we illustrated in the section on overlap in Chapter 7, when applying the brakes, a very strong hydraulic braking suspension will help the bike reach a steady attitude in a more controlled way than is possible with a weak braking suspension. In this case, the front end of the motorcycle will sink quickly, it is true, but then it will oscillate for some time before

stabilizing itself around its position of equilibrium.

Furthermore, on a dug-up road surface, the hydraulic system will make its pre-sence felt in a big way.

Traveling in a straight line over a series of hollows, first with standard settings and then with stronger compression braking, the attitude of the bike, you will notice, is slightly higher.

The influence of hydraulic suspension on the motorcycle's attitude is well-known to motocross enthusiasts, for whom the presence of deep holes and ridges across their path is the norm, both in straight-line motion and in corners.

To optimize attitude control, then, it is advisable to adopt:
- High stiffness on the suspension;
- Strong dampers.

Grip

In order to be able to transmit driving force to the ground both under acceleration and under braking, not to mention during fast cornering, there must be good adhesion between the tire and the ground.

If it were not for the presence of the suspension, passing over a small elevation of 4 centimeters, for example, at 50 km/h, would be enough to detach the wheel from the road surface, making transmission of power to the ground impossibile.

The parameter generally used to define adhesion is:

$$\textit{Adhension index} = F\left(\frac{\Delta N}{N}\right)$$

where:

ΔN is the relation between variation in dynamic load on the wheel and N is the static load bearing on its axle.

An increase in static weight bearing on a wheel can enhance the adhesion index, as we can see from the formula and from practical experience.

It is intuitively easy to understand that shifting your own bodyweight on top of the rear wheel when it is slipping on a surface with a low coefficient of friction will not succeed in transmitting the driving force to the ground.

The best settings to optimize grip depend on the type of road surface and the kind of bike, so it comes down to experimentation in order to discover them.

Speaking in general terms, we can say that the damping required for good adhesion is higher than the damping needed for a comfortable ride.

In this case, too, lighter unsprung masses improve the situation because the weight transfer (Ntrans) is reduced and the suspension is allowed to work well up to high frequency ranges.

COMPARISON BETWEEN CARS AND MOTORCYCLES IN TERMS OF SPRUNG AND UNSPRUNG MASSES

Dampers normally used for motorcycles are generally very sophisticated, more so than most automobile dampers. Indeed, the problems associated with two-wheel vehicles in this respect are quite delicate because of the fact that *the ratio between sprung and unsprung masses is smaller than in cars.*

Here is an example for the front end:

- Medium-powered touring-sport bike;
- Unsprung mass about 17 kg;
- Sprung mass on the front end with rider about 110 kg;
- Ratio between sprung and unsprung mass (110/17) = 6.48.
- Medium-powered car, eg. 1800 cc.:
- Unsprung mass about 25 kg;
- Sprung mass on the wheel in question about 300 kg;
- Ratio between sprung and unsprung mass (300/2)= 12.

The amount of difference in the ratio between sprung and unsprung masses typical of cars and motorcycles leads us to appreciate the extra care put into the design and construction of motorcycle suspensions.

HOW TO DETERMINE OPTIMUM SETTINGS

It happens quite frequently, as we have seen, that the suspension is called upon to perform incompatible functions:

- To obtain the best riding comfort you need limited damping and moderate stiffness;
- To keep the attitude steady, the stiffness and damping settings have to be high;
- As for adhesion, it may require a solution that lies between the other two.

This is why in the racing sector you often hear that during their test laps, the racers are in search of the best settings for their suspension.

In fact, on many racing bikes, being so light and powerful, the influence of the correct damping and spring stiffness settings are crucial and must provide a compromise between the search for the steadiest attitude and grip, with comfort only a secondary consideration.

In the end, it is the racer's sensitivity, along with his or her "tastes" and riding style that will define, in completely subjective terms, what settings are to be used for their own bike.

The only point that unites all the various demands to optimize the suspension behavior is the reduction of the weight of the unsprung masses.

And that is why sports applications are always looking for sophisticated technical solutions for keeping weight down to a minimum.

Even on sport production bikes, improving the weight problem requires a lot of attention to detail: the wheel spindles are bored, the light aluminum-alloy rims have a thin cross sections with hollow or very lightweight spokes, the brake discs are made as light as possible with aluminum carriers, etc.

THE SUSPENSION

CHAPTER 14
THE FRONT SUSPENSION

THE TELESCOPIC FORK

This is definitely the most widely adopted front suspension solution used in the world of motorcycles.

As its name suggests, a telescopic fork consists of two coaxial tubular components, one running inside the other, with sliding bushes placed between the inner and outer tubes to reduce sliding friction.

These tubes are attached at the top to the steering head tube by means of plates that are then joined to the handlebar. The steering head thus forms one piece with the suspension unit, guaranteeing maximum safety and direct linkage.

The fork tubes are connected together at the bottom through the wheel spindle.

The spring and damping system are housed inside the tubes.

The spring compression is equal to the displacement of the wheel (1:1 ratio).

During the compression phase the volume of air contained in the fork diminishes, thus providing a double function:

• That of another spring (made of air, obviously), characterized by a high progressive rate;

• That of creating pressure inside the fork, limiting cavitation problems and the formation of foam on the oil-to-air contact surface.

FORK FUNCTIONING

All the loads are transmitted from the inner tube to the outer tube (or vice versus) through the slider bushes placed between the two tubes.

The construction of these bushes is crucial for good fork functioning; the choice of material is an especially important factor, since it must offer a very low coefficient of friction and mounting tolerance.

The smoothness of the system depends, in fact, on the amount of friction forces developed during sliding movements and, especially, on the amount of stiction.

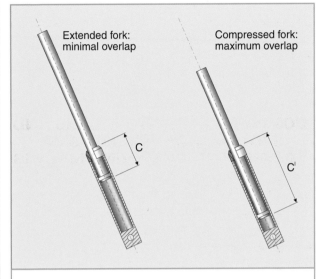

Fig. 14.1: telescopic fork:
a) fully-extended position—minimum stiffness.
b) fully-compressed position—maximum stiffness.

Stiction is at its maximum at "moto incipiente", when the movement between the surfaces initiates; in this phase it is called *static friction.*

In any case, no matter how much care is put into designing and fabricating the slider bushes, the problem of *sliding friction* always represents a weak point in the front fork.

Compare it, for example, to the rear suspension in which there is practically no sliding because the displacements consist of rotations around the bearings.

The suspension setting is obtained by the stiffness of the spring, and the damping provided by the hydraulic part, to which is added the resistance given by the sliding friction.

Because, as we have just seen, the sliding friction is not linear, it is difficult to predict a priori or even theoretically what the suspension behavior will be, and its proper functioning will always be conditioned by the presence of friction.

Limiting friction forces requires that the loads on the bushes be minimized during the design stage, thus enhancing the smooth movement of the unit.

A few simple observations about the fork may also be made concerning its stiffness:

• When the fork is fully extended, only a small segment of the slider tube enters inside the sleeve, so that at this stage its overlap is reduced to a minimum. This also constitutes the least rigid configuration of the whole system.

• At the end of its travel, instead, fork tube overlap is at its greatest, as is, therefore, suspension stiffness.

FORK STRESSES
AND DEFORMATIONS

• *Flexure due to vertical loads:*

This involves stresses brought on by the weight of the motorcycle and the rider, but especially those generated by road surface irregularities (like potholes, steps, ridges, etc.).

These stresses are anything but negligible: traveling in the city at less than 50 km/h, and coming up against a step that rises 4 to 5 centimeters from the profile of the road, 100% front overloading can easily be reached.

The vertical load applied to the wheel originates a moment of flexing or a bending moment that increases the more the fork is inclined.

Moreover, with the same applied force, the bending moment will be at its maximum when the fork is fully extended, and at its minimum with maximum compression (varying, obviously, with changes in the arm of the applied force).

The illustration shows how fork deformation occurs.

The closer the slider bushes are to the wheel spindle, the less the stresses will be, and, as is to be expected, the better the functioning.

• *Flexure due to braking force:*

Applying a braking force to the front wheel will result in the kind of deformation shown in Figure 14.3:

In this case, too, the longer the fork, the greater the bending.

A curious thing to note is that the deformation due to vertical forces is opposite to the deformation due to braking force.

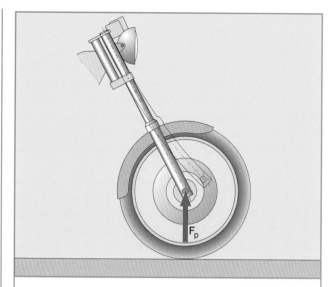

Fig. 14.2: fork flexure due to static load on the wheel.

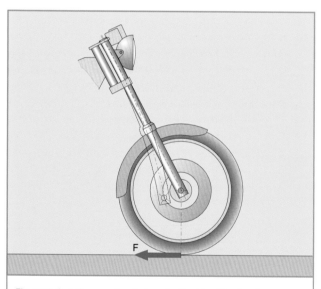

Fig. 14.3: fork flexure due to longitudinal braking load.

We have seen previously that during braking, because of the weight transfer effect, front end load increases; that is, there cannot be a braking force without an increase in vertical load.

The two effects, then, partially oppose each other, and within the deceleration range characteristic of a particular motorcycle, depending on its fork inclination, cg height, and wheelbase, fork flexing during braking is not as severe as one might think.

Let us pause for a moment at an example: with a

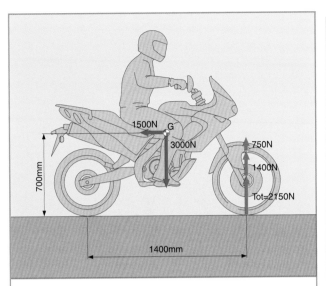

Fig. 14.4: example of a quantitative estimate of fork deformation due to braking force.

medium-to-high-powered streetbike that is decelerating quite decisively but not to its limit, such as a deceleration of 0.5 g, and imagining, as is usually the case, that we are braking with the front brake alone, all the braking force will act solely on the front wheel.

With the vehicle characteristics and calculations shown below, the resulting load is perpendicular to the fork, creating flexure, and is very limited, equal to only 50 kg.

Obviously, breaking conditions can vary greatly in reality, but the method of calculation used in the example may easily be extended to other cases.

Example:
Motorcycle specifications:

wheelbase (wb): 1400 mm
cg height (h): 700 mm
mass with rider (m): 300 kg
front load (N_a): 1400 N
deceleration (a): 0.5 g
rake angle (ε): 23 degrees

The situation described by our calculations is:

braking force applied to the wheel:

$$0.5 \; m \cdot t$$

$$(0.5 \cdot 3000) = 1500N$$

Beyond a static load of 1400 N, because of the weight transfer effect, another vertical component will act on the front wheel:

Weight transfer:

$$Braking \; force \cdot \frac{g}{wb}$$

$$\frac{(1500 \cdot 700)}{1400} = 750N$$

We thus find that:

Total front vertical load:
The net force applied to the front wheel will be 2620 N with an inclination of 34 degrees with

$$(1400 + 750) \; N = 2150N$$

respect to the vertical.

In fact:

Net force:
Angle with respect to the vertical:
The fork, then, is inclined at **23 degrees,**

$$\sqrt{(2150^2 + 1500^2)} = 2620N$$

while the net force is inclined at 34 degrees; the

$$arctan\left(\frac{1500}{2150}\right) = 34 \; degrees$$

difference between the two directions is only **11 degrees,** so the load *perpendicular* to the fork will be quite small, to be exact, calculable from the relation:

Perpendicular load:

$$2620 \cdot sin\ (11) = 500$$

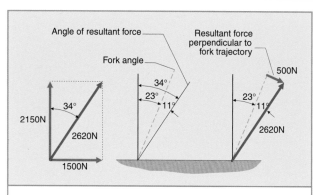

Fig. 14.5: fork deformation due to traction force.

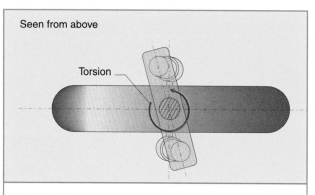

Fig. 14.6: fork torsion.

In conclusion:
Under braking, fork deformation is less than what one would expect, but it does exist and is very detrimental because it provokes non-calculated trail variations and has a bad effect on handling response, considering the delicate conditions under which the suspension functions.

Deformation due to torsional forces:
twisting forces derive from:

• Poor alignment between equilibrium forces and the fork axis (similar to what happens to the frame and rear fork);

• Components of equilibrium forces perpendicular to the fork axis and out of alignment with it;

• The couple applied to the steering head by the rider.

The consequent deformation is very detrimental to handling because the wheel no longer "goes" in the direction that the rider sets it in.

Influence of deformation on functionality:

Clearly, *the presence of fork deformation makes the proper sliding of the tubes inside one another more difficult (to the point of potentially impeding it).* Unfortunately, deformation is at its greatest at the most critical moments for the bike's motion, such as during braking and when entering a corner, when the rider most needs maximum road holding and complete control over the vehicle.

FORK DESIGN TYPES
One of the peculiarities of the telescopic fork, as we have seen, is the straight-line path of travel imposed on the contact point between wheel and ground, which places it in the category of pro-dive suspensions.

The greater the rake angle, the greater the compression (dive) effect will be.

Sportbikes with a small rake angle will experience less compression effect compared to custom bikes with large rake angles.

There are two main kinds of telescopic fork layouts used in practical applications:

•**Traditional** (or "standard"), with the internal tube (the one with the smaller diameter) in the upper position, fixed to the frame;

• **Upside Down** (or "inverted") with the internal tube in the lower position and fixed to the wheel.

The hydraulic and elastic elements of these two solutions may be perfectly comparable, so much so that, in order to verify the different responses of the same motorcycle equipped with the two different types of forks, some manufacturers have created a "cartridge" containing the hydraulic part that can be mounted onto each of the applications being tested. The first telescopic fork prototypes, which started to appear after the Second World War, were laid out with little attention as to whether they were in standard or inverted form.

Ever since the Sixties, however, by far the greatest majority of forks produced have been the traditional type, hence its name, while at the beginning of the Eighties, *the upside down* design came back into circulation for sport bike applications.

The debate on which of the two solutions is better continues to be a lively source of discussion.

Let us try to compare them, without taking into account the economic aspect, which lies out of the province of this book.

Traditional:

benefits:

• Fewer components, given that the wheel attachments and axle lug derive directly out of the lower stanchion, which also keeps weight down;
• Slightly reduced unsprung mass weight;
• Tubes slide in areas that are more protected from dirt and bumps.

Upside down:

benefits:

• Better torsional stiffness with the same weight, given that the tube has a larger diameter and is positioned in the upper area, which comes under greater stress from the bending moment;
• Sturdy attachment between the triple clamps and the tubes, given large tube diameters.

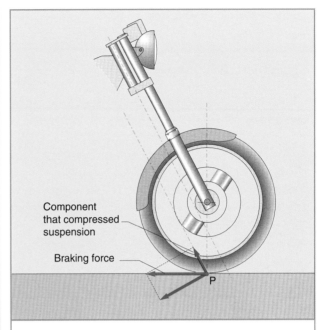

Fig. 14.7: pro-dive behavior of the telescopic front fork.

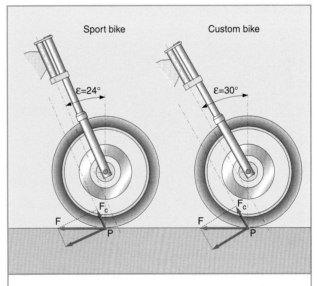

Fig. 14.8: with equal braking force (F), applied, the component that compresses the fork increases with increasing rake angle (ε).

There is no way, then, to insist that one solution is absolutely better than the other; at most, we could say that the *upside down* layout presents advantages in terms of stiffness, making it ideal for some sport-oriented applications.

147

It is clear that the two types of fork are characterized by:

- different stiffnesses;
- different weight distribution;
- different unsprung weight values;
- different center of gravity heights between the ground and the steering;
- different inertia values around the steering head axis.

All this justifies the fact that if you substitute a different fork onto the same motorcycle, but with the same stiffness and damping characteristics, the response of the motorcycle may be noticeably altered.

ALTERNATIVE FRONT SUSPENSIONS

There have been countless alternative new systems devised in the past and new ones continue to appear, but none of them have met with enough success and effectiveness to be considered real alternatives to the traditional telescopic layout.

Deficiencies always present in forks include:

- poor operating facility;
- inability to offer progressive stiffness and damping with changes in riding conditions;
- poor stiffness;
- inability to vary trail during compression;
- inability to provide any other wheel trajectory than parallel to the fork axis, which determines its pro-dive behavior;
- heavy weight, especially for the unsprung masses.

To be realistic, modern design experience and technological development of the fork do not completely justify the criticisms brought to some of its aspects.

- the use of progressive rate springs and the effect of the air chamber inside the stanchions make it possible to create a full range of elastic stiffness that is capable of satisfying all demands;

Take a look at Figure 14.9 that shows the typical

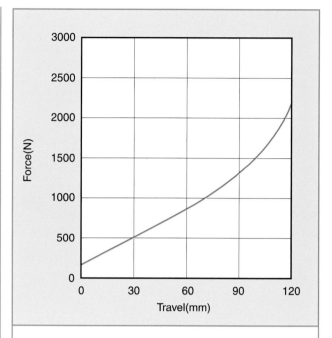

Fig. 14.9: example of typical stiffness curve of a modern fork.

stiffness curve of a modern fork.

You will observe that during the initial travel phase, it is practically linear, while, as the travel increases, the contribution of the air pressure increases, thus making the total stiffness of the fork *progressive*.

- much more rigid structures have been created by significantly increasing the diameters of the tubes and the wheel spindle; part of the internal sliders of the fork are also made bigger.

- as far as the pro-dive effect and reduced trail due to dive are concerned, the reader is referred to Chapter 7.

When the fork compresses under braking, trail is diminished because the rake angle is reduced by 3 to 4 degrees, but this can be a plus for ease of handling.

With the trail value what it is in a straight-line attitude, under braking, when the rear end rebounds to the detriment of the front end, the righting moment is very strong, making it very difficult to corner!

We are certainly not suggesting that the trail reduction brought on by the fork geometry is the best solution for the motorcycle's dynamic behavior; in any case, however, experimental

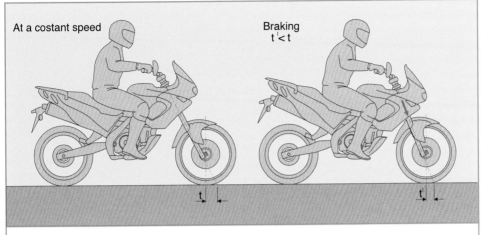

At a costant speed

Braking
t' < t

Fig. 14.10: under braking action, a reduced rake angle diminishes trail.

**a) with pivoted or swinging front fork;
b) with girders or parallelogram linkage;
c) with straight-line slider guides;
d) Paralever linkage.**

a) With swinging front fork

This is a very simple construction solution and, as such, it was used even on the earliest bike models.

In practice, it reproduces the rear-fork geometry, with an arm that rests on a fulcrum placed on the steering column, making the fork rotate in one piece along with the steering head.

They may be *leading link or trailing link front forks,* depending on the whether the arm is extended or compressed during braking.

In both cases the layout may be symetrical to the head angle with two arms, or it may have just one arm.

Pivoted front fork suspension is adopted for many scooter models, but it is almost non-existent on high-performance vehicles.

Characteristics:

• *smoothness*: very good, since the rotations are assured by rolling bearings, thus eliminating stiction; the shock absorber is analogous to the one used in the rear suspension;

• *stiffness*: better or worse depending on the design construction;

• *progressive rate*: connecting-rod linkage systems have never been used to obtain progressive rates, even if it is theoretically possible; it easy enough to obtain using progressive springs;

• *trail control*: is only possible by changing the wheel trajectory;

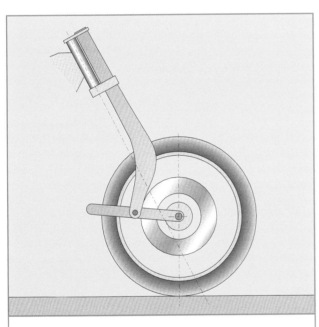

Fig. 14.11: leading link pivoted front fork.

studies have confirmed that the response tends to be a desirable one for sportbikes in particular.

So the true *limits of the fork include stiction problems, the heavy weight of the unsprung masses and the inability to control the path of travel as much as you may want to.*

There are a number of different, unconventional fork types.

For simplicity's sake, we will try to classify them into small groups, giving a list of their main char-

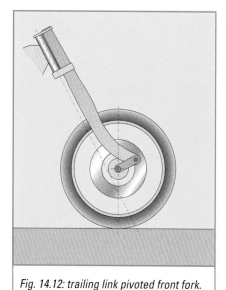

Fig. 14.12: trailing link pivoted front fork.

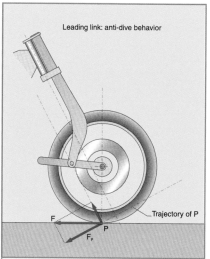

Fig. 14.13: anti-dive behavior of leading link fork.

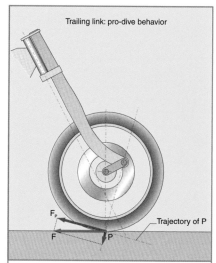

Fig. 14.14: pro-dive behavior of trailing link fork.

• *unsprung masses*: generally moderate weight, although this depends on the type of construction. In any case, it has high inertia around the steering axis.

A comparison between leading and trailing link types may be of interest at this point.

Leading link: during braking, it has a notable *anti-dive* effect (remember what we discussed in Chapter 7); that is, when a braking force is applied, it will tend to extend the suspension.

This effect may be reduced by linking the brake caliper to a torque arm connected to the steering; in this case, the instanteous center of rotation may be positioned so as to produce the desired anti-dive effect.

Trailing link: during braking, it has a pro-dive effect, similar to a traditional fork, but even more evident.

In this case, too, it may be desirable to introduce a brake torque arm, linked to the caliper, in order to obtain the desired effect when braking.

b) Girder or parallelogram linkage

Most recent linkage designs fall into this category, and, in fact, these sorts of solutions theoretically overcome almost all the traditional fork suspension limits.

• *smoothness*: excellent, since all the sliding friction is replaced by rolling friction (sliding movements are replaced by rotations around roller bearings); a shock absorber like the one used in the rear suspension can be used.

• *stiffness*: good or adequate depending on the design construction.

• *progressive rate*: a progressive suspension can be incorporated.

A suspension system similar to the rear suspension, with the characteristics described in the next chapter, can be used on swinging arms.

• *trajectory control*: good or excellent depending on the kind of solution adopted.

In theory, parallelogram linking makes it possible to obtain various types of wheel trajectories.

The trajectory may be perpendicular to the ground, thus maintaining the same wheelbase, or it may be inclined forward in order to obtain a certain degree of anti-dive, or even, in the first phase of travel, be pushed forward to create a pro-dive behavior.

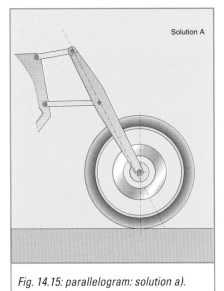

Fig. 14.15: parallelogram: solution a).

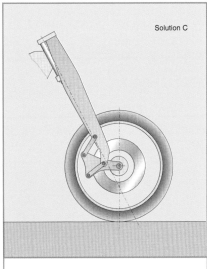

Fig.14.17: solution c)

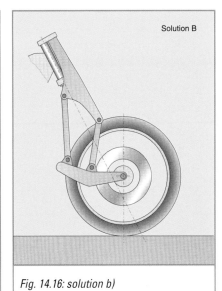

Fig. 14.16: solution b)

• *trail control*: good. Just as for the trajectory, it makes it possible to create constant trail geometry with varying travel, or else to have it increase or decrease according to the kind of riding behavior you want from the bike.

• *unsprung weight*: may be less compared to fork design, but the net weight of the suspension does not change dramatically.

The following section shows several of the most popular design solutions that have been used, along with a few remarks regarding each of them.

Solution a)

This is a very popular solution since it allows fork legs to be as long as needed with normal brake caliper mounting.

The link that holds the wheel can also be asymetrical, like a single-sided rear fork.

The steering must be controlled through appropriately positioned links.

Solution b)

Rarely employed, characterized by high steering masses and considerable inertia; less bulk, while the simplicity of its steering control is a plus.

Solution c)

Rarely employed, since the length of the legs is reduced, making for large wheel travel; with such short fork legs, moreover, there may be large kinematic loads.

As for case b), the steering is directly controlled.

Solution d)

Employed for light motorcycles after the Second World War, the simplicity of the steering control is a plus, but it imposes limits on the steering mass size and on the trajectories available to the wheel.

The stresses on the links due to ground forces are very strong, given that they are located so high up.

Solution e)

Used in the most advanced applications, it unites practically all the advantages offered by girder solutions.

It presents obvious similarities to automobile solutions.

In terms of looks, it has some drawbacks because the two horizontal arms have to be large enough to allow the wheel to be steered.

This may also strongly limit the maximum steering angle value, restricting the use of this solution to streetbikes.

The steering is controlled by links; it offers the valuable possibility to position the shock absorber

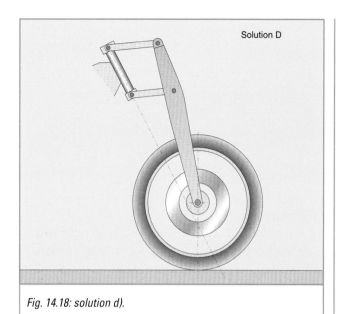

Fig. 14.18: solution d).

in areas that make the mountings sturdy and easy to fabricate; steering control may also be easily constructed through connecting-rod systems.

Solution f)

Similar to solution e), however it does not allow offset of the wheel with respect to the steering head axis (zero offset).

The wheel hub-center becomes somewhat complicated because it must have large diameter bearings in order to house the steering kingpin inside the wheel.

The illustration shows the Di Fazio hub-center design scheme (Figure 14.21).

As we have seen, many of the parallelogram linkage systems that have been proposed result in *indirect steering systems;* that is, the handlebar must linked to the wheels using connecting drag-links.

These crank mechanisms may create a number of problems:

• there must be *no play,* to avoid annoying "gaps" in the steering;

Car steering systems, which always use connecting-rod linkage to the steering column, offer special solutions for eliminating play that, in any case, is only noticeable when the vehicle is stationary.

Furthermore, when in motion, the attitude of a car is such that play in the universal ball joint is automatically taken up.

Play in the steering set is often avoided by the adoption of special solutions.

Figure 14.22 shows an example;

• *steering inaccuracy* problems; that is, variations in the steering angle must be avoided when the wheels is shaking. This effect is almost always present in cars and it is often used to improve carriage stability; for example, to assure straight-line stability the front wheels should tend to diverge during dive;

• *safety* problems: the steering must, of course, be reliable, and this means being able to posi-

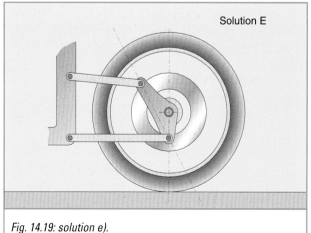

Fig. 14.19: solution e).

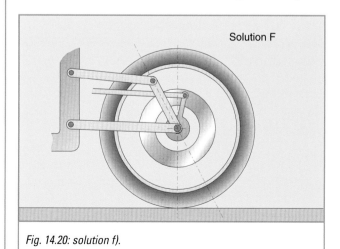

Fig. 14.20: solution f).

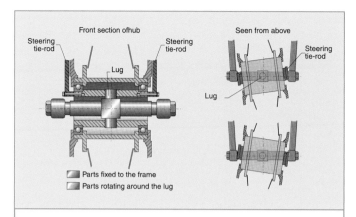

Fig. 14. 21: Di Fazio steering.

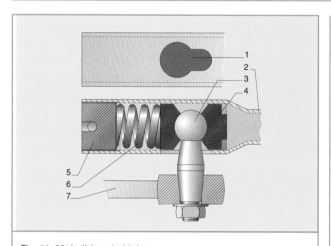

Fig. 14. 22: ball-headed joint.

tion the drag-links in impact-protected areas.

To satisfy all the complex and various demands made by girder linkage, motorcycles with this design scheme differ widely, as one would imagine, from traditional designs, taking on a very futuristic look that in some ways bring to mind automobile technology.

c) Straight-line slider guides

These suspensions are characterized by the same geometry as the rear fork as far as controlling the trajectory of the 0 point and trail are concerned. In practical terms, the cylindrical slider is substituted by a straight-line slider, as before, but of a rolling type.

The damping element in this case is represented by a classic shock absorber, while the rolling guide bearings are similar to ones used for sophisticated mechancal machining work.

Benefits:

• better smoothness;
• limited play and good stiffness.

Limits:
• the two brake discs are difficult to position;
• assymetry that, if overly so, may give rise to a very bothersome moment around the steering axis.

d) Paralever linkage

Schematically speaking, this solution can be thought of as a corrupted parallelogram linkage system.

Thinking of it this way, the upper linking bar is missing, and the function of the suspension is made possible by a slider derived from an intermediary part that becomes a sort of fork (see Figure 14.23).

Benefits:
• the sliding motion of the tubes is easier than for a standard fork, in that most of the loads are absorbed by the lower girder;
• the steering is directly connected to the tubes and is, therefore, completely secure; the transmission ratio is 1:1.

Limits:
• more mechanically complex than a traditional fork and generally more bulky because of the presence of the horizontal arm.

ANTI-DIVE ON THE FORK
In the racing sector, mechanical anti-dive type fork systems have been developed to limit their tendency to front end dive.

Figure 14.24 shows one such design scheme.

By means of a series of links, the braking force sustained by the brake caliper is transferred to the chassis, opposing its tendency to dive.

153

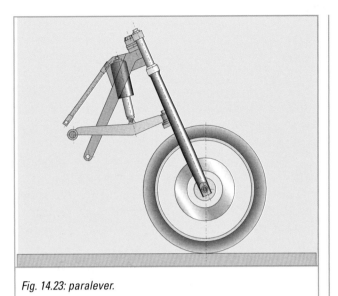

Fig. 14.23: paralever.

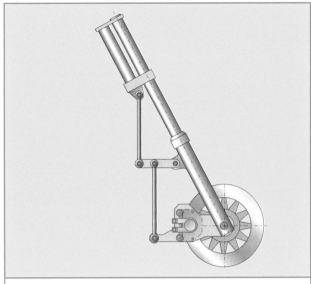

Fig. 14.24: mechanical anti-dive system.

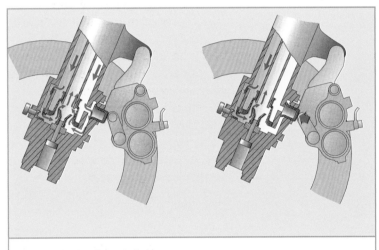

Fig. 14.25: hydraulic anti-dive system.

These systems have not been widely adopted because of the following problems:

• it is difficult to make the brake caliper mounting rigid enough, with possible braking power loss and the formation of micro-vibrations;

•- the system's weight;

• increased inertia around the steering masses;

• only moderate improvement of the vehicle's handling, as previously discussed.

Moreover, increasingly sophisticated hydraulic fork adjustments have surpassed the minimal benefits provided by mechanical anti-dive systems.

For the same reason, hydraulic anti-dive fork systems are increasingly rare; these act according to the principle of increased hydraulic braking when the brakes are applied, by blocking or closing the oil passages, as illustrated in Figure 14.25.

When the hydraulic brake is made too strong, it becomes difficult to absorb small irregularities in the road surface, especially during the delicate phase of entering a corner.

CHAPTER 15
THE REAR SUSPENSION

REAR SUSPENSION CHARACTERISTICS

In the world of today's motorcycle production, the universally adopted suspension design is that of the **swinging arm rear fork.**

This is a simple, sturdy solution, and for the moment there do not seem to be any valid alternatives.

In terms of kinematics, it is very simple to explain, in that the wheel center can only oscillate around the pivot point of the swingarm connected to the frame.

Consequently, the trajectory of the contact point with the ground, point P, will be tangential to the arc of the circle generated by the rotation of the swingarm around its pivot point attached to the frame.

Such simple geometry is altered, as we have seen in previous chapters, when horizontal forces are applied at the contact point.

When a resistance force is applied, the suspension will tend to extend, varying with the chain pull angle and opposing the weight transfer which tends, instead, to compress the suspension.

In the opposite case, when a braking force is applied, the suspension will tend to compress, also opposing the weight transfer.

Although the design layout of the rear suspension is common to all existing motorcycles, there do exist significant differences, determined by two important factors:

• **Ratio of wheel travel to shock travel;**
• **Variation of the ratio during vertical wheel movement.**

Let us analyze these factors separately.

RATIO OF WHEEL TRAVEL TO SHOCK TRAVEL

This is the ratio between wheel travel and the travel of the suspension spring.

In the solution adopted by vintage motorcycles,

with two shocks positioned vertically near the rear wheel, this ratio is given by the lengths **a** and **b** as shown in Figure 15.2.

Since the lengths are quite similar in this set-up, the ratio of wheel travel to shock travel may be taken as 1:1.

The next development was to incline the shock absorbers and move them forward with respect to the rear wheel axle; with this type of configuration things begin to change.

The initial static ratio is no longer 1:1 and, moreover, *it changes during vertical wheel movement.*

In particular, *when the wheel rises, the suspension becomes stiffer,* in that the resistance force increases, the shock absorber has a longer travel and therefore, the spring compresses more, thus increasing the wheel load.

Please note that when the *ratio of wheel travel to shock travel* varies, it also means, however, that *the hydraulic brake varies significantly* and, since the motorcycle is generally sensitive to even small percentage differences, this makes it a very important factor.

As we have seen, damping depends on the speed of extension or compression of the suspension, and speed is the derivative of displacement over time.

Later developments gave rise to a single shock, placed in front of the rear wheel.

Speaking historically, the first application of this type is the one shown in Figure 15.4; this

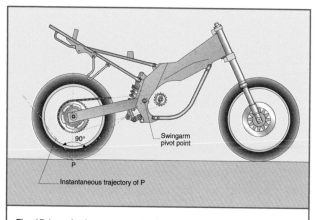

Fig. 15.1: swinging arm rear fork.

made it possible to construct a pivoted fork with a single shock absorber, using a simple, sturdy tube structure.

The ratio between wheel travel and shock travel was still given by the ratio between **a** and **b,** as in the previous case, varying along with the vertical wheel movement.

The main incentive to suspension development came during the 70's, out of the vitality of the motocross sector. The excellence of the new technical solutions applied to motocross bikes surpassed all the other sectors, initially spreading to enduro bikes and ending up on even streetbikes.

Extensive rear wheel travel was found to be crucial for easy absorption of surface irregularities: travel reached and surpassed 300 mm.

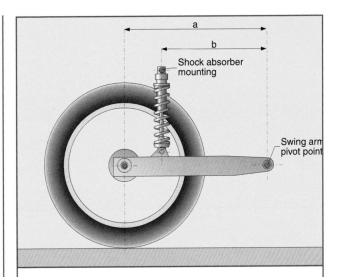

Fig. 15.2: arm forces on the wheel and force on the shock absorber.

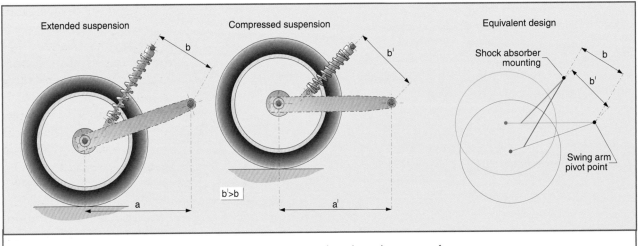

Fig. 15.3: progressive rate suspension: as wheel travel increases so does the resistance arm force.

When the shock is positioned near the rear wheel spindle to produce such kinds of travel, high construction costs and complexity are the inevitable consequences.

A logical evolution was to adopt *a single shock absorber with moderate travel, placed in front of the wheel,* and controlled through *appropriately positioned linkage systems* which permitted the creation of the desired ratios. Besides, every manufacturer could distinguish itself from the others according to the kind of design layout used for the linkage.

The positioning of the shock absorber in front of the rear wheel alters the way the bending

moment acts on the rear fork, making the bending moment very great and at its highest at the point of attachment between the connecting-rod system and the swingarm.

This made it necessary to construct more sturdy rear forks, in order to stand up to the bigger stresses due to vertical loads.

The need for high stiffness also derives from the necessity to reduce torsional deformation, which, as we have seen, has a bad effect on the bike's handling.

The present-day ratio between wheel travel and shock absorber travel on offroad and motocross bikes has settled at 5:7, while for enduro bikes, it

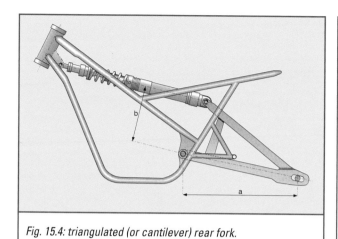

Fig. 15.4: triangulated (or cantilever) rear fork.

goes down a little with reduced travel.

For bikes designed for street use, which have smaller travel (we are talking about values between 120 and 160 mm), the ratio is usually about 3, and goes down to about 2 in Grand Prix bikes that have travel values around 120 mm.

The **monoshock** solution has become practically the universal choice, for the following reasons:

• The possibility to provide rather short shock absorbers, with limited travel with respect to wheel travel, making them lighter and easier to construct;

• The possibility of positioning the shock absorber further forward along the frame, all to the benefit of the strength of the shock's upper mount;

• Less bulk and inertia on the motorcycle: the shock is closer to the center of the bike and therefore, to its center of gravity;

• The possibility of creating desired ratio of wheel travel to shock travel and a progressive rate curve (extremely useful for all motorcycles, but especially for offroad bikes);

• Reduced cost, considering that a single shock, including the linkage, costs less than two shocks.

Furthermore, since the shock is often hidden from view, its finishing and visual appearance can be ignored, which saves generally high, extra costs.

This is a rare case in which a more sophisticated technical solution translates into practical solutions that are even more economical than their predecessors.

VARIATION OF THE RATIO WITH WHEEL TRAVEL (PROGRESSIVE RATE)

Suspension stiffness is maintained by differing values:

• *Wheel travel;*
• *Load conditions,* to be able to optimize riding comfort and grip.

During braking, with the suspension completely (or almost completely) extended, the stiffness must be soft enough to be able to absorb to surface irregularities and maintain contact with the ground.

Remember that adhesion (see Chapter 13) depends on the static load bearing on the axle and, therefore, the spring must be very soft to allow small dynamic load variations.

In straight-line motion the suspension stiffness must be, once again, quite moderate, even if it should be stiffer than during braking, given that the static load on the rear axle is increased.

When cornering, stiffer suspension is needed to avoid excessive rear end squat, and thus a steeper rake angle.

In the case, then, of a deep hollow or a jump, the suspension must offer high stiffness at the end of its travel to avoid abruptly bottoming out.

With a fully-loaded motorcycle, with two people and luggage, which, as we have seen, predominantly loads the rear end, the rear suspension should not squat too much, in order to limit attitude variations and, in this case, too, to make sure the suspension does not bottom out abruptly when it hits a bump.

So, as we can see, stiffness must increase as wheel travel increases;

The linkage, then, *makes the ratio of wheel travel to shock travel decrease;* that is, with the same wheel travel, the shock absorber and, consequently, the spring are more compressed.

By graphing the wheel-to-shock ratio as a function of wheel travel, we obtain a curve characterstic of each motorcycle.

THE REAR SUSPENSION

157

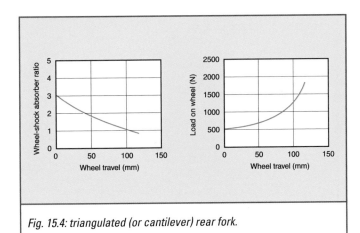

Fig. 15.4: triangulated (or cantilever) rear fork.

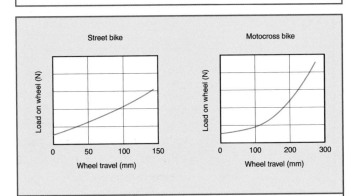

Fig. 15.6: wheel load curves as a function of wheel travel for streetbikes and motocross bikes.

This curve is called the progressive rate curve because it makes the load on the wheel increase progressively as the wheel travel increases.

This fact is easily observed in the graph above, showing the wheel load value as a function of wheel travel.

Every motorcycle has a progressive rate curve (reaching even 60%, for example, in motocross models) that varies according to the type of behavior you want from the bike.

Here (Figure 15.6) are two load curves as a function of wheel travel, characteristic of two extreme situations, that is, for streetbikes and motocross bikes.

One might object that a good amount of progressive rate can also be obtained by using springs characterized by increasing elasticity (based on what we discussed regarding variable rate springs), which, moreover, are easily constructed;

but, on the other hand, *with shock absorber linkage, the result allows us to very heavily modify the hydraulic rate as well.*

WORKING DESIGN OF SHOCK ABSORBER LINKAGE SYSTEMS

All linkage layouts are based on the working principle of a simple, or in rare cases, complex four-bar linkage, with familiar kinematics.

A simple parallelogram linkage system (see Figure 15.7) is composed of:

Element 1: the swingarm; can rotate around A, pivot point on the frame;
Element 2: lower crank; can rotate around B, its attachment point to the frame;
Element 3: connecting-rod; connected to 1 and 2, and capable of rotational and translational motion.

The shock absorber may rest on a fulcrum located on element 2 or 3.

Here are a few examples of linkages, classified on the basis of the above placement criterion:

• *Shock absorber attached to element 2:*

Figure 15.8 shows two working designs with the shock absorber resting on a fulcrum on element 2, that is, the crank, which is attached to the frame and which can only follow a circular path around the pivot point.

The desired progressive rate curve is obtained by designing the right lengths of the various elements and the angles between them.

• *Shock absorber attached to element 3:*

Figure 15.9 hows the shock absorber resting on a fulcrum placed on connecting-rod 3, which, being linked to 1 and 2, is characterized by *both translational and rotational motion.*

This makes it possible to create special, "imaginative" progressive rate curves, but, above all, it makes it possible to limit the longitudinal movement of the shock absorber without taking up a lot

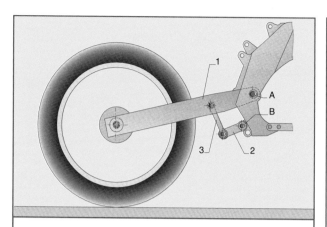

Fig. 15.7: shock absorber connecting-rod system.

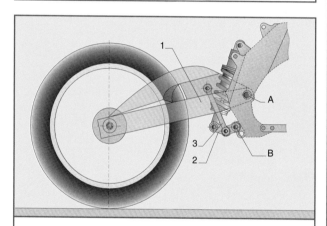

Fig. 15.8: shock absorber attached to crank.

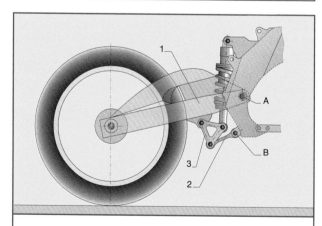

Fig. 15.9: shock absorber attached to connecting rod.

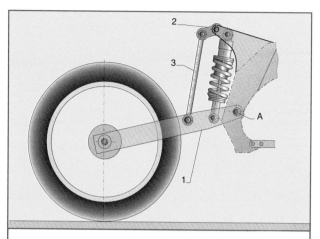

Fig. 15.10: design scheme for shock absorber that compresses at both ends.

can compress in a straight-line path without rocking during wheel movement.

In any case, *the two solutions* described here *are practically equivalent in terms of their performance* and the choice of one or the other depends on the particular application and the particular needs of the motorcycle it is intended for.

Thanks to today's improved shock absorber and tire qualities, progressive rate curves are becoming ever simpler, so the choice of the type of linkage scheme is determined by space considerations and the possibility of placing the attachment points in the desired locations.

In any case, there are many other linkage schemes that, for example, make use of a series of parallelogram linkages; this makes it possible to place the shock absorber in almost any position whatsoever and gives an enormous range of variable rate characteristics.

Another system that is quite widely employed does not have the shock absorber resting on a fulcrum on the frame, but rather, when the wheel moves closer to the frame, the shock is compressed at both ends. This layout obviously eliminates an attachment to the frame.

Figure 15.10 shows an example of this type.

With the appearance of shock absorber variable link systems, every motorcycle manufacturer has promoted their own design scheme, putting a name to it and equipping all of their models with it. Today, the adoption of variable linkage systems has become widespread, so each model is equipped with the one most suited to it.

of space on the motorcycle.

Using this layout makes it possible to create straight-line movement; that is, the shock absorber

INDEX